Siberia Today and Tomorrow

A study of Economic Resources
Problems and Achievements

Siberia Today and Tomorrow

A study of Economic Resources
Problems and Achievements

Violet Conolly

Taplinger Publishing Company
New York

First published in the United States in 1976 by
TAPLINGER PUBLISHING CO., INC.
New York, New York

Library of Congress Catalog Card Number: 75-26327
ISBN 0-8008-7182-0

contents

list of maps and illustrations

glossary

Okrug plural **okrugi** an administrative district in both Tsarist and Soviet Russia. Before 1917, it was inferior to a *Guberniya* generally translated as a Government and which was the largest of the administrative divisions in the eighteenth and nineteenth centuries. In the Soviet period *Okrug* is chiefly used in the phrase Natsional 'nyy *Okrug* National district, a subdivision designed for small minority peoples.

Ostrog plural **ostrogi** a type of fortress consisting of an outer wall, with towers at intervals, forming a rectangle within which were houses, churches, barracks and stores. It was essentially a frontier fortification.

Yasak a word of Turkic origin meaning tribute, but in Siberia it came to mean fur tribute. *Yasak* had been levied in furs by Tatars and Mongols before the arrival of the Russians. The Russian levy was on all able-bodied males among the native peoples, and was never payable by the Russian settlers in Siberia. The *yasak* was of two kinds: *okladnoy* which required a fixed number of skins annually, generally between five and ten; and *neokladnoy*, when the collector took what he could get. In order to emphasise that this was tribute, and not a tax, the Russians at first used to make gifts to the natives when the *yasak* was paid. But later this ceased, and *yasak* came to be paid often in money, and became very like other taxes.

Yurta plural **yurty** a hut, generally of circular plan, consisting of an outer covering supported by a wooden framework. It is used by many Turkic and Mongol tribes.

Zimov'ye a wintering cabin in the forest used by traders and hunters and generally made of logs.

As I could not improve on the definitions of these terms given by Dr T. Armstrong in his book *Russian Settlement in the North*, op. cit. p. 195, they are reproduced here with some slight amendments, with his kind permission.

list of abbreviations

ASSR	Autonomous Soviet Socialist Republic
BAM	Baykal-Amur Magistral (Trunk line)
CPSU	Communist Party of the Soviet Union
Glavneftesnab	Chief Administration for transport and supply of oil and oil products
GRES	State Regional Electric Station
Ekon. Gaz.	Economic Gazette
GOSPLAN	State planning committee
GOSSNAB	State Supply Committee
GOSSTROY	State Committee for Construction Affairs
HES	Hydro-electric Power-station
Iz.	Izdatel'stvo (Publishing House)
KRAYKOM	Regional Committee
Nar. Khoz. SSSR	National Economy of the USSR
. . . RSFSR	. . . of the RSFSR
OBKOM	Provincial Committee
OBLAST	Province
RSFSR	Russian Soviet Federal Socialist Republic
SSSR, USSR	Union of Soviet Socialist Republics
YASSR	Yakut Autonomous Soviet Socialist Republic

metric conversion table

1 desyatina, a former Russian measure of land =2·7 acres
1 hectare =2·471 acres
1 metre =3·281 feet
1 kilometre =0·621 miles
1 square kilometre =0·386 square miles
1 cubic metre =35·315 cubic feet
1 kilogram (me) =2·205 pounds
1 metric ton =0·984 tons
1 verst, a Russian measure of length =3,500 feet

foreword

Impressive progress has been achieved against great odds in the economic development of Siberia – the world's largest and richest developing country – since World War II and many exciting geological discoveries have enlarged its known natural wealth. But complex development problems are retarding the territory's further advance, though its economic potential is enormous. It would seem almost providential for the Soviet government at this stage, that injections of sophisticated technology and investment capital – both badly needed in some of Siberia's major industries – should be forthcoming as a result of the economic co-partnership deals now being negotiated with Japan and the United States for the development of Siberian natural gas and oil, in the first place, while further deals of the same nature may well follow.

Intriguing though they are, these multinational proposals are not the main concern of this book which was in fact planned long before they were announced. My purpose is rather to present a balanced account of the Siberian economy as it emerges from a critical study of the available Russian material. The territory's achievements and problems are analysed, considerable attention being devoted to the important energy industry in west and east Siberia and to Siberia's contribution to the all-Union economy, while the great future (as I see it) implicit in the development of Siberia's unusually rich resource endowment is outlined.

It is hoped that this book will fill a gap for readers interested in Siberian affairs but unfamiliar with Russian. With such readers in mind, it is not encumbered with footnotes, because my sources are almost entirely Russian. I have aimed at presenting as realistic a picture as possible of the performance and trends in the main sectors of the Siberian economy and the invidious role at times of the central planning authorities in Moscow. The text is often enlivened by graphic detail from the Soviet press which goes far to pin-point how things work or do not work on Siberian construction sites. In fact nothing of this local colour can be gleaned from the tidy totals of Soviet production statistics, or the final record of commissioned plants.

The reader should perhaps be warned not to take the almost incredible waste and muddle described in Soviet reports of construction projects too seriously. Such lapses are of course costly and time consuming and would certainly be seen as intolerable in a western private enterprise. But they never apparently finally wreck a project in Siberia.

It seemed a propitious moment after the celebration in 1972 of fifty years of Soviet power, to examine the state of development in Siberia, hitherto a close reserve of the Soviet socialist economic system. Now the invitations to Japan, the United States and perhaps Germany and other western countries, to cooperate in the economic development of Siberia could initiate a new economic era, with private enterprise working side by side with centrally directed state socialism, to improve and accelerate Siberian industrialisation. But the period I am dealing with (1917–1973) shows Siberia under undiluted state socialism, with its achievements and defects.

As these economic copartnership projects are still under discussion with the United States and Japan, their impact on the Siberian economy can only be very tentatively forecast. There seems little doubt however that Siberian industrialisation and the oil and gas industries in the first place could benefit enormously from the advanced technology they can offer.

A few words about the Russian source material on which I have worked seem called for, as the short reading list only contains works in English. This Russian material is fortunately both abundant and excellent. Siberian experts (mostly belonging to the Siberian Department of the all-Union Academy of Sciences) and special Soviet press correspondents on the spot, contribute to a flow of valuable information and for the most part express their views on economic problems with refreshing frankness and impressive knowledge.[1]

Owing to the constant shifts in Siberian construction, as projects move forward to completed plants, pipelines, etc., I have had continuously to revise and bring up to date much of the material written earlier. I hope synchronisation has not been impaired as a result. There is inevitably some overlapping in the discussion of intertwined subjects such as Energy (Chapter 5) and Copartnership (Chapter 12) or Government (Chapter 3) and Relations with the Native Peoples (Chapter 10), for which I ask indulgence.

Finally, I must draw the reader's attention to the Postscript which I added to embody the more important developments in Siberian affairs before the book went to press in mid-1974 e.g. the cancellation of the Irkutsk-Nakhodka pipe-line, the construction of the Baykal-Amur railway and the more recent trends in Soviet-US and Soviet Japanese copartnership projects.

My task in writing this book was greatly facilitated by many friends and former colleagues who allowed me to pick their brains. In particular, I must mention Mr. Quintin Bach, who was always most amiably at my disposal for help on technical points where I was at sea. Colonel Geoffrey Wheeler and the late Mrs. Jane Degras did me an invaluable service by reading my manuscript and offering their very expert editorial comments. Dr. E. J. Lindgren was as ever lavishly generous in lend-

---

[1] This book and the appended reading list are mainly concerned with Siberia since the 1917 revolution. The pre-1917 period was discussed in my earlier book: *Beyond the Urals*, Oxford University Press, 1967.

ing me special books from her splendid collection on Asiatic Russia, and has given me much other spontaneous help which I greatly appreciate. I am ashamed to remember how often I bothered Dr. Terence Armstrong with my questions on northern Siberian problems, and how indebted I am to him for his always prompt and definitive notes in reply. I am also most grateful to Dr. Werner Klatt for reading my pages on Siberian agriculture and for his advice. Finally, I must thank Mrs. A. Moody for the skill and patience with which she deciphered and typed my illegible first drafts. To E.M. who prefers to remain anonymous, I am glad to have this opportunity of expressing my affectionate gratitude for her constant encouragement in my frequent moments of gloom in writing this book.   *Violet Conolly*

chapter one

The Environment

The geographical situation of Siberia has inevitably exercised a decisive influence on its economic development. The environmental factors such as area, climate and topographical features are almost uniformly unfavourable and go far to explain Siberia's late emergence in the modern industrial world, in spite of its extremely rich source endowment. Across the Atlantic, the more favourable geographical situation of the U.S.A. has on the contrary facilitated the much more rapid modernisation of North America. This is of course not the only cause of America's rise to industrial power in the nineteenth century, but it is the only one relevant to this argument. What then are the main features of the Siberian topography and their relation to Siberian resource development?

First, the area. Taking Siberia in the traditional sense of the lands lying between the Urals and the Pacific, the area of 125 million sq. km. is larger than that of the China Peoples' Republic with 9.5 million sq. km., or the U.S.A. with 9.3 million sq. km. It is more than twice as large as European Russia (5.57 million sq. km.) The distances from east to west and from north to south in Siberia are also enormous and with the prevailing harsh climate, greatly complicate the construction of a well organised communications system. Moscow is separated from its Far Eastern naval base at Vladivostok, for example, by 5,732 miles via the Trans-Siberian railway, while it is some 2,000 miles from the Arctic north to the more temperate southern zones of the Soviet Far Eastern Region.

Siberia is now divided into three economic regions: west Siberia, east Siberia and the Soviet Far Eastern Region. And it is therefore convenient to discuss the Siberian environment, which varies so considerably from region to region, on this basis. All three regions are very large by European standards and the largest, the Soviet Far Eastern Region, is five times the size of France and larger even than the entire continent of Australia.

There are many climatic variations within the three Siberian regions. All have relatively hot summers and extremely rigorous winters with varying degrees of frost, and an annual mean temperature of 0°C. The Siberian climate thus presents some surprising anomalies. In Verkhoyansk within the Arctic Circle for example, and one of the coldest places in the world, there are wide differences between the hottest and the coldest days, and the summer can be as hot as the south of France or Italy. But the mean for the coldest month is − 50°C.

The permafrost (permanently frozen ground), one of the characteristic features of Siberia, extends from the Arctic and sub-Arctic zones of west Siberia, mostly east of the Ob' river, with varying degrees of depth to almost the whole of Yakutiya and the northern Siberian extremity of Chukotka. In east Siberia only small patches of ground are free of it.[1]

The existence of this frozen sub-soil creates many technical problems for the construction of civil engineering industrial projects, such as pipelines or hydroelectric power stations in the Arctic and sub-Arctic regions. Any major structure, unless precautions are taken, causes the soil temperature to change, with serious effects on the settling of foundations so that damage, up to and including the collapse of the structure, may result.[2]

Permafrost assumes not only different depths but also different forms. In some areas there is not a continuous, solid mass of frozen earth, but alternate layers are frozen and not frozen, the latter being maintained at a higher temperature by circulating underground water. Since the frozen layers are impermeable, the upper layers of earth cannot absorb the rainfall precipitation and swamps occur where the permafrost is near the surface. Modern buildings, as a result of much careful local research, especially in the Permafrost Institute in Yakutsk, can now be constructed on piles, driven deep through the earth into the frozen ground, which provides rock-like foundations. Good examples of such constructions are to be found in Yakutsk and Noril'sk and hydro-power stations such as the Khantayka or Ust'-Ilimsk stations now being built in permafrost ground.

Throughout the permafrost areas of northern Siberia, only moss and lichen can grow in the tundra and survive the ferocious winds and frosts. This is the summer home of the reindeer, whose natural fodder is this moss and lichen. But even they move south to the cover of the taiga in winter. These chilly territories are very thinly populated, mostly by small settlements of native fishermen and hunters. Where minerals have been found, as at Noril'sk, new towns and settlements have grown up and in spite of all the difficulties of establishing civilised life there, it has been proved that it can be done. But there are still many unsolved problems arising from this environment. Not surprisingly, there seems a good deal of local steam behind the recommendation that a special Soviet ministry, on the analogy of the Canadian Ministry for the Development of the North, should be established to concentrate particular attention on Siberian permafrost and other problems peculiar to the Soviet north; this measure was suggested in 1970 by *Stroitelinaya Gazeta* (24.5.1970) the official journal of the State Committee for Construction Affairs of the U.S.S.R. and other interested parties. In view of the size and peculiar problems of the Soviet north it is surprising that no special body exists to coordinate northern activities. It is interesting to note that the Soviet North (including the European as

---

[1] See map on opposite page.
[2] I am indebted for much of this information to Dr. Terence Armstrong's article 'The Soviet North', Survey, no. 67, April 1968 and to Dr. James S. Gregory's *'Russian Land and Soviet People*, Harrap, 1968.

Principal zones of Permafrost

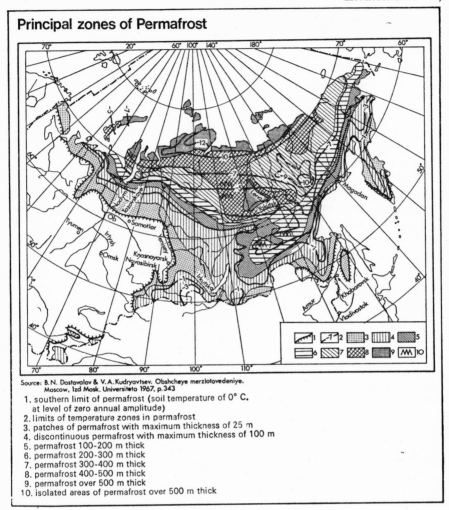

Source: B. N. Dostovalov & V. A. Kudryavtsev. Obshcheye merzlotovedeniye.
Moscow, Izd Mosk. Universiteta 1967, p.343

1. southern limit of permafrost (soil temperature of 0° C.
   at level of zero annual amplitude)
2. limits of temperature zones in permafrost
3. patches of permafrost with maximum thickness of 25 m
4. discontinuous permafrost with maximum thickness of 100 m
5. permafrost 100-200 m thick
6. permafrost 200-300 m thick
7. permafrost 300-400 m thick
8. permafrost 400-500 m thick
9. permafrost over 500 m thick
10. isolated areas of permafrost over 500 m thick

well as the Siberian and Far Eastern northern territories) extends over nearly half
the total area of the Soviet Union or more than ten million square kilometres. It is
the largest northern area in the world, larger even than Canada.[3]

The Arctic tundra is succeeded in west Siberia by the wooded tundra and the
great belt of coniferous forest stretching thousands of miles eastwards through east
Siberia to the Soviet Far East. These forests, still largely within the permafrost
zone, are interspersed with large areas of bog and marsh which are impassable in
summer. Valuable oil deposits have been found in these swampy wastes of west
Siberia but the unstable nature of the marshy terrain has greatly complicated their
exploitation. It has been graphically described by Dr. Gregory: '. . . Between the

[3] The Canadian journal *North/Nord* (March-April 1973) published a special issue on the
Soviet North with some excellent articles in which useful comparisons between the Soviet
and Canadian North were made (and on which I have drawn here).

confluences of the Irtysh and the Vasugan rivers, a wide expanse of lowland extends westward across the Irtysh to the Tavda river. The western and northern parts constitute an immense, virtually uninhabited, wilderness, where water and forest are inextricably mingled in a complex of streams and countless lakes. South of the Ob', the Vasuganye swamp includes large tracts of bog and moss-covered land with few trees.'[4] This formerly desolate, grim, Vasuganye swamp is now being activated by all the mechanical impedimenta of a modern oil industry working under great difficulties.

The southern areas of west Siberia, where there are large expanses of wooded and true steppe, contrast sharply with the frozen northern scene. The best agricultural land in Siberia is to be found here and the famous black earth or *chernozem* soils produce high quality grain crops. Harvests in this area are, however, constantly threatened by endemic, sultry winds and droughts and the danger of flooding from the local rivers such as the Ob' and the Irtysh. These steppe lands merge southwards into the extensive Kazakh steppes, where cultivation has been greatly expanded in recent years following Khrushchev's Virgin Lands campaign.[5]

West Siberia, consisting mainly of the so-called Siberian Depression, or Lowland, is one of the world's largest areas of unbroken flat land. It extends across the country from the Urals foothills to the east Siberian highlands, and is 1,200 miles from north to south and 900 miles wide across the southern boundary with Kazakhstan. In the middle Ob' region, south of the permafrost zone and extending far north to the permafrost territory of the Yamalo-Nenetskiy national okrug, huge oil and gas fields have been discovered. The exploitation of these deposits in such difficult and very sparsely populated terrain presents many complicated and new problems to the Soviet energy industries.

East Siberia lacks the favourable basis for agricultural development of west Siberia. It is traversed by many mountain ranges, permafrost is widespread throughout the region and the climate is more continental than in west Siberia. The best agricultural lands are in the eastern hinterland of Irkutsk and the southern mild zone round Minusinsk. Agriculture is well developed there and livestock thrives in the hills and valleys of Khakassia. The highlands and prairie-like country of eastern Transbaykaliya, from the point of view of soil and climate, also favour livestock breeding which is relatively well developed there, but suffers from a lack of fodder. East Siberia has a great wealth of timber, much of it still virgin forest. The timber industries have been expanding since hydro-electric power from Bratsk and other local stations has become more generally available but the climate and primitive state of transport are still obstacles to greater exploitation of the local taiga.

Siberia is traversed by many of Russia's greatest rivers. The chief are the Ob', the Irtysh, the Yenisey, the Angara, the Lena, the Yana, the Kolyma, which are powerful sources of hydro-electric power and useful seasonal means of transport. All flow northwards to the icy coasts of the Arctic, where they discharge an enormous volume of water. Commercially, this is a great disadvantage, especially when compared with the geographical situation in North-eastern America, for example.

[4] cf. Gregory, op. cit. p. 540.
[5] For details of Siberian agriculture see chapter 7 *The Land*.

There, the waterways flowing into the Atlantic favoured the establishment of settlements and trading posts and maritime development of the greatest importance to American economic progress.[6] Though the natural conditions on the lower courses of the north Siberian rivers preclude developments similar in scope and scale to the American, a great deal has been done to take advantage of the short open navigation periods before the rivers are frozen solid in winter, so as to collect local raw materials such as minerals or timber at the river ports, to distribute supplies down stream, and to develop the Northern Sea Route.

Nearly a century ago, an intrepid British captain, Joseph Wiggins, proved that it was possible to navigate the perilous waters of the Kara Sea, pass upstream along the Yenisey and distribute cargo at Krasnoyarsk. This has now become a regular route annually for Soviet shipping, including hydrofoils, though foreign ships are not allowed beyond the Yenisey timber ports of Dudinka or Igarka. The Yenisey's fairway is now being deepened between Krasnoyarsk and Igarka. It is anticipated that by the summer of 1973, thousands of tons of rock and soil will have been removed from the river bed, so as to allow a much increased volume of freight to be shipped on the river. Another measure aimed at increasing the seasonal usefulness of Siberian rivers is the use of helicopters to remove ice blockages, by landing demolition teams on thick ice-floes and by the destruction of thinner ice-floes from the air. In many areas lacking other means of communication with European Russia, these collecting-distributing river services are invaluable. The Lena river, which is an essential communications link between the rail-transhipment point Ust'-Kut and Yakutsk, is exceptional in that its lower reaches and enormous delta are not navigable.

A scheme to divert some of the immense volume of water annually discharged into the Arctic Ocean by the Siberian rivers, so as to fructify the waterless deserts of Central Asia, was put forward some years ago by a Soviet engineer J. Davidov. In fact, this project was the brain-child of another 'daring engineer' Yakob Demchenko nearly a century earlier. He was clearly ahead of his time in his understanding of the technical needs and possibilities of diverting the flow of the Siberian rivers and his project was rejected at the time as 'fantastic'. In much the same way, Davidov's proposals originally met with more scepticism than support, but they have now been revived with official support. A Soviet government decree in 1971 authorised the necessary scientific research and surveying work for such a diversion project. It is hoped, if the project matures, to irrigate 4,000,000 ha. of land in the Syr-Dar'ya and Amu-Dar'ya area of Central Asia (which were fertile in antiquity), starting with the diversion of the Irtysh waters.

Irrigation should also be improved in Siberia by regulating the floods of the Ob', Tom and Chulym rivers. According to an interview given by I. A. Gerardi, the Technical Head of the project, care is to be taken to avoid some of the dangers implicit in such a complicated undertaking. 'All factors are to be taken into account which could to any degree affect the climate of the area or the conditions of the development of the flora and fauna', he stated. The project aims to take off not less

[6] *American Economic Development*. By A. M. Sakolski and Nyron L. Hock. Thomas Nelson and Sons N.Y. 1936.

than 10% of the flow of the rivers of the Kara Sea basin and Soviet experts believe that this will not affect the thermal balance of the Kara Sea and its coast. In a pioneering project of this magnitude which is still in the planning stage, it is impossible to foresee the outcome. It was announced in 1973, that the first stage of hydro-geological surveying work has been completed along the route by which water is to be diverted from the Siberian rivers to the basin of the Aral Sea and that a 4,000 km. gravity-flow canal will be built across the Kazakh steppes. .

The expert comments on the original Davidov plan by Sir Olaf Caroe, who had wide experience of this type of irrigation in India, may usefully be recalled in this connection. He warned of the dangers of damming and serious water-logging in a flat country like Turkestan. 'A great accession of water into the Turanian basin might make of the desert a saline marsh', he cautioned.[7]

Since the thirties, the Soviet Government has expended much money and scientific effort on the development of the Northern Sea Route between northern European Russian ports and Soviet Pacific ports. The aim has been to ensure safe passage through the perilous Arctic waters for ocean-going ships by better ice-forecasting, ice-breakers, improving navigating aids, ports, and so on. The Northern Sea Route is much shorter than either the Suez or Black Sea routes. From Archangel'sk to Vladivostok it is 7,000 sea miles via the Bering Strait, while it is 10,800 sea miles from Odessa and 14,700 from Leningrad via the Suez Canal.[8] The old dream of a North-East Passage is now a practical proposition as hundreds of Soviet ships annually pass through, aided by powerful ice-breakers, during the short navigation season. In this way, much needed supplies can reach the coastal settlements and be sent up stream by barge and river craft to many of the new mining settlements in the north. Heavy minerals may in turn be collected for processing or use in distant industrial centres, in Siberia or European Russia. In a vast area lacking either railways or good roads, the Northern Sea Route is thus an invaluable complementary means of transport to the widespread Soviet air service which cannot deal always, as the N.S.R. can, with the heavier type of cargo.

Extending over such a vast area from north to south and east to west, it is not surprising that the Soviet Far Eastern Region has a wide range of climates and soils within its boundaries. The permafrost area reaches far south from the Arctic and sub-Arctic zones, with temperatures and soils that preclude any substantial development of agriculture. By careful husbandry, livestock can be raised, in conjunction with fur farming, even in the region of Verkhoyansk – though Verkhoyansk and Oymyakon contend for the honour of being the 'cold pole' of the northern region.

The high and difficult Cherskiy and Verkhoyansk mountains in north-east Yakutiya were long an insuperable barrier to exploration of the hinterland. A belt of gold and tin is now being developed there and this so-called 'Golden Arc' extends to the north-eastern massif of Chukotka, also very rich in gold and tin. The nature of the terrain changes to the south in the Kolyma river basin. The area here is low

7 *Soviet Empire*, pp. 207-8. Macmillan. 1953.
8 *The Northern Sea Route.* By Terence Armstrong, Cambridge University Press. 1952.
 . 106.

lying and often little above sea level with large swamps and many shallow lakes. This is gold mining territory, where the reindeer plays an essential part in supplying meat for the miners, as well as the many other commodities and transport for the native inhabitants.

In the Soviet Far Eastern Region agriculture can only be practised with any degree of success in three areas: (a) the upper Amur-Bureya-Zeya district adjoining the southern Sino-Soviet border; (b) the Olekminsk district of central Yakutiya which produces good crops of wheat and potatoes in a grain deficient land; (c) the Lake Khanka district and the Ussuri valley, specialising in sugar beet, soya beans and rice. Great efforts are being made to extend the cultivation of vegetables, dairy farming and some crops in the vicinity of Yakutsk. But there the possibilities are limited owing to the northern climate and permafrost soil.

More temperate zones are found in the Amur basin, the Ussuri valley and the Primor'ye coastal region, where semi-tropical, humid conditions are found. These areas of the Soviet Far East would lend themselves, under more efficient management, to more intensive agricultural development and better all-round farm production. The soil and climate are relatively propitious, though the prevalence of monsoons and flooding are disadvantages.

The lands of the extreme Soviet Far East, Kamchatka, the island of Sakhalin and the Kuril Islands, suffer from serious natural handicaps. Kamchatka has many active volcanoes on the east coast and there are frequent earthquakes and tremors in this volcanic soil. On the whole, the monsoon climate is somewhat milder than on the opposite Okhotsk coast, but the Kamchatka peninsula also suffers from dense sea fog. Owing to the mountainous nature of the country, many places are cut off from each other and can only be reached by water. A large area of Kamchatka is covered by forests and peat bogs: there are no railways and only a few good arterial roads. Kamchatka's seas and rivers abound in fine fish (including salmon and crab, for which Kamchatka is world famous), but otherwise most of its food must be imported. Sakhalin and the Kuril islands are also afflicted by earthquakes, dense fogs and very severe winters with ferocious winds and blinding snow storms.

There are now some forty seismic stations in the Soviet Far East, working on problems arising from volcanic conditions and aiming at carrying out automatic processing of seismic information so as to avoid, as far as possible, the present unpredictable disasters. The conditions round the often fog-bound Kuril Islands are, however, propitious for seal hunting and fishing, but it is primarily their strategic significance that is important for the Soviet Union, which has built up their population and defences since their annexation from Japan in 1945.

This brief survey of the characteristic features of Siberia's environment should underline the extent to which it complicates economic development. Nature has indeed been lavish with natural resources in Siberia, but she has also more often than not located them in most inhospitable, remote areas. The challenge to Siberia's developers today from the environment is thus much greater than was faced a century ago by America's pioneering colonists. It is also faced by a serious problem of conserving its natural wealth from pollution, which was no concern of the American pioneers.

The pollution-conservation problem has begun to rear its hydra head in Siberia as in most parts of the twentieth-century world, developed and undeveloped. It certainly has long existed in Siberia and elsewhere in the Soviet Union but has only recently been given any publicity. An astonished Soviet public learned from a letter in *Komsomol'skaya Pravda* (10.5.1966) that effluence from pulp mills, to be built on the southern shore of Lake Baykal, might pollute waters famous for their purity.

The mills were built after assurances were given that an efficient purification system would be installed. But it is not at all certain that this was satisfactorily done, judging from later reports. Similar complaints were made about the pollution of the Amur river from the Komsomol'sk chemical plant and of other Siberian rivers. 'Long stretches of our rivers and waters can no longer be used as a source of drinking water or for fishing,' according to an official report in 1968. 'Even in great rivers like the Volga, the Kama, the Belaya and the Irtysh, fish life is rapidly becoming extinct.' Siberia's great timber wealth has, it seems, encouraged wanton wastage and even destruction of many forests, according to complaints in the Soviet press. Soviet conservationists are doing their best to change this attitude. But, the Ministries concerned with timber processing and timber felling should, it is alleged, be more active in organising both efficient felling and forest protection measures and so put an end to this evil.

Possibly as a result of the outcry about the threat to Lake Baykal, a new government agency has been established, within the Ministry of Agriculture of the U.S.S.R., with the task of examining all proposed factory sites from the point of view of pollution. The exact powers of this new Agency are far from clear or to what extent it is entitled to control any harmful activities of industrial enterprises in this respect.

The many warnings from conservation experts and others of the threat to the Soviet environment from pollution culminated in 1972, in an official acknowledgement that the existing Soviet legislation on pollution was inadequate to deal with the prevailing evils. This was followed up by an energetic drive against pollution in all forms. The Supreme Soviet set up a Preparatory Commission to prepare new and more precise legislation to protect the environment from the effects of mining etc., and to make stricter demands on 'those who approach the country's natural wealth from the point of view of consumption alone', 'guided by immediate considerations and departmental interests'. New and detailed legislation was therefore adopted in 1972 to counter pollution and to protect the environment and wild life. It remains to be seen how effectively it will be enforced by the hitherto lax local officials and industrial enterprises. In the words of a western expert analyst of Soviet conservation: 'The record of the Soviet Union's fifty years would seem to suggest that the centralised planning of an economy *per se* provides no necessary guarantee that pollution of the environment will not occur. As in the United States, numerous agencies to control these phenomena exist, but extravagances, wastes and environmental contamination still occur. The problems of economic expediency, bureaucratic inefficiency, pressures from "above", overtly lenient enforcement, neglect of intangibles and externalities, fallacious concepts of inexhaustibility and public indifference remain unsolved in the Soviet Union, or at best only partially solved, even as they do in the United States.'[9]

This indictment of Soviet quasi-official indifference to the environment was written before the start of the current fight against pollution, but it was borne out by the disclosure, months after the establishment of the Supreme Soviet Commission, late in 1972, of the threat to the Tyumen' tundra and its wild life food by the impact of caterpillar tractors in summer, especially at the maximum thawing period of the permafrost. 'Construction firms should consider the manufacture of means of transport which would not destroy the thin vegetation cover on permafrost and thus threaten the food resources of northern wild life', stated the head of the Laboratory of the Extreme North of the Botanical Institute of the Academy of Sciences.

In the last few years, accounts of the way in which both natural life and its environment in Siberia are ravaged by unscrupulous and extremely ingenious poachers have frequently appeared in Soviet sources. Apparently, the sable is now threatened by these intruders in some of its best natural habitats, from Transbaykaliya and the Sayan mountains to the Primor'ye, while valuable fish like the salmon, likewise suffer from their ruthless overfishing. Apparently, this is not only the work of ordinary citizens but high Soviet and collective farm officials are also occasionally involved. It is curious that in the Soviet socialist society high profits can be made on the black market from these nefarious practices and that there should be no more care for socialist property among Soviet poachers, than there is for private property among their opposite numbers in capitalist society.

[9] *Conservation in the Soviet Union.* Philip R. Pryde. Cambridge University Press. 1972.

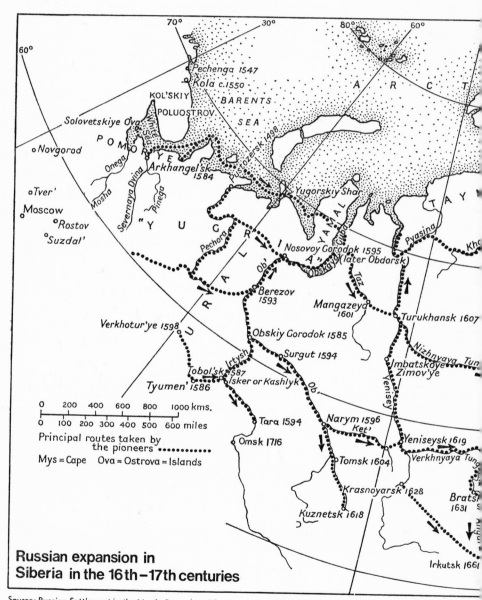

**Russian expansion in
Siberia in the 16th–17th centuries**

Source: Russian Settlement in the North. Reproduced by permission of Dr T Armstrong

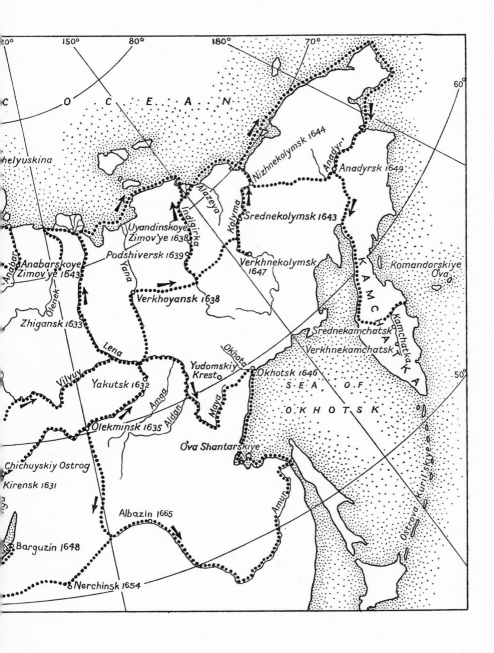

chapter two

The Russian Conquest
of Siberia

It might seem from a glance at the map of Asiatic Russia as
if Siberia, being geographically a natural extension of the great Eurasian plain, had
also always been Russian territory. But a brief survey of Russian expansion since
the sixteenth century belies any such assumption. From the last decades of the
sixteenth century, the frontiers of the small Grand Duchy of Muscovy expanded
rapidly across the Urals, and in the short space of about fifty years Russian pioneering Cossacks had pushed the frontiers of Russia eastwards, from the Urals to the
Pacific Ocean. It was a tremendous enterprise requiring great boldness and endurance.

Before advancing through Siberia in the fifteenth–sixteenth centuries, Russians
had no idea of the extent or nature of the vast lands lying beyond the Urals, or
whither their forward thrust would lead. All they knew of Siberia was the White
Sea littoral, or Pomor'ye, and the Yugrian and lower Ob' areas to which Russians
had voyaged for centuries, in search of the highly valued fur-bearing animals of the
region. But these were private ventures of Russian trappers and traders, unconnected
with ideas of conquest or permanent settlement. Further south there had also been
intermittent contact between the Russians and the Tatar Khanate of Sibir' which
controlled the native tribes in the Ob'-Irtysh area for some years before the conquest, and the local Siberian Tatar Khan Yediger Taybugid had recognised Ivan IV
(1533–84) as his vassal lord. By the time the Russians advanced into Sibir', this
Khan had been ousted by Kuchum, of the Bukharan Shaybanid family, who broke
off the tributary relationship with Moscovy in 1572. Kuchum was thus a hostile
force to be reckoned with by the Russians.

The fall of Kazan' to Ivan IV (the Terrible) in 1552 was a crucial event in the
Russian conquest of Siberia. The Muslims of Kazan' had long barred the easier
passage to Siberia *via* the Volga and this route now passed under Russian control.
The first to take advantage of this opportunity was the great merchant family of the
Stroganovs, anxious to extend their trade and fur trapping from their upper Kama
estates where the fur-bearing animals were declining, to Siberia.[1] They equipped

[1] For a fuller treatment of the question of the Russian conquest of Siberia, consult T. Armstrong's fine study *'Russian Settlement in the North'*. Cambridge University Press. 1965.

Yermak, a Don Cossack, to lead an expedition of Cossacks against Kuchum and his followers, in 1581. Having defeated Kuchum and seized his headquarters in Kashlyk (Sibir'), Yermak himself was drowned in 1584. Though the Bukharan Siberian chief Kuchum survived Yermak's campaign and continued to harass the Russians, a small local nucleus of Russian power was established by Yermak from which his inflated title of 'Conqueror of Siberia' originated. But his victory over Kuchum meant the end of the local Siberian Khanate.

Following Yermak's success for the Stroganovs, the Muscovy government soon realised the great economic value of this footing in Siberia for the lucrative fur trade and the further conquest of Siberia became a matter of government policy, conducted by mixed forces of military and Cossacks.

The *yasak*, or fur tribute, formerly taken by the Tatar khans was in turn imposed by the Russians on all the native peoples of Siberia, beginning with the chiefs of the Vogul (Mansi) and Ostyak (Khanty) tribes of west Siberia. Though in constant revolt against their new conquerors, they had no chance of success with their primitive weapons against superior Russian fire power. The Russian advance eastwards continued with great rapidity in spite of constant attacks from native peoples and difficult supply problems over immensely long stretches of country.

The whole area abounded in valuable, fur-bearing animals such as the sable, the ermine and squirrel, and these were the lure which drew the Russians ever further through the wide forest belt of Siberia.[2] Porterage between the great Siberian rivers and their tributaries largely determined the direction of their advance, as there were, of course, no maps or charts to guide the pioneering Cossacks. The desire to avoid the harassing tactics of the native Tatars and Bukharans in west Siberia and conflicts with the Tungus, Buryats and Mongols in the Yenisey-Baykal area, kept the direction of this advance in a more northerly direction than might otherwise have been taken. This is reflected in the dates of the establishment of the first Siberian towns. One of the first *ostrogi* or stockaded wooden forts (containing their houses, stores, etc.) built by the Russians was Tyumen' (1586), on the site of a former Tatar settlement and end-post of the Bukharan trade with Siberia; then Tobol'sk (1587), Surgut on the middle Ob' (1594), followed. From west Siberia, the advance in a north-easterly direction was marked by a further series of *ostrogs* (all later sites of towns): Tomsk (1604), Turukhansk (1607), Kuznetsk (1608), Yeniseysk (1618), Krasnoyarsk (1627), Yakutsk (1632), Okhotsk (1647), Nizhneudinsk (1647), Barguzin (1648), Irkutsk (1651), Chita (1655).

It is notable that Omsk was not established until 1716, when the Russians were advancing up the Irtysh towards the Jungarian lands of Central Asia. This great eastwards trek reached its limits when the Cossack Semen Dezhnev and his companions brought their little ships to the 'end of the Eurasian land mass' and through the narrow Straits separating the Eurasian mainland from Alaska, in 1647-49. But they were subsequently named not after Dezhnev, but Bering's expedition, eighty years later. The great mainland outpost of Kamchatka was annexed in 1697 by

---

[2] The predominant role of fur in the Russian conquest of Siberia is analysed in a masterly work by Raymond H. Fisher: *The Russian Fur Trade, 1550-1700.* University of California Publications in *History*, 1943 . . . to which I am greatly indebted.

Vladimir Atlasov, whose brutality and rapacious demands terrified the helpless natives.

This great Russian exploration adventure reached the Aleutians at the end of the eighteenth century and the first Russian colony was founded on Kodiak Island east of the Alaska Peninsula, in 1784. In 1799, the Tsar Paul I granted a charter to the Russian-American Company (a misleading title, for the company was wholly owned by the Russians) to operate a trading monopoly over Alaska, the Aleutians and the Kuril Islands. Russian America as this large area was then named, was annexed to the Imperial Crown, until sold by Alexander II in 1867 to the United States for the paltry sum of $7,200,000.[3]

When the Russians reached the Yenisey area, they were met with such strong opposition from the native princes and chiefs of the Buryat, Mongol, Tungus and other local peoples, that they thought it wiser to advance in a more northerly direction along the basin of the Lena towards Yakutiya, and wait until they were in a stronger position to deal with this opposition. The establishment of Yakutsk (1632) and Okhotsk (1647), before the less remote sites of Irkutsk (1651) and Nizhneudinsk (1647), was the result of this fierce native opposition to the Russians in the Buryat lands. Yakutiya was not occupied either without opposition, but it was less well organised and effective than the fight put up by the peoples round the southern shores of Lake Baykal and reaching into Mongolia where some of the tribes were 'vassals' to Mongolian feudal lords.

It may be interesting to note in passing that the current Soviet historical explanation of these bloody encounters with the Tungus, Mongols and other opponents of Russian subjugation at this time, is that this opposition stemmed from the local chiefs and princes, in an attempt to regain power over the 'native masses whom they were ruining' and who were seeking safety in 'Russian protection'. While it is true that there was a good deal of switching of allegiance from native overlords, such as the Mongols, to the Russians and back, in accordance with the fortunes of war, it is more plausible to regard this situation not as a case of 'the masses' rising against their chiefs, but of the shifting alliances of certain local chiefs and princes vis-à-vis the Russians, who showed considerable skill in winning them over, if only temporarily, with presents and other honours.

From the earliest days of the advance through Siberia, food supplies posed problems of the greatest difficulty and urgency for the Russians. With the exception of small pockets of arable land where grain was grown in west Siberia, Buryatiya and the Amur basin, Siberia was not a grain-growing country in the early years of Russian occupation. Grain however was an essential food stuff for the new inhabitants, the military, the official administration and the Cossack settlers. Peasants were therefore brought in from European Russia and settled within or round the *ostrog* to till the soil in the wake of the advancing forces. The need for grain was so great that natives growing grain were often relieved from the obligation to pay the fur tribute.[4] Grain was also exported from European Russia at great expense and

[3] For fuller details of this Russian-American Company see T. Armstrong, *Russian Settlement in the North*, op. cit. pp. 26-31.
[4] These problems are analysed in detail in James R. Gibbon's excellent study: *Feeding the*

with long delays, often resulting in terrible hardship for the settlers, along the unpredictable Siberian forest trails and rivers as far east as Okhotsk. The situation continued to be critical until agriculture was more widely and adequately developed by intensive peasant colonisation, from the end of the nineteenth century.

It was the rumour (allegedly from some Tungus) that good supplies of grain, as well as fur-bearing animals, gold and silver, might be had for the asking, that first attracted Russian attention to the still unexplored lands of Amuria. By the end of the seventeenth century, the Russians had traversed the entire expanse of north Asia to the Pacific where there were enormous stocks of valuable pelts and large mineral and forest resources. Siberian furs had become the most important single item in Russia's home and foreign trade, and the main source of revenue in the Russian treasury in the sixteenth–seventeenth centuries. But the great Far Eastern lands traversed by the Amur still awaited Russian exploration and conquest. This was nominally Chinese territory and therefore to be approached more cautiously than the Siberian tribal lands, so as to avoid a confrontation with Peking which might jeopardise the much prized Sino-Russian trade.

The first attempts to explore the Amur country came from Yakutsk in the north and not from the nearer, but still insecure, Russian outposts among the Buryats and Mongols. A small band of Yakutsk Cossacks under Poyarkov carried out a hazardous investigation along the Aldan–Zeya route to the mouth of the Amur in 1643–45 and returned to Yakutsk with alluring tales of grain, furs and other valuable commodities to be found in the Amur country. Poyarkov was followed by another expedition (1649–50) under the Ataman Khabarov (after whom the present town of Khabarovsk is named) and who, some Tsarist sources claim, was 'successful in establishing Russian power on the Amur'. This is an inflated claim, because both Poyarkov and Khabarov were strongly resisted by the local Dahurs and Duchers and their expedition resulted in a Manchu force being sent to the Amur to drive out Khabarov and the Russians. As the Manchus were armed with cannon and muskets they represented a much more formidable foe than the native Siberian tribes with their primitive weapons. Both Poyarkov and Khabarov had disgraced themselves and Russian power, as they moved along the Amur, by their high-handed extortions of grain, furs and anything else they fancied, and atrocious cruelty to the native peoples of the region. This brutal behaviour turned the native inhabitants against the Russians and led them to seek the protection of the Manchus (who were the rulers of China from 1644), thus introducing a new and decisive element into the progress of this stage of Russian expansion.

The struggle for control of the Amur continued for some forty years, with swaying fortunes between the Russians and the Manchu forces. The Manchus were not the militant party, but tried by various stratagems to achieve a settlement by negotiations rather than by force of arms.[5] During this time, the Russians set up a number of

Russian Fur Trade, 1639-1856. University of Wisconsin Press 1969. See also relevant section on 'Fur' below.

[5] For a detailed analysis of the Manchu attitude to the Russian intrusion into the Amur lands, cf. Marc Mancall's *Russia and China, Their Diplomatic Relations to 1728.* Harvard University Press, 1971.

peasant agricultural settlements and trading posts along the Amur: and a sort of shadow administration of this new province was established in 1658, at Nerchinsk. These attempts to colonise and annex the Amur lands were throughout resisted by Peking. In order to strengthen their position, the Russians established a fortified base at Albazin, in the centre of this agricultural area, and the former capital of a native prince and tribute-bearing vassal of Peking. With the aid of this Albazin base, it was hoped to protect the supply of Amur grain for the hard-pressed, grain-hungry colonists in Yakutsk. According to the latest official Soviet *History of Siberia*, the position of the Tsarist forces in these 'annexed lands' was 'complicated by the activisation of the aggressive policy of the Manchurian dynasty'. Neither then nor now has the Kremlin recognised that these were traditionally tribute-bearing territories of the Manchus, who thus were not strictly aggressors in defending them, and not a sort of no-man's-land which could be freely entered and annexed. After many skirmishes, expulsion and much parleying of peace, the Russian advance was temporarily halted by the destruction, by the Manchu forces, of the Russian fort of Albazin in 1685.

At this time the Manchus, now firmly established in Peking, militarily and diplomatically proved equal to a successful confrontation with the Russians, who were in a very weak position, thousands of miles from their main sources of supply and also fearful of a hostile attack in their rear from the Mongols. After a successful Manchu siege of the re-built Albazin fort, negotiations for peace started near Nerchinsk in Transbaykaliya and were concluded by the Treaty of Nerchinsk, in 1689. By this Treaty, the Russians had to abandon their settlements on the Amur and the Zeya, and all ideas of annexing these lands, for nearly two centuries. It delimited the Sino-Russian frontier along the Amur while the Russian possessions in Yakutiya and northern eastern Asia remained undisturbed. This was the first treaty to be signed by China with any foreign power. As the geography of the area between the Uda and the Amur was only very vaguely known to both sides, the delimitation of this frontier in the Treaty was far from accurate or precise and the ill-defined topographical provisions later led to much confusion and controversy.

By the supplementary and much more comprehensive Bura-Kyakhta Treaties in 1727, the 1,200 mile stretch of Sino-Russian frontier west of the Argun river (between Transbaykaliya and Mongolia), which had not been defined by Nerchinsk, was now defined, while detailed arrangements regulating the important Russo-Chinese caravan trade through Kyakhta were included in the Kyakhta Treaty. It was mutually agreed to leave the Uda-Gorbitsa territory undefined, until its geography was better known to both sides. Major frontier trading posts for the Sino-Russian caravan trade with Peking were established at Kyakhta (on the Siberian side) and, opposite, at Mai-mai-ch'eng (Trade Town) in Mongolia and continued to operate after the 'entire caravan trade died a natural death', in the middle years of the eighteenth century.

In the recent polemics with the Chinese about the Amur frontier, the Russians insist that the Treaty of Nerchinsk was concluded under duress and is therefore classified as 'unequal', while this is the only Sino-Russian Treaty not regarded as 'unequal' by the Chinese. There is little doubt that in 1689, the Chinese were in a much stronger military position than the Russians. Nerchinsk was an unfortified town and they could expect no further military help in this exposed place which the Chinese threatened to storm if the Russians did not sign. But, in fact, it suited both sides to come to agreement without having to resort to a prolonged armed struggle. Whether 'unequal' or not, and in the nature of things treaties cannot be expected to bring equal advantages to both sides in a quarrel, Nerchinsk was not only a most important event in Sino-Russian relations, establishing peace on the Amur frontier for nearly two hundred years, but it also concluded the first stage in the Russian conquest of Siberia.

Russia's initial opening up and acquisition of large areas of the Siberian mainland, starting in the sixteenth century, had its counterpart in the movement of other European powers outwards to equally unknown lands, but across the uncharted seas. Columbus, for example, had discovered America in 1492, about a century earlier than Yermak's Siberian expedition. Then there was the arrival of the Dutch in South Africa and the great trek northwards in 1652, and the planting of the British flag in Australia in the same century. The age of what is now known as 'Colonial-Imperialism' had begun. Russia was an active participant in this enterprise, but her colonies were on her doorstep, not across 'uncharted seas'.

In the mid-nineteenth century there was a new period of Russian expansion aiming at the final inclusion of the Amur lands in the Russian Empire. The moment was propitious for Russia. China, strong and secure at the time of Nerchinsk (1689), was now torn by civil strife and unable effectively to oppose the Russian plans for the annexation of the Far Eastern territory, from which the Russians had been expelled by the Manchus in 1689. The then Governor-General of Siberia, Count Murav'yev (Amurskiy, as he later became), acting more or less on his own initiative, seized this moment of China's weakness to extend Russian sovereignty throughout the entire length of the Amur and southwards to Vladivostok. Murav'yev was deeply convinced of the great future which awaited Siberia and the importance for her trade and development of access to the sea, through a port at the mouth of the Amur. Russia's national interests were paramount with him in this matter and he was not a man to be deterred by any moral scruples about ways and means, or China's territorial rights. Cossack posts and free colonists were arbitrarily settled from about 1855 along the Amur and the Ussuri rivers without regard for the reactions of the Chinese or the native inhabitants. The effects of this Russian colonisation movement on the native peoples in the years 1855–56 was poignantly described by a learned representative of the Russian Imperial Academy of Sciences Dr. Leopold Shrenk, in the following words: 'The indigenous peoples of the Amur are at present in the same process of degeneration as the Siberian natives and it may proceed more rapidly with them as a result of the fact that colonisation in the Amur kray is being tackled more energetically than anywhere in Siberia'. From the time of the unification of the Amur kray with Russia, its ethnographical features quickly changed, reported Shrenk. 'Now along the entire Amur and Ussuri river banks you can meet post stations and villages of Cossacks or free colonists every 20–30 versts.'

Before the protracted Sino-Russian frontier negotiations started (1857–58), the

Russians had forestalled the later treaty arrangements by including the lower Amur region in the Imperial administration and designated Nikolayevsk-na-Amure as the provincial centre of the new Russian Primorskiy (Maritime) Province. Two subsequent Sino-Russian treaties formally consolidated these Russian Pacific acquisitions. By the Treaty of Aigun (1858), China reluctantly ceded to Russia the left bank of the Amur, up to its confluence with the Ussuri, and both banks thence to the Pacific estuary of the river. Two years later, the Treaty of Peking rounded off this process of Russian Far Eastern territorial aggrandisement by the cession to her of the whole of the newly named Maritime Province, down to the Korean border. To crown these successes, Murav'yev named the new Russian city on the Korean border Vladivostok (Conquer the East). Neither of these treaties, which added some 40,000 sq. miles of Chinese territory to the Imperial Russian Empire, mentioned the island of Sakhalin. But, in 1875 by the Treaty of St. Petersburg, Japanese rights in Sakhalin were exchanged for Russian rights to all the Kuril islands, north of Etorfu. Unlike the rigid post-World War II exclusion of the Japanese from Sakhalin and its vicinity, the Treaty of St. Petersburg allowed Japanese fishermen to continue to fish off the coast of Sakhalin, and fishing, trade and navigation in the ports of the Sea of Okhotsk. They were also compensated for the loss of immovable property and allowed to open consular offices in Korsakov.[6]

The Soviets, like their Imperial predecessors, tend to regard these nineteenth-century treaties as merely a legal confirmation of a position established in the pre-Nerchinsk (1689) period, while in the Chinese view they belong to the long list of 'unequal treaties' arbitrarily imposed by Russia and other stronger powers in a period of Chinese weakness.

Nearly a century later, after World War II, Soviet Russia further expanded its Far Eastern possessions, this time at the expense of the Japanese. The whole of Sakhalin, formerly a condominium shared with Japan, passed into Soviet hands and all the Kuril Islands. These new Soviet possessions were of great strategic importance, while the economic resources of Sakhalin, notably its natural gas and oil, timber and fish, were also of no mean significance locally.

As already suggested, the Imperial Russian and Soviet approaches to the incorporation of Siberia and its native inhabitants in Russia differ sharply in some respects and are not at all so apart in others. Like the other colonial powers, Great Britain or France, pre-Revolutionary Russia saw nothing shameful or derogatory in the concept of a colony in which primitive or 'barbarous' peoples were subjugated to a power physically and culturally superior to them. Thus, a remarkable official publication 'Aziatskaya Rossiya' published in St. Petersburg in 1914 frankly stated: 'The lands of Asiatic Russia are an indivisible, inseparable part of our government and our only colony . . . Acquaintance with them and the glorious history of their acquisition is the inexhaustible source of the proud and joyous realisation of the greatness of Russia . . . Old Russia,' continued this patriotic tribute, 'with its outward austerity and abundance of untapped resources is being reborn in our Asiatic border lands.'

[6] cf. John J. Stephen's excellent account of Russo-Japanese relations in Sakhalin. *Sakhalin, A History*. Clarendon Press Oxford, 1971.

The voluntary submission to Russian power and acceptance of Russian sovereignty by the native inhabitants of Siberia, which has increasingly become the keynote of Soviet historiography, finds little or no echo in the more realistic pre-revolutionary histories of Russian expansion. The new Soviet *History of Sileria* (1968–69) repeatedly emphasises the lack of conflict between the Siberian aborigines and their Russian rulers, old and new, and their welcome to 'Soviet institutions'. This line overlooks the many bloody clashes between the Chukchis, the Yakuts and other native peoples and the Tsarist authorities, apart from the later difficulties experienced by the Soviet government itself, in imposing 'Soviet institutions' in native areas of Siberia.

Whatever the actual historical circumstances, passing under Russian rule, at any period, is now regarded by Soviet commentators as 'historically progressive' for all the peoples of the Soviet Union and security for 'the local peoples' is generally equated with submission to Russia. The present Soviet position has thus shifted far from Lenin's analysis, which was dominated by the 'evils of Tsardom' and the opposition to it of the subject peoples. According to *Narody Sibiri* (The Peoples of Siberia): 'The Russian state, growing economically and fortifying itself politically, required to expand and strengthen its frontiers. The annexation of Siberia, discovered by Russians, completely coincided with this aim. In Siberia, which was the natural continuation of the territory of the Russian state beyond the Urals, and which had great natural wealth and was so sparsely populated, the Moscow government saw a major source of territorial and economic development for Russia.' All this is true of course, but the *apologia* comes strangely from a communist country, so loud in its condemnation of other states for colonialist ventures, which could be justified in much the same terms, while ignoring negative aspects of the situation.

Tsarist Colonisation Policies. During the first 300 years of Russian rule in Siberia, the Russian immigrant population inevitably grew slowly, owing to the immense difficulties of transport and supply over the great distances separating the immigrants' homes and supply base in European Russia from the Siberian territory. These new Siberian settlements consisted for many years of small isolated groups of Cossacks, soldiers, traders, government officials and peasant farmers. All were encouraged to grow grain and keep cattle in cleared land round the new Russian settlements, so far as possible, to ease the always precarious food situation, especially in the many areas where the native population were neither grain nor cattle farmers.

At the end of the eighteenth century, the Russian population was roughly estimated at 575,000 and the native peoples at 363,000. Convicts were deported to work at hard labour in the forests and mines from the seventeenth century but, contrary to a widespread myth, they never formed a majority of the Russian population in Siberia. There were also penal colonies in Siberia, where exiled people lived a relatively free life but were prohibited from returning to their homes.

The population situation changed dramatically and rapidly at the end of the nineteenth century. The immediate cause was the replacement of the old and very primitive Siberian Trakt (or Great Siberian Post Road) by the construction of the nearly 6,000 mile long Trans-Siberian railway, connecting Moscow with Vladivostok. This trunk line facilitated a great peasant influx into Siberia aided by government grants for transport, housing, etc. Simultaneously, a new era of prosperity based on the successful expansion of agriculture began. The percentage of Russians and other migrants was constantly growing compared to that of the various groups of native peoples. By the time of the 1897 census Russians formed 82% of the total population, or 4,415,829 souls, and the indigenous peoples numbered 816,070. By 1911, the Russian population had leaped to $7\frac{1}{2}$ million or 86.5% of the total, with the native share at 10.9%, or 927,000.

Total Population of Siberia : Russians and other Migrants

1897	4,889,633
1911	8,393,469

(Source: Aziatskaya Rossiya pp 66-67, vol 1)

By 1911, the native population of Siberia was swamped in 'a Russian peasant sea'. Official settlement policies were heavily slanted in favour of the Russian peasant element. This had a double object, to relieve the poverty-stricken and overpopulated rural districts of European Russia and to provide a reliable, permanent basis for satisfying the acute and increasing food requirements of Siberia. Siberia thus became a predominantly peasant land and indistinguishable in its cultural-religious institutions from 'Mother Russia'. On the fringes of this Russian society lived the various native peoples, who maintained their own primitive cultures and hunting and fishing skills. Both the government agents and private operators squeezed and cheated them for pelts. Though the Speranskiy laws (1819) should have protected them from the depredations of unscrupulous traders and officials, they were for the most part ignored in practice, because so difficult to enforce at great distances from European Russia and the central administration, and because of the prevailing corruption in all planes of society.

The concentration on the peasant as the main element in the colonisation of Siberia, greatly restricted and impeded the economic development of Siberia under Tsardom. As a result of this policy, the population lacked many other useful elements such as tradesmen and members of essential professions, e.g. engineers, architects, lawyers, etc., who were only represented in relatively small numbers. They could have added much-needed variety and depth to the predominantly agricultural development of nineteenth-century Siberia and its social structure.

In another respect, Siberian development was hampered by official restrictions. In the United States of America and Australia, economic development proceeded at a much swifter rate and on more sophisticated lines than Siberia in the same century, largely due to the 'open door' immigration policy ensuring a valuable flow of multinational peoples with a great variety of skills – refugees from Russia and Poland, sturdy farming stocks from Germany and Scandinavia, professional elements (doctors, engineers, business managers, etc.) from all over Europe. Russian colonisation of Siberia, on the contrary, was exclusively drawn from rather limited domestic and peasant sources. Nevertheless, the great services rendered to the exploration and development of Siberia by Polish émigrés, Russian revolutionary exiles like Kropotkin and even Swedish prisoners of war, should not be overlooked. The restrictive official practices of the Russian government in regard to the colonisation of Siberia undoubtedly go far to explain the relative under-development of the country compared to America, up to the 1917 Revolution, even taking into account the more difficult geographical-climatic Siberian conditions.

On the other hand, great credit is due to the Russian peasant colonists of Siberia for their labours in creating a prosperous agriculture in their new homesteads, in the nineteenth century. Unshackled by the bonds of landlordism of European Russia, where they originated, they made a signal success of grain, butter and stock farming in the best Siberian lands. They also displayed an eager interest in the organisation of creamery and agricultural credit cooperatives, in the spread of education for their children and the acquisition of the most modern machinery for their farms. In all these initiatives they showed a degree of enterprise unknown among their fellows in European Russia. As a result, Siberian farms were better supplied with agricultural machinery and tools in 1914 than central Russia or the Ukraine and the numbers of stock, per hundred of the population, greatly exceeded that in European Russia.

No butter or other agricultural products now reach England or other foreign markets from Siberia. Yet, in the pre-Revolutionary years, Denmark and Britain among other countries imported large quantities of Siberian butter. The Danes had their own creameries in Siberia and some English firms importing butter from Siberia aided the cooperatives with credit to purchase equipment and refrigeration for the export of butter.

It was not only colonisation that suffered from the often ill-informed controls imposed by the bureaucrats of St. Petersburg. The administration of Siberia was seriously undermined by widespread incompetence and corruption. Incensed by the harm done to this potentially rich country by misgovernment, some patriotic well-educated Sibiryaki formed a loosely organised 'regionalist' group known as the 'Oblastnichestvo' in the early nineteenth century. They vaguely thought in terms of regionalism or separatism for Siberia. Their views were expounded with great vigour by one of their leaders, N. M. Yadrintsev, in a long work Sibir kak Koloniya (St. Petersburg 1882). He painted a deplorable picture of the state of affairs in Siberia at this time and though his account is possibly exaggerated, he pointed to many real grievances. In the first place, he violently denounced the Siberian administration and the merchant class for their ruthless wanton exploitation of Siberian land, forests, fur-bearing animals and other natural resources and their total indifference to the oppression of the labourers and the lives of the native peoples. The plundering of natural resources had gone so far as to lead in some parts of Siberia to the virtual extinction of valuable animals, like the sable and the squirrel in the Far East. Another feature of Siberian life that aroused Yadrintsev's ire was the extremely low prices paid by Russian merchants for Siberian raw materials, for which they were the only market, and the exorbitant prices extracted in return for all manufactured goods, including the same Siberian raw materials processed in various forms in European Russia.

The lack of development in Siberia, in spite of its great latent wealth, was most unfavourably contrasted by Yadrintsev with the situation in the 'developing countries of America and Australia'. One of the reasons for this disparity, he thought, was that no solid bases of industry had been established by the Russians, who only diminished or exhausted the land's productivity and showed no trace of humanity towards the workers. Exceptionally, Yadrintsev had some words of praise for the generosity of those Siberian merchants who had contributed lavishly towards the establishment of Siberia's first University in Tomsk, in 1886. Finally, Yadrintsev regarded union with Russia as 'an historical misfortune for the native peoples of Siberia' bringing them only oppression and misery. Siberia, he believed, had developed by 'special paths' and should therefore pursue a 'separatist path' from European Russia, if it was to attain the prosperous future it merited from its immense natural riches. It should not be overlooked that the Siberia of Yadrintsev's censure was the country before the advent of the Trans-Siberian railway.

Not surprisingly, these criticisms of the *Oblastniki* failed to impress the Russian bureaucracy either in Siberia or St. Petersburg. But they hit many rotten nails on the head in their time.

The Establishment of Soviet power in Siberia.[7]

The transition from Tsarist to Soviet power in Siberia and the Far East, following the Bolshevik revolution of 1917, was a complex and protracted business. Soviet rule was not easily established and civil war broke out after a confused interregnum in 1918. The peasants, who formed the great majority of the population, were not drawn to the Bolsheviks, as they had been in European Russia, by their land programme. There were no landlords in Siberia and the peasants were prosperous and amply endowed with land and farm animals. National groups like the Buryats, who had many old scores to settle with their former masters, also emerged demanding their independence of Russia, while the Yakut revolt was not finally quelled till 1923. The Bolsheviks also had trouble with Russian 'regionalists' who like their nineteenth-century predecessors the *Oblastniki*, wanted to run Siberia free from the bureaucratic controls of St. Petersburg or Petrograd.

By mid-1918, Allied and American intervention had become a factor in the Siberian opposition to the Bolsheviks and Admiral Kolchak's White armies had reached western Siberia from Vladivostok, while the Japanese were moving along the Trans-Siberian railway to Lake Baykal. At the same time, the Czech Legion, made up from former prisoners of war, was obstructing the eastwards movements of the Red Army by its efforts to control the Trans-Siberian railway, so as to ensure the safe evacuation of its men through Vladivostok. Kolchak, with his headquarters established in Omsk, was recognised by the Allies as the 'Supreme Ruler' of Russia on the rather slender basis of his opposition to the Bolsheviks.

By 1919–20, as the struggle was fought out with swaying fortunes between the Red Army and Kolchak's Whites, it was clear that the lack of unity in the anti-Bolshevik front, Kolchak's reactionary and anti-nationalist policies, plus dis-

[7] As this is not a political history of Siberia, the events leading to the establishment of Soviet power in Siberia are only very briefly noted in this section. Fuller information may be found in works quoted in the Bibliography.

reputable elements in his entourage and the often cruel depredations of his armed forces, had badly alienated the local populations. Hard pressed by the much more disciplined but no less brutal Red Army, reinforced by local bands of partisans, Kolchak was finally defeated near Irkutsk and shot in 1920. With his disappearance, the anti-Bolshevik front in Siberia collapsed and opened the door to the establishment of Soviet power from the Urals to Irkutsk.

East of Lake Baykal, where Japanese influence was still strong, a curious situation existed between 1920–22. With the approval of the Soviets and the Japanese, neither of which at this stage was anxious for an armed confrontation, a Far Eastern Republic was set up in Chita with a mixed communist-bourgeois government, a curious and unstable institution. It lasted until 1922 when it was absorbed 'by mutual consent' in the R.S.F.S.R., as the Japanese finally left the Russian mainland. The occupation of Sakhalin by Japan lasted until 1925. Soviet power may then be said to have been officially established from the Urals to the Pacific when the Japanese withdrew and Sakhalin became Soviet territory by agreement with Japan.

Though the Bolsheviks had routed their armed opponents in this Siberian civil war, they had by no means subdued the Siberian peasant masses. This was not accomplished until the collectivisation campaigns of the thirties which destroyed the former thriving Siberian agriculture and the more prosperous thrifty Siberian farmers were eliminated as being socially undesirable elements, or kulaks. Siberian agriculture has not yet recovered from this catastrophe.

chapter three

Government and Administration

The vast Siberian territory is governed by the same centralised State power and Party organs as exist throughout the rest of the Soviet Union and notably the Supreme Soviet of the U.S.S.R. and the Congress of the C.P.S.U. The main features of this all-Union system of dual controls may be assumed to be to some extent familiar to the general reader. Specific mention will therefore be made here only of certain features peculiar to Siberia and of how the system operates there. Though widely used and historically important, the term Siberia has no administrative significance. For planning purposes however Siberia is divided into three regions: west Siberia, east Siberia and the Soviet Far East. Geographically, the area known as Siberia is a part, and by far the largest part, of the R.S.F.S.R. to which it is politically subordinated.

Siberia is also divided into a number of administrative units: autonomous republics, autonomous oblasts, national okrugs, krays and oblasts. And in the formation of this administrative structure, the traditional habitats of major national groups of Siberia like the Buryats or Yakuts have to a large extent been maintained.

The highest unit in the Soviet state hierarchy in Siberia is the autonomous republic. Constitutionally, autonomous republics (A.S.S.R.) have the right to their own constitution 'which takes account of the specific features of the Autonomous Republic', with the overriding restriction that it must be drawn up in full conformity with the Constitution of the Union Republic to which it is subordinated, in this case the R.S.F.S.R. Moreover, all laws and regulations of these Siberian republics must be approved by the R.S.F.S.R. They neither have the right of secession which is granted (if only theoretically) to the Union Republics like the R.S.F.S.R. or the Ukraine nor, even more important, is there any Constitutional provision by which they may eventually attain the higher status of Union republic, and thus have the right, *inter alia*, of 32 rather than 11 deputies in the Council of Nationalities. In fact their political rights are extremely limited.

There are three autonomous republics in Siberia: the Buryat A.S.S.R., the Tuvinian A.S.S.R. and the Yakut A.S.S.R. That these peoples, and not some others, were selected for this precedence among the native peoples of Siberia was, presumably, because all three form compact groups in their historic homelands, but, with the exception of the Tuvinians, they are now outnumbered at home by the Russians. Two groups of Buryats have been separated from the Buryat A.S.S.R. and attached respectively to the Irkutsk and Chita oblasts: the Ust'-Ordynskiy Buryatskiy national okrug and the Aginskiy Buryatskiy national okrug, respectively. This separation of Buryat tribal groups probably had its origin in the historical hostility of the Buryats to the Russians and was regarded as a means of weakening them in case of trouble. Among other national okrugs are the Taymyrskiy (Dolgano-Nenetskiy), Evenkiyskiy, Koryakskiy and the Chukatskiy national okrugs.

There are also three autonomous oblasts: the Gorno-Altayskaya, the Jewish, and the Khakasskaya. Thus, the names of the larger of the many national groups in Siberia have been singled out as the titular designations of their individual administrative units, while other native peoples are anonymously included in the various krays and oblasts of Siberia. This is primarily true of the 'little peoples' of the Soviet Far North and Far East such as the Yukagir, Gol'd, Samoyed, Ket or Eskimo. They are obviously regarded officially as too small numerically to merit a separate administrative national unit.

Some of the largest territorial units in the Soviet Union are in Siberia, e.g. the Tyumen' oblast, with an area of 1,435.2 th. sq. km., the Krasnoyarsk kray, with 2,401.6 th. sq. km, or the Magadan oblast, with 1,199.1 th. sq. km. Magadan, by a rather crude administrative decision, contains the historic homelands of the Chukchi people (organised as a national okrug in 1920), though the new town of Magadan exists only since 1939 and the Magadan oblast since 1953. Its area largely coincides with the former notorious *Dal'stroy* concentration camp territory.

Siberians (*Sibiryaki*) of all races enjoy the same political rights as the other citizens of the Soviet Union. Thus, all the inhabitants of Siberia who have reached the age of eighteen are entitled to vote without distinction of race, sex, ethnic or social origin. Any citizen of twenty-three or over can be elected a deputy of the Supreme Soviet, the supreme organ of state power in the Soviet Union, in which is vested the 'exclusive' power of legislation. The Supreme Soviet is a bicameral institution and Siberians, like all Soviet citizens, reach its two chambers by two different voting procedures. Voting for the Council of the Union is by electoral districts, on the basis of one deputy for every 300,000 of the population. Here the numerically predominant Russians have a clear majority of deputies, or 455, while most of the native peoples of Siberia who do not number 300,000 have no representation in this Chamber at all. With a population of 812,000, Buryatiya has now made the grade, owing to the large Russian influx, while Yakutiya with a population of 664,000 is also eligible, largely for the same reason: but the Tuva A.S.S.R. with less than 300,000 citizens does not yet qualify.

The Council of Nationalities is elected on an entirely different basis. Irrespective of the size of the local population, the national administrative units have the right to send a fixed number of delegates to this Chamber. Thus, the Union republics elect 32 deputies each (formerly 25), the Autonomous Republics 11 deputies, the Autonomous oblasts 5 deputies and the national okrugs 1; such in brief outline is the pattern of Soviet central government in Siberia.

Below the central government representation, the 'local organs of state power' are the local Soviets, or councils, which are to be found throughout Siberia in the krays, oblasts, autonomous oblasts, the towns and villages. Their business is to deal with the local problems of public health, schools, roads, protection of citizens' rights and maintenance of public order, etc. etc., in their respective areas. Political-constitutional questions such as a change of constitutional status from autonomous republic to Union republic are not within their competence but should they be raised would get short shrift from higher authority. Discussion and decision on such matters are strictly a monopoly of the Supreme Soviet in Moscow. Though these Soviets are essentially executive organs of the central Government and decisions by, and elections to, them are strictly controlled by the Party, they provide many of the native peoples of Siberia with a new and useful experience in participating in local activities and voluntary service to the community. They vary greatly in size, from 25 for a village, to 100 deputies for a kray such as Krasnoyarsk, or a large oblast such as Irkutsk or Chita. Each Soviet elects an executive committee which is responsible not only to the Soviet which elects it, but also to the executive committee next above it in the government hierarchy. This system of subordination and supervision is aimed at keeping the local Soviets on their toes and preventing any deviation from central government plans in their areas. Deviations and scandals are none the less frequent and are reported in the metropolitan press, without sparing the culprits.

The system of national representation in the Council of Nationalities is, as far as Siberia is concerned, highly selective. While compact, settled groups like the Buryats, the Yakuts and the Tuvinians have their own autonomous republics, even this relatively exalted status presents a delicate issue for Soviet constitutional lawyers, who are at pains to gloss over the constitutional disabilities of these largely nominal republics. Their citizens cannot be represented in the Presidium of the Supreme Soviet (formed by the chairmen of the Union republics), which has important legislative-diplomatic functions between sessions of the Supreme Soviet.

That half-way constitutional institution the Autonomous Oblast, the status held in Siberia by, for example, the Khakassy and the Jewish peoples, in fact has little or no genuine autonomy. Before becoming effective, all their decisions are subject to the jurisdiction of the Krasnoyarsk and Khabarovsk krays, respectively, to which they are constitutionally subordinate.

The following table gives the total number of deputies from Siberian constituencies in the Council of the Union (8th Session 1970). The Council of the Union is elected by electoral constituencies on the basis of one deputy per 300,000 of the population, irrespective of nationality. There is, however, a fixed norm of deputies for the different national divisions of the Council of Nationalities irrespective of the numerical strength of these individual units however small, e.g. an autonomous oblast or a national okrug.

Analysis by nationality of the total number of deputies elected by Siberian national divisions to the Council of Nationalities throws up some interesting discrepancies which are not immediately obvious. It must not, for example, be presumed that all these deputies belong to the titular nationality in question. For example, the Buryat republic as an Autonomous Republic has the right to send

Number of Deputies elected to the Council of the Union from Siberia

Autonomous republics	Population	No. of deputies
RSFSR	130,049,000	423
Buryat ASSR	812,000	3
Yakutsk ASSR	664,000	2
Tuvinsk ASSR	231,000	1
Krays		
Krasnoyarskiy	2,962,000	10
Altayskiy	2,670,000	9
Primorskiy	1,721,000	6
Khabarovskiy	1,346,000	4
Oblasts		
Amurskaya	793,000	3
Irkutskaya	2,313,000	7
Kamchatskaya	288,000	1
Magadanskaya (including Chukotskiy nat. okrug)	353,000	1
Kemerovskaya	2,918,000	10
Novosibirskaya	2,505,000	8
Omskskaya	1,824,000	6
Sakhalinskaya	615,000	2
Tomskaya	786,000	3
Tyumenskaya	1,406,000	4
Chitinskaya	1,145,000	4

11 deputies to the Council of Nationalities, but according to a Soviet analysis of the composition of this Chamber by nationality (in 1970), only 7 of these 11 delegates were in fact Buryats. In the case of the Tuvinian A.S.S.R., out of its 11 delegates again only 7 were native Tuvinians. The Yakut delegation of 11 contained only 5 Yakuts.

It is not possible to break down the national composition of the constituent divisions of the Council of the Union in the same way. But the total Siberian representation by nationalities in both chambers of the Supreme Soviet is shown in the table below.

Composition by Nationalities of the Supreme Soviet (1970)

Council of the Union		Council of Nationalities	In Joint Session
Russians	455	102	647
Buryats	2	7	9
Tatars	6	12	18
Tuvinians	1	7	8
Yakuts	1	55	6
Altaytsy	—	3	3
Jews	2	4	6
Khakasy	—	3	3
Koryaki	—	1	1
Nentsy	—	2	2
Dolgany	—	1	1
Khanty	—	1	1
Chukchi	—	1	—
Evenki	—	1	—
Eveny	—	1	—

The above-listed Siberian peoples have a constitutional right either to representation in the Council of the Union, or the Council of Nationalities, or both Chambers.

There are however many small peoples in Siberia and especially in the Soviet Far East, such as the Yukagiry or the Nanaytsy, who constitutionally are denied representation in either Chamber. They are too small for a seat in the Council of the Union and are not eligible for the Council of Nationalities because they lack a titular national status, such as an okrug.

Towering numerically over all nationalities in the Council of Nationalities come the Russians, with 102 delegates, though as a Union Republic their quota is only 32. The explanation of this anomaly is of course that the Russians are spread pretty thickly throughout the Soviet Union and, in view of their prominence in all spheres of public life in the various national units, are often elected by them as part of their delegations to the Council of Nationalities. There is no constitutional ruling on the nationality of the individual members of the delegations to either the Council of Nationalities or the Council of the Union. A Tungus, or a Buryat, living in Yakutiya might well therefore form part of the Yakut delegation to the Council of Nationalities, or serve as a delegate to the Council of the Union from one of the Irkutsk or Krasnoyarsk constituencies. It is interesting in this connection to note that there are 55 Yakut deputies in the Council of Nationalities although the Yakut Autonomous Republic, as such, is only entitled to 11 deputies. The other Yakuts in this Council have therefore been elected by other constituent members than the Yakut A.S.S.R.

Though the proportion of Russians is high in the local organs of state power in the native areas of Siberia, the native elements are also quite well represented in these bodies. Soviet statistics for 1965 show that among the deputies of all nationalities to these bodies there were: 6,457 Yakuts, 4,671 Buryats, 1,647 Tuvinians, 946 Altayitsy, 704 Khakasy and more than 3,900 representatives of northern Siberian peoples: Evenki (traditionally better known as the Tungus), Chukchi and others. Among these delegates elected to local Soviets in 1965, collective farmers were a conspicuously small number, or 15.6%, while the corresponding figure for workers directly engaged in production was 42.6% and for women 42%. The proportion of delegates who were members and candidate members of the C.P.S.U. was 42.5%.

The local Party apparatus[1] in Siberia is organised on roughly the same territorial basis as the administrative sub-divisions of the country: krays, oblasts (in which for Party purposes are included the autonomous republics and the autonomous oblasts), and okrugs (or circuits). At a lower level there are numerous city, urban and rural district Party organisations. There is also the functional organisation of the Party, with primary party units in industrial enterprises, state and collective farms, and government, educational, cultural, scientific, and trading institutions.

It has been officially claimed that between 1959 and 1966, the Party ranks in Siberia grew from 948,000 to 1,400,000. This included Party members from among the settled Siberian population and those joining the Party from other parts of the country. Not surprisingly, the strongest party organisation was in the highly

---

[1] For a succinct account of the Party-Soviet organisation cf., L. Schapiro, *The Government and Politics of the Soviet Union*. London, 1965.

A more detailed analysis of the Communist Party is given in T. H. Rigby's *Communist Party Membership in the USSR 1917-1967*. Princeton. 1968. I am much indebted to both works.

industrialised oblast of Kemerovo, where there was a 40% increase between the twenty-second and twenty-third Party Congresses of the C.P.S.U. Favourable official reports of the growth of the Omsk and Buryat party organisations were also given.

A close analysis of the Party position in west Siberia, east Siberia and the Far Eastern Region, reveals other, less promising, aspects of the Party in these areas.[2] West Siberia, though one of the most important industrial regions of the U.S.S.R. and containing a relatively small rural population, had a party membership continuously below the national average of 4.5% in 1961. As in the Donbas, mining and metallurgy are the key industries in west Siberia, and this shows in Dr. Rigby's expert opinion that 'intensive industrial development of this kind is not particularly conducive to high party membership'. The situation is much the same in east Siberia, which had a −12% under-representation in the C.P.S.U. in 1961. But in the Soviet Far Eastern Region, the situation was very different. In 1939, it contained more party members in relation to population than any other region in the country. 'This undoubtedly reflected the large concentrations of military, naval and corrective labour camp personnel in the area. By 1961, it had slipped back to the third most party-saturated region, presumably due to the drastic contraction of the corrective labour camp system, but its party membership level still contrasted sharply with those in the rest of Soviet Asia' where they are notably low.[3]

The recent Russian *History of Siberia* (vol. V, p. 379) described the relations between the Party and the Soviets in Siberia as follows:

'The Party organs basically conduct their work through the Soviets and the public organisations, striving not to replace them in direct practical activity.' But, it admitted 'that although the role of the Soviets and public organisations increased during the period under investigation (up to 1966), some habits of the past and forces of inertia were not entirely overcome. . . . The Party organs sometimes took decisions of a narrowly economic character, thus replacing the economic and administrative directors.' Indeed, in view of the leading role assigned to the Party cadres to stimulate increased productivity and all aspects of plan fulfilment, it is easy to understand how they often overstep their role as a sort of ginger group and become directly involved in management.

In some of the national areas responsible posts are held by natives, but this is far from always being the case. It seems to happen more frequently in Yakutiya than elsewhere. But native or Russian, it is remarkable how critical some of the leading Party officials from important bodies like the Krasnoyarsk kraykom or the Irkutsk *obkom*, for example, can be of the policies enforced by remote 'armchair economists' and industrial ministries in Moscow (many instances of which are given throughout the following pages). Being so much closer to their local bailiwicks than centralised economic organs like *Gosplan* or *Gossnab*, or the relevant ministries, they often do not hesitate to indict them by name for their planning blunders and other deficiencies harmful to local Siberian interests. If long enough in the saddle, they seem to

[2] These statistics are confined to 1961 because according to Dr. Rigby, 'there is not enough information to extend this analysis beyond 1961'.
[3] T. H. Rigby, op. cit. p. 505.

develop a definite feeling of local patriotism for their particular areas. Indeed, some have paid the penalty of demotion, or worse, for too blunt but seemingly well justified criticism of Moscow's Siberian planning.

For the purpose of economic administration (apart from Soviet-Party organisation), Siberia is divided into three main regions: west Siberia, east Siberia and the Far Eastern Region. Over the years, there have been a bewildering number of changes in the internal sub-divisions of these Regions, such as the shifting of the Tyumen' oblast from the Urals Region to west Siberia, or the Yakut A.S.S.R. from east Siberia to the Far Eastern region in 1966. As of 1972, the regional structure was as follows:

West Siberian region

Altayskiy kray
including the Gorno-Altayskaya aut. oblast
Kemerovskaya oblast
Novosibirskaya oblast
Omskaya oblast
Tomskaya oblast
Tyumenskaya oblast including: the Khanty-Mansiyskiy nat. okrug Yamayo-Nenetskiy
    nat. okrug

East Siberian region

Krasnoyarsk kray
including:
Khakasskaya aut. oblast
Taymyskiy (Dolgano-Nenetskiy) national okrug
Evenkiyskiy national okrug
Irkutskaya oblast
including: Ust'-Ordynskiy Buryatskiy national okrug
Chitinskaya oblast
including: Aginskiy Buryatskiy national okrug
Buryatskaya ASSR
Tuvinskaya ASSR

Far Eastern Region

Primorskiy kray
Khabarovskiy kray
including Jewish aut. oblast
Amurskaya oblast
Kamchatskaya oblast
including the Koryakskiy national okrug
Magadanskaya oblast
including Chukotskiy national okrug
Sakhalinskaya oblast
Yakutskaya ASSR

Industry and agriculture within these regions are administered by either Union Republican or all-Union ministries, all with their headquarters in Moscow. This is also true of the authoritative State Committees: the State Planning Committee (*Gosplan*); State Committee for Construction Affairs (*Gosstroy*) and other top level organs responsible for basic decisions on Siberian development. Thus, the overall planning and administration of Siberia's main resources is in the hands of State agencies, often thousands of miles away from the mining and other industrial projects involved in their decisions. This frequently leads to differences of opinion between remote Moscow's top brass and the regional party leaders and industrial bosses on the spot, about financial and other points in these decisions.

Though all major decisions regarding the economic development of Siberia and the related investment policies are taken by the higher Party organs in Moscow and unfailingly approved by the Supreme Soviet, this does not mean that these policies are imposed without consultation with local Siberian officials and experts whose views of course may be overruled in the process, or on the contrary they may effectively procure adjustments in draft plans more favourable to Siberian interests. The interventions of the Siberian delegates from the larger units at the Supreme Soviet sessions are as often as not extremely businesslike, pointing to the need for additional budgetary subventions for one project or another, or a criticism of some item in the draft plan which in their view should be revised. There is plenty of evidence to show how active Siberian representatives can be, in lobbying influential people in Moscow, so as to ensure financial or other support for locally favoured schemes, when plans are being drafted. They do not always get their way, but especially when not involving major expenditure, proposals put forward by Siberian deputies at meetings of the Supreme Soviet seem on the whole to be duly noted and implemented in the final draft of the plan.

Some of the most primitive territories of Siberia and the Soviet Far East have been the scene of spectacular recent discoveries of natural wealth. Thus, much of the great reserves of natural gas and oil in west Siberia have come to light in the traditional lands of the Khanty-Mansi people. The new Soviet diamond fields were discovered in virtually uninhabited western Yakutiya; further east, among Chukchi, Yukagir, Eskimo, still semi-nomadic reindeer breeders, hunters and fishermen, enormous resources of gold, tin, tungsten and other precious metals are now being exploited. There was no question at any period of consulting the local peoples about these mining developments. Legally, as all land and natural resources in the Soviet Union are nationalised, the Government is not obliged to consult them. This does not of course preclude reactions (however impotent or passive) among the native peoples of the North (or elsewhere) about the resulting drastic changes in the environment of their natural habitats, involving a threat to the wild life on which, as fishermen and trappers, they have traditionally depended.[4]

The realities of the power situation in the native areas of Siberia and the Soviet Far Eastern Region thus emerge more sharply in the decisions of the all-Union government in Moscow, than in the very original and complex framework of local government so skilfully drafted by Soviet constitutional lawyers, the positive aspects of which are regularly stressed by the Soviet media and other commentators, to the exclusion of more critical interpretations.

[4] This subject is further discussed in Chapter 10: *Soviet Policies and the Native Peoples of Siberia.*

chapter four

The Economy

The natural resource base of Siberia and the Soviet Far East is exceptionally rich and varied. And in regard to metals and energy, Siberian reserves are probably unique in the world today. In fact the Soviet clichés 'immeasurable', 'incomparable' or 'inexhaustible' are scarcely hyperbolical in this case. Among the few deficient minerals are high quality bauxites, an expansion of the known iron ore deposits which are scarcely adequate for the expanding local heavy industry, and manganese. The intensive post-war exploitation of Siberia's great energy reserves, coal, oil and natural gas and water-power, has been a providential asset for the deficit energy balance of European Russia and the Ukraine, as well as giving a great boost to regional industrialisation.

Official Soviet estimates credit the Siberian landmass with nine-tenths of the Union's bituminous coal reserves, two-thirds of its iron ores, four-fifths of the total timber stands, the largest national oil and natural gas deposits (both possibly also the largest in the world), enormous water power potential and very rich reserves of gold, tin, copper and other non-ferrous and precious metals.[1] Intensive geological prospecting, originally inspired by Khrushchev's ambitious Siberian plans, is constantly expanding these known resources and checking estimates of reserves. Thus it was only in the late fifties that Siberia's rich deposits of oil and natural gas were discovered and in the same decade the great copper porphyry of Udokan came to light.

In spite of this successful record, much of Siberian territory still awaits the geologist's revealing hammer. No complete geological map of Siberia yet exists, though it is in the making. If the future course of events runs true to that of recent years, further useful and profitable mineral finds may be expected to enrich the Soviet treasury, including even bauxites, so badly needed by the huge new Siberian aluminium industry now dependent on local nephelines.[2]

The development of Siberian economic resources has up to the present been

[1] cf. *Istoriya Sibiri* (History of Siberia), 1969. vol. V.
[2] A more detailed analysis of the different branches of the economy only generally surveyed here, is given in the following chapters.

basically a domestic Soviet responsibility, involving neither foreign capital nor labour (though this situation is now changing with the multi-national cooperation projects). In this respect, it has been in striking contrast to the early development of the United States, Canada and Australia, in which foreign capital and labour played an important role. The motive power propelling Siberia into the modern world of industrialisation by large injections of capital, labour and technology is in Moscow, while the native inhabitants have little or no say in these decisions.

After the revolution, attention was first directed in a practical way to the development of Siberia by Stalin's early five-year plans in the thirties. This move was in accordance with Lenin's emotive ideological dictum, stressing the importance of developing the former underdeveloped areas of Tsarist Russia and the need to create industries nearer the sources of raw materials in the Eastern territories. But in the case of Siberia, the first Soviet stage of industrialisation was inspired not so much by ideology as by the basic strategic aim of creating a second metallurgical base far from the vulnerable Donbas–Leningrad areas, where Russia's chief metallurgical-defence industries were then situated. Great iron and steel plants were built in the Urals and the Kuzbas, fed by a shuttle-rail service, bringing Kuzbas coal to the energy-poor Urals and the high quality Urals iron to the new plants in the Kuzbas. On this basis, the heavy industry of central Siberia expanded in many directions and proved invaluable when the German invasion of 1941 overran the defence industries of southern Russia and the Ukraine.

More comprehensive plans to develop Siberian resources date essentially from the post-war period and Khrushchev's eastwards drive, beginning with his ambitious 'Virgin Lands' scheme (1953–54) in southern Siberia and north-west Kazakhstan. A considerable impetus to the diversification of industry had been given by the evacuation to Siberia of plant, mostly engineering, with some light industrial factories, from areas in European Russia threatened by the German advance during World War II. A good deal of this plant, and some of the workers evacuated with it, remained permanently in Siberia. Relatively little attention was, however, paid to Siberia in the post-war period, until Khrushchev awoke to its importance and made this plain in a major speech at the Twentieth Party Congress in 1956[3]. As a result of his interest, large investment funds were allocated to Siberia to fulfil the often excessive targets set for the region by the sixth and seventh five-year plans (and which were eventually cut down). A section of the new Party Programme in 1961 defined in general terms Siberia's economic role 'within the next twenty years' as: 'the creation of new large power bases using deposits of cheap coal or the water power of the Angara and Yenisey rivers; the organisation of big centres of power-consuming industries and the completion in Siberia of the country's third metallurgical base, the development of new rich ore and coal deposits; and the construction of a number of new large engineering centres; the rapid development of the power, oil, gas, and chemical industries and the development of ore deposits'. In fact, as emphasised in this programme, Siberian industrialisation in the decade since 1961 has been consistently dominated by the energy, extraction and heavy industries, while light industries have received relatively little attention. Essential

[3] cf. Chapter 12.

domestic-consumption goods such as clothing, footwear and household utilities as a result of this neglect, have to be largely imported from European Russia.

Siberian post-war industrial expansion is reflected in the rapid growth of the older urban centres while completely new towns are constantly arising around mining and hydro-power sites in formerly uninhabited taiga and tundra, extending to the bleak shores of the Arctic. Noril'sk, Mirnyy, Zelenyy Mys, Cherskiy, Lensk, Aykhal, are some of these mushroom growths, others are not yet identifiable on Soviet maps. A look at the map, however, shows the great distances separating the larger towns like Krasnoyarsk or Irkutsk and the extent of the area still very sparsely inhabited in spite of the growth of urban centres.

Population of some larger Siberian Towns

	1959	1970
Abakan	56,000	90,000
Angarsk	135,000	204,000
Bratsk	43,000	155,000
Irkutsk	366,000	451,000
Kemerovo	289,000	385,000
Khabarovsk	322,744	437,000
Komsomolsk-na-Amure	177,000	218,000
Krasnoyarsk	412,000	648,000
Magadan	62,000	92,000
Nakhodka	64,000	105,000
Novokuznetsk	382,000	499,000
Noril'sk	118,000	136,000
Novosibirsk	885,000	1,161,000
Omsk	581,108	821,000
Tyumen	150,000	269,000
Vladivostok	290,608	442,000
Yakutsk	53,000	108,000

Source: Nar. Khozyaystvo RSFSR v 1969

Over the last thirty years, as a result of the growth of productive forces in the regions east of the Urals, the 'economic proportions' between the western and eastern territories have significantly changed. The eastern regions have increased their contribution to the all-Union economy primarily in regard to energy and energy resources: 40% of all coal output, more than one quarter of the natural gas and one quarter of the electric power produced in the country originates there, and the proportion is constantly increasing. The largest oil and natural gas reserves being operated at present in the Soviet Union are in western Siberia. Siberian oil and natural gas are now reaching energy-deficient European Russia and it is hoped eventually to be able to extend the long high-power transmission lines to supply the central regions also with Siberian electricity. The location of a new aluminium industry in eastern Siberia, based on cheap local water power, has resulted in 'great expansion of all-Union aluminium production'. The formerly underdeveloped northern regions of Siberia have been found to be extremely rich in valuable minerals, e.g. nickel-copper, gold, tin, oil and natural gas. According to Academician Nekrasov some 25 milliard roubles had been invested in developing the resources of north Siberia up to 1969. Some Soviet specialists have criticised this policy on various grounds. Thus, there seems a good deal of support for the view that the range of industrial activity in the North has become far too wide and that it should be limited to basic production, while auxiliary technical facilities now widely established at great cost of labour and money should be provided by the older industrial towns in the south of the region. These facilities include such side-lines as repair shops making spare parts and other equipment and even consumer goods. In Magadan oblast, for example, for every employee in the specialised sectors of the non-ferrous and fishing industries in 1969, there were more than five employees from the service sectors. This uneconomic division of labour has obviously grown up as a result of local frustration with the delays and inefficiency of the central supply organisations in satisfying the requirements of industrial enterprises in the North, and is unlikely to disappear until the supply situation improves.

There also seems to be a good deal of steam behind the view that there should be a higher government organ, either a Ministry or a northern department of *Gosplan*, solely concerned with northern affairs. Such a department might be expected to avoid some of *Gosplan*'s costly miscalculations if given adequate authority and based in Siberia and not thousands of kilometres away in Moscow.

After a period of rather haphazard industrialisation in Siberia, in line with the then prevailing eastwards trend of Soviet policy, when relatively little attention seems to have been given to considerations of profitability or 'efficiency', or the advantages or disadvantages of the location of particular industries in Siberia rather than in European Russia, a more 'rational' approach to these questions has been noticeable in Moscow since the fall of Khrushchev. At the theoretical level, a voluminous literature exists on the subject of the location of industry in Siberia, in which the pros and cons of the long-term prospects of the industrialisation of the region are debated with a good deal of loaded and often mutually contradictory arguments. In this controversy two schools of thought have emerged. The pro-Siberians contend that the economic possibilities of European Russia are exaggerated and that the 'western' profitability case is based on relatively short-term advantages. They sharply criticise the further location of various energy-consuming enterprises in energy-deficient European Russian areas, which have the effect of actually increasing this critical deficit while Siberia still has enormous latent power resources. And there is incidentally no concealing the fact that industrial ministries and ministerial departments, with an understandable preference for the easier construction conditions of the European urban centres, have successfully evaded the Party rulings restricting further industrial construction in and around Moscow and Leningrad. Thus, in spite of its great natural wealth, the eastern zone of the R.S.F.S.R. still accounts for only 10% of the industrial output of the U.S.S.R. and this is found to be wholly inadequate by the Siberians who agitate for higher investment in Siberian projects.

The opposing school of thought, or the so-called 'Europeans', have doubts about further industrialisation of the Eastern regions and press for greater concentration on developing mineral and other resource reserves in the Western regions, at much less cost. The Minister of Geology, A. V. Siderenko, for example, backed this case with the significant weight of his academic and ministerial authority in the leading Party journal *Kommunist* in 1970 (no. 18). One of the main arguments used to halt this eastward drive is that the average indices of output to input are lower in the eastern regions, while higher construction costs require larger capital investments, owing to the harsh climatic conditions, higher wages, etc.

These points are disputed by the Siberians, who argue that it is incorrect to use average regional indices for this comparison, as the rate of output to input depends primarily on the 'branch structure' of the region's industry and could vary as it developed. It is also contended that the industrialisation of the eastern regions had long been dominated by the extraction industries (and the associated ferrous and non-ferrous metallurgical, chemical and construction branches), all marked by a high ratio of investment to output. Nor should the general comparison of a ratio of output to investment be indiscriminately used to prove the comparative efficiency of capital investments in the west, as opposed to the east, of the Soviet Union. There must be 'differentiation', according to this argument, in appraising the situation in the various eastern areas. Though costs of construction are undoubtedly higher in certain remote areas this is not always so in the southern zone of Siberia. Moreover, the higher costs of construction, where they exist, are generally compensated for by much more favourable natural features in, for example, mining and energy; the construction of hydroelectric power stations in Eastern Siberia, in terms of kilowatt capacity, still costs about one half that in the European parts of Soviet Russia, and in spite of the extremely unfavourable conditions that dominate oil and natural gas production in the north Tyumen oblast, capital outlay in both cases is lower than the corresponding averages for European deposits, according to Siberian experts.

It is implicitly admitted by both sides that a more intensive study of the situation is necessary, before final conclusions can be reached on the advantage of locating particular industries in the eastern regions of the R.S.F.S.R. It seems to be agreed, however, that in view of the cheapness of all types of energy in Siberia, priority should be given there to the power-intensive branches of industry, while labour-intensive sectors, such as the intermediate processes of the chemical industries, should not be located in Siberia. This view has now been endorsed by the directives of the ninth five-year plan (1971–75) which ruled 'that there must be further improvement in the siting of productive forces in the Soviet Union. In particular, taking account of the cheaper power resources in Siberia (Kazakhstan and Central Asia) that energy-consuming industrial production should be located mainly in those areas.'

It is too often assumed in the West that, because the familiar problems created by a conflict of interest between capital and labour do not exist in the Soviet Union, no other conflicts of interest arise in Soviet industrial society. This is certainly not so in Siberia, where, apart from the Siberian versus European Russian competition for capital investment funds, controversies regarding development frequently arise. Over and over again, for example, the so-called 'narrow departmental interests' of the all-powerful, centralised ministries in Moscow are severely criticised in economic journals and even in the metropolitan press, for obstructing the coordinated development of a particular Siberian area or enterprise. Among many such attacks, that of V. Dolgikh, the then Krasnoyarsk Party Secretary (a man with exceptional experience of Siberia) is particularly revealing. Writing in *Pravda* (26.3.1971) he described the harmful lack of cooperation between eight all-Union ministries at the big Maklakovo-Yeniseysk group of wood-working enterprises. 'Each of them worked independently', he reported, 'constructed its "own unit", and as a result there was a great lack of coordination and disproportion in the development of the wood-felling and wood-working industries. New equipment was little used in the timber combines, mountains of waste products grew, and no associated timber processing enterprises were established. Narrow departmental interests like an impenetrable wall stood in the way of creating unified engineering installations such as water fences, thermal springs, industrial sewage, etc. There is not even one modern town there; instead they divided the area up into factory housing estates.'

The damage done to the economy by this kind of 'narrow specialisation' is aggravated by erratic, seemingly senseless, bureaucratic methods of work within the departments of the important Ministry of Erection and Special Construction Work, employing 14,000 people in the Krasnoyarsk kray alone and responsible for 190–200 millions of roubles of work annually in that kray. Only two of its 22 trusts engaged on Krasnoyarsk constructions are located in Krasnoyarsk, the rest are scattered throughout Siberia from Chelyabinsk to Angarsk and thus direct their work in Krasnoyarsk from distances ranging from 800 to 6,000 kms. And not one directorate is located there. 'It is easy to imagine the waste of precious time necessary to decide any production or financial question arising on the job, under these circumstances', wrote a critical *Pravda* correspondent. Moreover, each trust jealously guards its own special sphere of work and has its own production base, with the result that there is no one body responsible for the job as a whole on a site. Not surprisingly, the Krasnoyarsk *kraykom* appealed to *Gosstroy* and the Ministry of Erection and Special Construction Work to put an end to this frustrating state of affairs, in 1971. Up to 1972, at least, their proposals had apparently been ignored.

After a period of trial and error, the high cost of creating the necessary infrastructure for individual new enterprises in the less accessible areas of Siberia has inspired a new policy of 'territorially coordinated production complexes' as the directing guide-line, as far as possible, of future construction projects. This should eventually mean a shift away from the former type of 'isolated individual enterprises' for which a whole expensive infrastructure might have to be built. This happened originally at the Bratsk H.E.S., which for some years existed in an industrial vacuum, with a great wastage of surplus energy. Now the situation is entirely different and Bratsk is the centre of a large 'territorial-industrial complex' with aluminium, metallurgical, timber-processing and some light industries, while radiating its energy north and south through its high-power long transmission lines. It is also hoped to increase the range of processing of primary raw materials in these large multi-sectional, territorial-production complexes by combining, to a much greater extent than formerly, extracting with manufacturing industries.

Siberian economists tend to criticise the present production structure by which so many unprocessed products or semi-finished articles (timber, semi-finished chemicals, wood, and ore concentrates) are shipped hundreds of miles away to other industrial centres. It is too early to say how far this new system will succeed in eradicating the present imbalances and achieve its general aims.

In its projection study of the economic development of Siberia and the Far East up to the year 2000, the Siberian department of the U.S.S.R. Academy of Sciences approved this 'territorial production complex' principle as the most efficient method of exploiting the natural wealth of the region. It will be the guideline from the start of the construction of the largest H.E.S. in the world (6.4 ml. kw. capacity) now getting under way at Sayan in Eastern Siberia. Here, according to the ninth five-year plan, reserves of coal, asbestos, iron, non-ferrous and rare metals are to be developed, simultaneously with the Sayan hydropower station, to form a big new industrial centre in the unindustrialised Khakas steppes.

Though this territorial-production principle seems to be generally approved, the over-all planning for Siberia is locally seen as still far from perfect and requiring more precise formulation and tailoring to promote Siberian development. From many published criticisms it would seem to be still a rather crude, immature instrument for dealing with the many complex problems of the region. Speaking at the Twenty-fourth Party Congress, the first Party secretary of the important Kemerovo *obkom* plainly expressed his dissatisfaction with the local plan. 'The development of Siberia has its own special features and difficulties,' he said. 'In order to extract and place the riches of this region more effectively at the service of the people, a more profoundly thought-through, specific, approach is necessary as well as a complex plan of development of this extremely rich region. This plan must take into account local natural-climatic and mining geological conditions and the special need, as V. I. Lenin stressed, to exploit the wealth of Siberia by the use of the most up-to-date equipment with the minimum use of labour. The time has come to solve the many-sided problems of Siberia according to a unified plan, centralised on a strictly scientific basis. The most effective way to utilise the wealth of Siberia is by complex development' (*Pravda* 6.4.1971). A more serious criticism of the techniques of planning and design employed in Siberia is, that they are chiefly based on technical norms devised for European Russia and largely unsuitable for Siberian conditions:

'They do not correspond to the specific conditions of Siberia, especially in its northern regions. . . . Siberia needs basically new technical means and work organisation methods that meet the regional conditions of management,' according to V. P. Popov, a distinguished specialist at the Siberian Department of the U.S.S.R. Academy of Sciences. On the basis of these various criticisms, there seems little doubt that the organisation of Siberian resource development could be basically improved by more direct and efficient coordination of central planning with local conditions and requirements.

Clearly, a 'correct strategy' must be evolved if full national advantage is to be gained from the development of Siberia's great natural wealth. However, the detailed and very critical information abundantly supplied by serious Soviet sources shows how defective and wasteful Soviet planning has been in many spheres of Siberian development. Constructional work should be adapted to the severe natural and climatic conditions, the isolation from transport and lack of roads, sparse population, etc. etc., all of which inevitably increase costs of construction. But, in fact, the differences between conditions in the more developed and inhabited areas and in remoter Siberia have not always been properly taken into account in planning, often with costly and even disastrous results.

In Siberia, the labour problem is acute both in industry and agriculture, though nominal wages (at least in industry) are higher than in the European and Central Asian zones of the Soviet Union. The regional wage coefficients vary from 15% in the southern zone of western Siberia up to 70% in its northern regions, and even 80–100% in the north-east. There is also a system of northern benefits. Nevertheless, in 1959–68, western Siberia lost 282,000 inhabitants; the migration exodus was about 40% of the natural increase. Over the same decade, eastern Siberia had a negative population balance of 147,000. It is now recognised, officially and unofficially, that living conditions and, primarily, housing must be radically improved in order to check the exodus of workers from Siberia.[4] Mechanisation is also strongly advocated as a solution of the acute labour shortage. And the Siberian Department of the Academy of Sciences, in urging more mechanisation, has pointed out that 'tightness of labour throughout the Soviet Union' precludes the possibility in future of relying, as hitherto, on labour from the relatively well-populated regions of European Russia.

Quite apart from the labour problem, Siberian industries have for years been pleading for specialised equipment that can withstand low temperatures and high wind velocities.[5] The incredibly slow response of the *Gossnab* and the centralised industrial ministries to this obvious need might have been equated with 'economic sabotage' in other days and has already caused big economic losses in northern Siberia, in both the mining and the oil and gas industries. The production of new machines and materials adapted for use in Siberian climatic conditions seems now to be at last getting under way, but slowly. One quasi-explanation preferred for this unsatisfactory state of affairs is, that the designing and organisation of mass output for such items are impeded by the remoteness of the producer from the customer and the lack of contact between them.

Siberia is so vast that the flow of news items about new developments in various parts of the region may be at once fascinating, accurate, and quite misleading. This is strikingly so in the case of the last plan period (1966–70), when the press was full of new mineral finds, expansion of existing mines, new power stations, in various stages of activity at such difficult sites as Vilyuy, Bilibino, Kolyma, Ust'-Ilimsk and construction of many new towns. All this was exciting to read about, yet the overall statistics of the rate of industrial growth in our three areas of western Siberia, eastern Siberia and the Soviet Far East in each case were lower than for the previous 1961–65 plan period.

Nevertheless throughout the two periods listed, growth rates, except in the Far East in 1966–70, were higher than the average U.S.S.R. rate. As the following table shows, the share of Siberia and the Far East in total U.S.S.R. output of some leading items of production was on the whole stationary between 1965 and 1970.

[4] The Siberian labour problem is discussed in further detail in Chapter 10.
[5] This subject is further discussed in relation to different industries in the following chapters.

Industrial Growth by Region (%)

	1961-65	1966-70
USSR	51	50
West Siberia	79	51
East Siberia	61	59
Soviet Far East	59	49

Source: Nar. Khoz. SSSR v 1970g

The only items to show a significant rise were oil and natural gas, while meat production, for which Siberia was famous in pre-revolutionary days, fell from 11% to 10% of U.S.S.R. production. The picture would no doubt be altered in Siberia's favour if Soviet statistics included production of precious and non-ferrous metals (gold, tin, copper, etc.) and diamonds, in which Siberia's contribution to all-Union production is high.

Siberia and Far East as Percentage of USSR Output

	1965	1970
Electric Power	17	18
Oil	1.4	9.5
Gas	negligible	5
Coal	30	32
Iron	7	8
Steel	7	8
Rolled Ferrous Metal	8	9
Mineral Fertiliser	6	4
Commercial Timber	30	33
Sawn Lumber	26	26
Paper	8	8
Cement	12	12
Cotton Fabrics	4	4
Woollen Fabrics	1	1
Silk Fabrics	4	4
Leather Footwear	5	5
Meat (industrial output)	11	10
Butter (industrial output)	12	12

Source: Nar. Khoz. SSSR v 1970g.

Agricultural production in Siberia between 1960–69 was disappointing and below its potential as a food producing area. Falls were registered in the areas sown with wheat and vegetables and in the irrigated lands of west Siberia. The Far East achieved comparatively better results (at very high costs) with rises in the sown area and in wheat deliveries. But both the Far Eastern region and east Siberia remain heavily dependent on food imported from other parts of the Soviet Union and on occasional shipments of grain from Canada and the United States.

Against the industrial background described above, it is not surprising that the current ninth five-year plan (1971–1975) showed a certain slowing down on the construction of new enterprises in Siberia. The present emphasis is rather on the completion of unfinished enterprises like the long-lagging Third Metallurgical Base, the *Zapsib* (west Siberian) metallurgical works near Novokuznetsk, the Bratsk aluminium works, the new Achinsk oil refinery and the Krasnoyarsk aluminium works. As there is no mention of the Tayshet iron and steel plant, originally designed to form the third leg of the Third Metallurgical Base, it may be presumed to have been dropped for the present. It is also noticeable that Siberia was not assigned any of the new Soviet iron and steel works planned for this period. The emphasis is on maintaining high growth rates in the major branches of the ferrous, non-ferrous, chemical and other industries already in existence. Nevertheless, a large number of new industries are to be centred round the Sayan hydroelectric power station (now under construction), including coke-chemical, engineering and synthetic fibre plants, but it is unlikely that this comprehensive scheme will get off the ground until at least the end of the next five-year plan.

Not for the first time in recent years, the plan links the need for 'a further influx of population to the Far East and east Siberia' with the creation of the conditions necessary for 'fixing cadres' and a speed-up in the construction of housing and social-cultural facilities.

More permanent 'fixing of cadres' will certainly be an important factor for achieving the 'accelerated development of the production forces in the Far East and, in particular, the increased extraction of coal, tin, tungsten, mercury, gold and diamonds' called for by the plan. No output targets or precise geographical locations are indicated for any of these items but it is of course normal Soviet practice to withhold, under the classification of state secrets, production statistics of gold, non-ferrous metals and diamonds.

These provisions of the current ninth plan and subsequent events would seem to undermine the fairly widespread notion in the west, that tension on the Sino-Soviet frontier has adversely affected economic development plans for the region, but it may well have been responsible for curtailing published information about planned economic development to the minimum. It is notable that, while Sino-Soviet hostility continues unabated, the long-outstanding problem of the development of Yakutsk natural gas now seems to have been decided in principle. This is a most costly and complex development project and the Soviets seemed understandably hesitant to undertake it alone. Negotiations had been dragging on inconclusively for some years with the Japanese regarding technical and financial aid to develop this gas when, in 1972–73, an American consortium consisting of the Occidental Petroleum Corporation and El Paso Natural Gas expressed eager interest in participating in this project and signed a letter of intent with the Soviet government in June 1973 for this purpose.[6] The Japanese then agreed to cooperate with the Americans in a sort of triangular Soviet-Japanese-American deal to develop Yakutsk natural gas. Some weeks later a somewhat similar letter of intent was signed by another American group to produce west Siberian natural gas and export it to the United States.

It is still early days to try and assess in any detail how these and other multi-national projects will work out in Siberia. If successful they should in many ways radically alter the picture given in this brief survey of the Siberian economy. The large injections of investment capital and technical assistance expected from the American involvement in Siberian resource development should go far to raise former technological and production levels in those industrial branches concerned

[6] Japanese and United States copartnership in Siberia is discussed in detail in Chapter 13 below.

and even dispel, to some extent, that economic stagnation which originally prompted Brezhnev to seek economic aid from the west.

Capital Investment. Leninist ideology requires Soviet investment policy to be directed towards the twin goals of 'accelerated development' of those eastern regions of the R.S.F.S.R. that are west and east Siberia and the Soviet Far East, and the simultaneous elimination of economic disparities between the industrial advanced European Russian areas and the under-developed eastern lands. This enormously complex *mot d'ordre* has involved the Soviet State in a continuously expanding development programme and vast capital investment in Siberia, since it was first proclaimed. But, ideology notwithstanding, in the first decade after the Revolution, the claims of European Russia had priority on tight investment funds over under-developed Siberia and the Far East. Thus, it has been estimated that only 14.1% of all-Union capital investment between 1918-41 was allocated to the eastern regions.

The first indication of a shift in investment eastwards came in the early thirties with Stalin's decision to establish a second metallurgical base in west Siberia at Stalinsk (now Novokuznetsk) for which further development of the adjacent Kuzbas coalfields was necessary. This project absorbed some 67% of the total Soviet investment in Siberia under the second five-year plan. In the Far East, investment was concentrated mainly in the construction of the new town of Komsomol'sk and the Amurstal' plant, the first steel and rolling mill in the Soviet Far East. In the late thirties, the military threat posed by Japan in Manchukuo caused investment to rise steeply in the Far Eastern region, on military preparations. By 1940, it was estimated that capital investment there was almost five and a half times the Soviet average.[7] Some of this investment must also have gone to finance the various expensive mining enterprises being developed at this time, with concentration camp labour, in the Far North by *Dal'stroy* (the Far Eastern construction organisation specially set up to administer these camps).

The German occupation of the great Soviet industrial base in the Ukraine during World War II (in 1941) caused a rapid speed-up of industrialisation in western Siberia, based on the evacuation of entire factories and their workers from the Ukraine and other German occupied areas. To cope with this emergency, the level of capital investment rose 74% above the pre-war level. After the war, attention was diverted from Siberia towards the restoration of the war-devastated areas of Russia and the Ukraine and the level of investment in Siberia fell accordingly. But from the fifth five-year plan (1951–55) onwards, Siberian requirements were increasingly considered in the allocation of investment funds. The level of industrial growth in Siberia was, however, relatively slow in the fifties, compared with the rise in capital investment.

Khrushchev's dramatic recognition of the economic importance of the eastern regions at the Twentieth Party Congress (1956) culminated in the decision to double capital investment there under the sixth five-year plan. Following the scrapping of this plan in 1958, however, the rate of capital investment in both east and west

[7] cf. Paul Dibb, *Siberia and the Pacific*, London, 1972.

Siberia slowed down between 1958–64 and was actually less, according to Soviet sources, than the amount nominally allotted by the Seven Year Plan; considerable reductions being made in the allocations to some of Siberia's main industries e.g. ferrous and non-ferrous metallurgy, the chemical industry and wood-processing industries. Nevertheless, state capital investment in Eastern Siberia and the Far East during the Seven-Year Plan (S.Y.P.) was almost 10% of the total State investments. This proportion is virtually 80% larger than the region's small share of the Soviet population, whereas western Siberia only received 25% more than its population share.[8] It is officially claimed that State investments in Pacific Siberia (i.e. eastern Siberia and the Far East) during the S.Y.P. equalled the sum of all State investments (at comparable prices) in the previous 40 years. A large share of the S.Y.P. investments, particularly in eastern Siberia, went into such very expensive constructions as the giant Bratsk H.E.S. and the large Shelekhovo aluminium plant, which absorbed about 65% of State capital investment in eastern Siberia in this period.

The planned aim of achieving a faster pace of industrial growth in Siberia during the S.Y.P. (1959–65) than the all-Union planned average of 14% was not achieved. The annual rates actually attained were 11.1% for western Siberia, 14% for eastern Siberia and 12.7% for the Far East. As the claimed level of growth for the U.S.S.R. as a whole of 12% was also below that planned, in fact both eastern Siberia and the Far East did comparatively well.

Throughout the sixties, the per capita investment allocations to east Siberia and the Soviet Far East, with their relatively very small populations, are estimated to have been generally higher than in most other regions of the R.S.F.S.R. or the U.S.S.R. as a whole.

Critics of the high capital cost of major construction schemes in Siberia (and they were many in the Soviet Union) were at pains to stress the large amounts of capital tied up in protracted, unfinished constructions like the Bratsk hydroelectric complex, or the Shelekhovo aluminium plant, the inflated level of construction costs in Siberia resulting from higher wages than in European Russia and the 'flight of labour' and the long delays beyond planned economic commissioning periods. These factors may have tended to reduce the attraction of Siberia as an investment area, in spite of the much lower costs of fuel and power, compared to the levels in the Urals or European Russia. It should be noted, however, that protracted, unfinished construction is not confined to Siberia. It is an all-Union phenomenon and very costly. According to Prime Minister Kosygin, the volume of Soviet unfinished construction had risen to 70 billion roubles by 1972 and represented about 76% of the total capital investments for that year, in the Soviet Union.

Following Khrushchev's removal from office, his emotional attraction to Siberian development was replaced by cooler considerations of profitability and economic advantage for the Soviet Union, as criteria for capital investment in Siberia and the Far East. The conflicting claims of the Siberian and the European 'lobbies' for tight Soviet capital were and are openly aired, experts of the Siberian Department

---

[8] I have drawn on Mr. Paul Dibb's lecture paper *Soviet Siberia and Australia*, Wagga Wagga, Area of Humanities Paper no. 2, for some statistical information in this section.

of the all-Union Academy of Sciences backed by many high ranking regional Party bosses, often making the economic case for the Siberians. In spite of the relative ease of construction in European Russia compared to Siberia, both the level of industrial output and of investment in the eastern regions of the R.S.F.S.R. continued to rise and only east Siberia fell below the U.S.S.R. and R.S.F.S.R. averages for investment increases in 1966–69:

Industrial Output (Gross) % increase

	1961-1965	1966-70
USSR	51.0	50.4
W. Siberia	49.8	51.4
E. Siberia	60.8	59.5
Far East	59.0	49.0

Source: Narkhoz SSSR v 1970g. p. 139.

RSFSR State and Co-operative Investment (excluding Kolkhozes)

	1966-69 as % of 1961-65
RSFSR	108.4
USSR	110.2
W. Siberia	113.4
E. Siberia	101.2
Far East	118.2

Source: Narkhoz SSSR v 1970g. p. 478.

Though the bulk of capital investment still goes into the older, highly-industrialised European regions of the Soviet Union, this percentage has been falling since 1918, while that invested in developing new resources in Siberia and the Far East has risen slowly but steadily, as the following investment data for 1918–70 show (U.S.S.R. = 100%):

	1918-1941	1941-1950	1951-1960	1961-1970
European regions	70.7	67.7	65.4	63.3
Siberia and the Far East	14.1	14.5	15.9	16.2

Moreover, to speed up the development of Siberia and the Far East, it was stated that 25% of the R.S.F.S.R. capital investments would be allocated to these regions, in 1972.

The actual volume of investment in millions of roubles over the period 1961–70 is shown in the following table. As a result of the large capital investment in the new oil and gas fields, west Siberia was the major recipient in the eastern regions of the R.S.F.S.R. A later report (1972) claimed that the Krasnoyarsk kray occupied second place in the R.S.F.S.R. investment, probably owing to the large capital funds sunk in the Krasnoyarsk H.E.S., and the Sayan hydroelectric industrial complex, among other projects.

	5 FYP (1951-1955)	6 FYP (1956-1960)	7 FYP (1961-1965)	8 FYP (1966-1970)
	In millions of roubles			
W. Siberia	4,710	9,416	13,915	20,319
E. Siberia	3,513	7,456	11,965	15,783
Far East	3,955	6,210	9,492	14,758

These global statistics of the volume of investment in the individual regions of Siberia do not reveal how the respective funds are shared out among the various sectors of the regional economies. Such information is not regularly published in the U.S.S.R. and is only very occasionally discussed by local experts. This dearth of information is all the more frustrating as investment allocations to industry, agriculture or transport may be regarded not only as criteria of the 'rationality' of Soviet regional investment policies, but also as useful pointers to the financial capacity of these economic sectors to fulfil plan assignments. Fortunately, the investment situation in east Siberia has been examined in some detail[9] including a break-down of the assignments to the various sectors of the economy (1971) and suggests that the 'irrationalities' found in regard to capital investment in east Siberia may also be prevalent to some extent in west Siberia and the Soviet Far East.

According to this analysis, the allocations of investment funds in east Siberia are 'irrational' because they do not correspond to the basic requirements of the region, as a whole. In particular, there are unjustifiable 'disproportions' between the share of capital investment assigned to the productive (industry) and non-productive spheres of the economy. Thus, the lion's share of capital investment went into the productive sphere in 1966–68 or 78% and only 22% into the non-productive sphere (which includes the housing and domestic-welfare sectors). This is a much higher proportion than the average national indexes for this period or indeed throughout 1961–70. Within the productive sphere, the proportional amount of capital investments in east Siberian industry was almost 100% higher than for the country as a whole, while the capital invested in agriculture was 100% lower and remained almost constantly at this level.

In east Siberia where the lack of transport is a serious handicap to economic development, and the building industry is under heavy pressure, capital investment in transport construction and in building in 1966–70 declined relatively and even absolutely, compared with the previous planned period (1961–65). These economically ill-advised discrepancies in capital investment allocations are stated to be the result of the determination of individual departmental ministries, in Moscow, pursuing an entirely 'one-sided policy' to promote a sort of forced development of their respective inefficient sectors of national specialisation, regardless of the effect of these investment practices on the whole infrastructure of the region. In fact, these practices have led, in the words of this Soviet report, to 'a freezing of capital investments during the construction stage, an obsolescence of equipment which has not even been put into operation, the incomplete use of production capacity and a substantial lag in the actually achieved indices behind the indices envisaged in the technical and economic studies and plans.'

This unbalanced investment policy not only fails to contribute to raising the effectiveness of social production, but also defeats its own object, according to Filshin's report. Thus, the inadequate development of the infrastructure and agricultural production, in turn creates great difficulties in retaining industrial personnel

[9] G. I. Filshin, *Ekonomika i Organizatsiya Promyshlennogo Proizvodstva*, no. 2, 1971, pp. 39-42.

(for whom regular agricultural supplies are among the essential conditions for settling in their Siberian jobs. As a result of the poor state of transport, the low level of mechanisation of freight handling and the lack of rolling stock etc., millions of tons of goods produced at the Siberian enterprises were allegedly not delivered to the consumers. The supply of housing and social-domestic services lags behind the growth of population and is another main cause of the 'mass exodus of the labour force'. In particular, unless these policies are reversed, they must adversely affect the great Sayan H.E.S. scheme, in the south of the region, which has been planned as a model of industrial-territorial integrated construction policies. The effect of the failure to establish a sufficiently large construction base here and of the discrepancy between the productive and non-productive sectors is such that, while the big Abakan railway-car building complex is regarded as a sound proposition, from 'the sectional position', it will scarcely be possible to build simultaneously the many other enterprises planned for the use of local raw materials and the large volume of Sayan hydro-electrical power, e.g. a ferro-alloys plant, an electro-metallurgical plant, an electro-chemical combine, etc.

The decline in the financing of the construction and of the building materials industries in east Siberia since 1962 is attributed in this report to 'an increase in the capital investments for the expansion, reconstruction and technical re-equipping of operating enterprises, as well as for the completion of nearly completed projects concentrated chiefly in the European sector of the U.S.S.R.' It seems particularly unfortunate, if well founded, that such basic sectors of the Siberian economy as the construction and the building materials industry should have suffered because of the preferential treatment given to projects in the European U.S.S.R.

The many discrepancies in the planned allocation of capital investment in the productive and non-productive sectors of the east Siberian economy originate, according to this analysis, in the 'decisive influence' on planning of the branch industrial ministries and their departments in Moscow. Their 'narrow specialisation' attitude to regional development being thus directly contrary to the principle of the 'unified, integrated and completely balanced territorial plan' favoured officially since 1970 as a solution to Siberia's problems of development.

chapter five

Energy

Siberia has very rich reserves of the main types of energy: coal, water power, oil and natural gas. They are all rather unevenly distributed throughout this enormous territory and the almost inaccessible northern regions contain most of the known oil and gas deposits. But so many new sources of energy have been discovered in recent years by Soviet geologists, that it would be premature to regard current estimates of these Siberian resources as either precise or definitive. In fact, no complete geological map of Siberia yet exists.

Coal. The most important bituminous coal fields now being operated in Siberia are in the Kuzbas (Kuznetsk Basin) which includes the gigantic Leninsk-Kuznetskiy, Prokop'yevsk and Novokuznetsk mines. These mines, which were known and worked before the revolution, have been subsequently greatly expanded and modernised. This basin is estimated to contain reserves four times larger than the Donbas, the largest coal field in European Russia. The high-quality coking coal, which can be opencast mined in very large seams, is also much cheaper to produce than Donbas coal. Moreover, according to Soviet estimates the specific capital outlays per ton of coal mined are 43% lower in the Kuzbas than in the Donbas, because of more favourable mining-geological conditions which apparently compensate for other factors increasing costs in Siberia.

The Kuzbas planned production target for 1975 is 135 million t., a steady but not spectacular increase over its 100 million output in 1965. If achieved, this would represent 17% of the total Soviet coal production, but the Donbas would still be the leading producer and the Kuzbas in the second place. Many new pits have been opened in the post-war period and Kuzbas output has not yet been affected by the all-Union shift away from the former lop-sided dominance of coal in the national fuel balance over oil and natural gas, of the sixties. Its range of consumers extends to the Urals, Moscow and even the Ukraine. But there is a movement to reduce the percentage of Kuzbas coal exported to the Urals and further west by the use of cheaper Siberian oil and natural gas. And this is probably the way the situation will ultimately develop, though Kuzbas coal will long remain indispensable in central and eastern Siberia, and is likely to become increasingly in demand for the metallurgical industries of European Russia and the Urals.

The Kuzbas is the fuel source of the great industrial centre which has developed round the second metallurgical base, established in the Kemerovo oblast by Stalin. Production increased considerably in the Eighth F.Y.P. period (1966–70), without expanding the labour force, as a result of higher productivity, mechanisation and automation. But mechanisation in the Kuzbas mines still leaves much to be desired in regard to the type of equipment supplied and operated. Local reports in the press insist that much better results could be obtained if the right machines were installed. But the Kuzbas miners, 'the step-children of mining science', have to use machines designed for the Donbas and Moscow coal basins, though conditions in the Kuzbas are seldom similar to either. This predicament is attributed locally to the lack of coordination between the scientific research and construction institutes concerned with equipment problems. Criticism of another aspect of Kuzbas mining comes from the Party Chief of the Kemerovo coal industry. 'Can it be considered normal', he asked in a press article, 'that up to the present no scientific base for opencast coal output exists in Siberia although the target for opencast coal in the Kuzbas is 40,000,000 t. in the current F.Y.P ?'. From this and similar comments the impression remains that the local managers of the Kuzbas coal fields are far from satisfied with the way their problems are handled by Moscow's high level planning and scientific authorities. Nevertheless, labour productivity in 1972 in the opencast workings was 3–4 times higher than underground and the cost twice as low.

Beyond the Kuzbas, in east Siberia, the huge Kansk-Achinsk brown coal mines stretch for hundreds of miles along the Trans-Siberian railway, left and right of Krasnoyarsk. Though this region is still not sufficiently developed to absorb more than a fraction of the Kansk-Achinsk potential output, among the few important consumers now operating on this coal are the Nazarovo G.R.E.S. (2.4 million kw. capacity) and the Achinsk alumina plant. Other enterprises reported to be under consideration for construction here are the East Siberian construction engineering works, a ferro-concrete works and a branch of the Krasnoyarsk combine-harvester plant. The advantage of the very low price of Kansk-Achinsk coals at the pit-head, compared to either those of the Kuzbas or the Donbas, is largely outweighed from the export angle by the fact that they are not economically transportable over long distances, owing to their low calorific content. Their main use would therefore seem to be as fuel for pit-head thermal electric stations and future industrial enterprises, once the technology of transmission over long distance has been mastered.

The most important of the other smaller, but locally useful, coal deposits in east Siberia is at Cheremkhovo, once of major importance for fuelling the Trans-Siberian railway and the Angarsk synthetic fuels plant – functions it has lost since the electrification of the railway and the replacement of coal by oil at the synthetic fuels plant. Further north, the much larger Azey brown coal deposits are now being operated. Both coking and steam coals are found at Noril'sk, part of an enormous Tungus field stretching far east to the Lena and Yakutiya, but as yet undeveloped. They are used locally for bunkering, and in the Noril'sk metallurgical smelters and heat and power stations. With the introduction of more electric furnaces at Noril'sk, coal will be used more efficiently and there will be no incentive for further development until the railway, planned to link Noril'sk with other Siberian industrial centres, revives interest in this fuel. A number of small mines in the Chita province supply sufficient coal for local needs and to supplement the inadequate resources of the Buryat A.S.S.R.

The Soviet Far Eastern Region is well supplied with high quality coal reserves. The remoteness from populated centres and lack of industrial demand has prevented large and rich reserves in the north of the area from being exploited up to the present. The main producing mines are in the Amur oblast at Raychikhinsk with 40% of the region's output. These brown coals from opencast mines are largely used locally to fuel the small electric power stations of the area. Owing to their relative cheapness they are also used extensively in the adjacent Khabarovsk kray. The Primor'ye has a number of good brown and hard coal mines, which will provide adequate fuel for the new Primozskiy thermal electric station now under construction and eventual electrification of the Khabarovsk-Vladivostok sector of the Trans-Siberian railway. The old Suchan hard coal mines near Vladivostok, worked since 1888, are now eclipsed, owing to high operating costs in the underground mines, by the new open pit deposits in the Ussuri area.

Serious allegations of inefficiency and bad planning in the Primor'ye coal mines were made at the Twenty-third Party Congress (1966) and as a result of this mismanagement local requirements had to be met by dearer imported coal. It is not clear how the situation has developed subsequently. The big Chul'man mines in southern Yakutiya, which include good coking deposits, offer very promising possibilities for future development. They are situated near the important Aldan ore mining area and provide useful fuel for the local Chul'man power station, but only a fraction of their capacity is now exploited. The Japanese have shown interest in developing them and they are frequently mentioned in Soviet sources as the best fuel base for the proposed Far Eastern metallurgical plant. The lack of road and rail communications in the area has hitherto prevented their exploitation. The local Yakut Party representative urged the Twenty-fourth Party Congress to include the construction of the Bam–Tynda–Chul'man railway in the ninth F.Y.P., so as to facilitate development of the Chul'man coal mines. c.f. Postscript for 1974 Soviet-Japanese Copartnership Agreement for development of these South Yakut coal mines.

A minute part of the extensive geological coal reserves of northern Yakutiya, estimated at a third of the total Soviet reserves, more than half brown coal, is now being worked. At a Soviet estimate of 2,647 milliard tons, they are considered to be the largest reserves in the world, but statistics based on geological measurements do not yet exist. Neither these fields, nor the very extensive Tungus coal basin, stretching far west to the Taymyr peninsula and Noril'sk, can be exploited to advantage until there is greater industrial demand for this fuel. In both cases, it is estimated that production would be extremely costly. The small Magadan coal field is officially scheduled to produce 2,800,000 t. of coal by 1975 and to raise opencast mining by 35% but these are ambitious targets in the harsh Magadan climate. Small though these local Magadan coal deposits are, they are most useful for bunkering and the rapid development of the area, which is otherwise remote from sources of fuel and depends at present, to some extent, on imports from Sakhalin.

There are good quality brown coal fields on the west and east coasts of Sakhalin. About 6,000,000 tons were produced in 1970, but the cost of this coal is high owing to the difficult geological conditions in some of the mines. It suffices for the island's requirements and, when the seas are not frozen, small quantities are exported to Kamchatka, Magadan and other ports on the mainland. One enthusiastic Soviet press man has even claimed that Sakhalin coal is of better quality and cheaper than American, but lamented that more attention was not given 'by the Soviet economic organs' to the workers' demands for better living conditions and to supplying much-needed pitprops. Though there has been some reconstruction of the coal pits and introduction of new mining equipment, the replacement of old equipment needs to be speeded up, according to the same journalist.

Oil and Natural Gas. The huge marshy wilderness of the west Siberian Depression was until recently one of the most unattractive, underdeveloped areas of Asiatic Russia. Since the depletion of the rich fur trade in the eighteenth century, it was shunned by migrants from European Russia and only very thinly inhabited by its native Khanty-Mansi people. Yet it was in this wilderness, now forming part of the Tyumen' oblast, that Soviet geologists, doggedly searching for new energy resources, discovered in the mid-1950s, what will probably prove to be one of the world's great reserves of commercial oil and natural gas. These dedicated Soviet geologists and their supporters, far from being officially encouraged in their well-founded scientific confidence in the existence of Siberian oil, were in fact long opposed as 'Siberian fanatics' and even at one juncture largely deprived of the necessary funds and supplies to continue their researches. Influential groups at the 'Centre' were sceptical about this Siberian oil and regarded allocation of money and supplies to the geologists as a waste of State funds, 'throwing money to the winds'. As a result of this influential scepticism, noticeably in *Gosplan*, oil prospecting in western Siberia was hampered for years.

Soviet critics also stress the lack of coordination between the various bodies involved in early development plans for this industry and the 'narrow sectional approach of government departments to the use of capital investments and manpower' which resulted in great losses of energy bearers. The schemes for building up the oil fields were worked out without considering measures for collecting and processing the oil-well gas which was flared off, while oil extraction was forced up, without regard for the prevailing lag in the development rate of pipeline transport and the capacity of the oil refining and petrochemical industries in Siberia.

River transport in the Ob'-Irtysh basin was crucial (pending the construction of the Tyumen'–Surgut railway) for the planned deliveries of building materials, equipment, pipe, etc. Yet the technical facilities necessary to improve river transport were not installed as planned and supplies were unduly delayed, as a result. Moreover, in many places access was only possible by helicopter because of the marshy terrain and tracks could only be used in winter. Yet, in spite of much bungling and costly 'hitches', the richness of the actual deposits and the relatively

Blocks of flats in the new oil
town of Surgut (West Siberia)

more sophisticated equipment now available has resulted in some striking developments in Siberia's oil and gas industry.

It took more than a century, originally, to bring Russian petroleum extraction up to 350 million tons, but western Siberia is expected to reach this volume of output 20–25 years after the beginning of extraction in the region. In 1970, total natural gas output in the U.S.S.R. reached 200 billion cu.m. Western Siberia, where the output of natural gas began only a few years ago, should now reach this figure by the beginning of the 1980s. The optimistic conclusion is that 'similar scales of tapping natural resources have not been found in any other regions of the country.' There are various reasons for this rapid development. In the first place the heavy capital investment into this oil-gas industry, was as much, it has been estimated, as the total oil-gas investments of the U.S.S.R. in the early sixties. These Siberian oil and gas reserves are now recognised as of the greatest importance for the national fuel balance of the Soviet Union, and also internationally, because they are a major source of supply for the East European countries and important earners of hard currency from customers in W. Europe and possibly in future from the U.S.A.

The proven oil reserves of west Siberia have recently been estimated at 1,000 million tons and the North Tyumen' natural gas reserves at approximately 23 trillion cu.m. Both oil and gas production in west Siberia have risen spectacularly since the first output figures released in the early sixties. Oil production rose from 1 million tons in 1965 to 31,400,000 t. in 1971 and 85.5 million t. in 1973, and natural gas from 2.5 billion cu.m. in 1965 to more than 10 billion cu.m. in 1970, and 11.6 billion cu.m. in 1972. The targets set by the Twenty-fourth Party Congress for west Siberian oil and natural gas by 1975 are 120–125 million t. of oil and gas processing works with an annual capacity of 5–6 billion cu.m. of processed gas. These newly opened up energy reserves came at a most propitious moment for the Soviet fuel balance. The former major sources of oil in the Volga-Urals fields and other areas of European Russia were in the later stages of exploitation, while the fuel deficit in the highly industrialised area of Russia and the Ukraine loomed ominously on the horizon. At the same time, the national requirement for natural gas was expanding faster than could even be supplied by the addition of large new Central Asian supplies to the previous sources.

The comparative costs of developing Tyumen' natural gas and oil, in the forbidding natural conditions in which both are found, compared to deposits in more moderate climates, is a matter of continuing controversy in the Soviet Union. The largest gas wells now being operated lie well within the Arctic Circle and the permafrost zone, where the costs of geological research, labour and transport are very high. Nevertheless, some top-level Soviet analysts maintain that specific capital outlays for extraction of this natural gas are still a quarter lower than in the Volga region, for example, and that the average capital outlay for the eastern regions as a whole is almost a third lower than the average for the European gas-producing regions. The Siberians also argue that capital outlays on the extraction of petroleum in western Siberia are only half as high as in the north Caucasus, and exploration costs per ton of oil in the Ob' basin 5–10 times lower than the Union average. Some of the points used in this argument are, (a) the high concentration of the oil deposits

Site of the Zeya Hydro-power
station (Far Eastern region)

in relatively small areas of the middle-Ob' with the exception of the Shaim field; (b) the high level of exploration-surveying ('finding') work; (c) the relatively low costs of the preparation of the reserves. These favourable aspects of the oil industry also apply to the gas deposits which, in addition, are characterised by the shallow bed of the productive strata, their great power, good collector qualities and also the exploitation of very powerful reserves.

The west Siberian oil fields stretch from the Shaim field in the western sector of the Tyumen' oblast, north-east to the largest known concentration of reserves in the middle Ob' basin (where the exceptionally rich Samotlor deposit is situated) and south-east into the Tomsk and Novosibirsk areas. Production is now concentrated in three main oil-bearing areas; Shaim in the foothills of the Urals, the Surgut and Nizhnevartovskiy regions situated in the Ob' river basin. All differ sharply in their geological structure and in the type of oil produced. The administrative centre for this industry is in the old town of Tyumen', where the new all-Union Institute of Oil Engineering is also located. The discovery of the 'giant Samotlor' oil field (some 20 miles north of the Nizhnevartovskiy oil centre) put paid to the ill-conceived ministerial ideas of restricting geological research to the Ust' Balyk area. Now, Samotlor has already become a kind of heroic legendary theme, with a poem in its honour featuring in *Pravda* (17.10.1971). It is estimated to be one of the largest if not the largest oil concentration in the Soviet Union. By 1972, it was producing almost half of the west Siberian daily output and the production target for 1975 is 78,000,000 tons, or about a third of the planned Soviet oil production. Subsequently, it is expected to produce 100,000,000 tons of oil for annually.

The west Siberian natural gas fields cover an even larger area than the oil deposits. The major fields now being operated lie in the far north of the Tyumen' oblast, within the Arctic Circle. Here, at Novyy Port, Medvezh'ye and Urengoy and other deposits in the Taz and Pur river basins, there is a most important concentration of high quality natural gas characterised by uniquely large wells. The great Urengoy field, for example, is reliably estimated to be the largest in the world, with reserves of about 6 trillion cu.m. It is claimed by Soviet sources to be much larger even than the world famous 'Texan field', and covers an area of 2,000 sq. km. South of the middle Ob' oil fields, gas has also been found in the desolate swampy area of Vasyugan and north of the Tas-Pur fields, at Messoyakha.

The result of little more than a decade of active prospecting and exploitation of the western Siberian energy reserves is that the Soviet Union could become the richest country in the world today for prospected reserves of oil and natural gas and raw material for the Soviet petro-chemical industry. This is indeed an accolade for those 'Siberian fanatics' led by the redoubtable Academician A. A. Trofimuk who refused to be sidetracked from their quest for Siberian oil.

West Siberian oil and natural gas are indeed flowing, but there are still many complex problems confronting this industry. An indispensable industrial infrastructure has to be built up in this very difficult terrain. 60–90% of the oil-bearing areas are covered with bogs and marshes and many of them are annually threatened by the spring flooding of the Ob' river. The most prolific gas fields lie well within the Arctic Circle and largely in the permafrost zone. Reasonable living conditions have to be created from scratch for the oil and gas workers and roads and railways built where none formerly existed. From the early days of the exploitation of these oil-gas reserves, the retention of an indispensable corps of skilled and unskilled workers has presented the industry and government with formidable problems. The failure of the responsible Soviet authorities to solve these problems is reflected in the high level of departing workers. This 'flight of labour' not only disrupts production but is also causing great energy and financial losses to the State. It is variously reckoned that it costs between 16,000–20,000 r. to settle a worker-family in the Tyumen' oblast. And these high costs have put some steam behind the move to mechanise production more rapidly. The reports of expert Soviet observers on the unbelievably bad housing conditions in the oil-gas fields, with the inevitable corollary that the situation must be radically improved if a stable labour force is to be created, have been common form for nearly a decade now. Judging from the most recent comments, the position though definitely improving still remains unsatisfactory.

In a series of remarkably frank articles on conditions in the Tyumen' oil fields, *Pravda* in 1971 declared that normal timber, brick or heated prefabricated houses were urgently needed and not unrealistic plans for towns with glass cupolas and covered streets in places like Surgut, Uray or Nadym, which reached 'the limit of constructive fantasy'. In view of the expense and difficulties of creating decent housing and domestic amenities in the harsh climate of the north Tyumen', the idea has been put forward of setting up temporary hostels (for the construction workers) and small compact dormitory 'shift' settlements for the extraction staff, near the remoter oil-gas units to which the workers could be flown by helicopter for 7–10 day shifts. Their families and permanent homes would be in towns like Tyumen' or Surgut where the various social amenities, schools, hospitals, club, etc., would be situated. No general decision seems to have yet been taken on this proposal and objections are raised on the score that places of residence and employment should not be separated – unrealistic though this seems in the Far North of Siberia. A more plausible practical reason for delay in extending this so-called 'expeditionary' housing is the number of helicopters, or other air transport machines suitable for landing in all weathers, that would be required in this harsh natural environment. The need for more large-panel prefabricated houses is urged by all concerned with labour problems in the Tyumen' oblast. The central ministries and in particular *Gosplan* and *Gossnab* come in for frequent criticism for their bureaucratic attitude to local housing. By holding up the necessary construction equipment, they are alleged by Soviet sources 'to have prevented prefabricated housing enterprises in Tyumen' and Surgut building thousands of sq. metres of living space properly adjusted to northern conditions, while the funds for construction are given in driblets'.

Meanwhile, thousands of workers have had to shift for themselves as best they can, either to live in deplorable conditions or depart. Over a seven-year period from 1963, one Soviet expert estimated that some 80% of incoming migrants left the Tyumen' oblast, primarily on account of the shortage of decent housing and normal living conditions. High pay will evidently not stop the 'drain', as the pay scales throughout Siberia have for some years been substantially higher than in European Russia. 'High pay attracts in the first stage', commented *Voprosy Ekonomiki* (no. 9, 1969), 'but it will not retain migrant workers if other conditions are not satisfactory. Poor living conditions, unsatisfactory food and goods supplies, poor cultural amenities and overall inadequate wages in terms of local prices were responsible for the high turnover of workers'.

In view of the importance and magnitude of the north Siberian housing problem, it is not surprising to learn that Soviet delegations visiting the Canadian Far North take a special interest in the progressive types of housing created there for northern industrial workers. And the Soviet press warmly commends Canadian mobile housing 'on wheels' as a 'model for Tyumen' '. The air is thick with informed criticism, disturbing facts and recommendations. But the housing and labour problems are still acute in the oil and gas industry and await much more effective action from Moscow, including much more precise and coordinated planning than hitherto.

The lack of coordination between the relevant official bodies which has hampered housing construction in Tyumen' has become even more crucial in regard to technical matters and lowered efficiency in the extraction and transmission of the region's oil and gas. Undue haste originally, in plunging into production before the physical peculiarities of these oil and gas deposits had been properly studied, exacerbated the situation, and proved very costly for the Soviet government. But in spite of these difficulties and costly wastage, oil and gas production has risen rapidly and the ground work for the transmission of this energy to the Urals and European Russia is being laid by the construction of a network of pipelines.

The first of these pipelines to be constructed connected the Shaim oil field with the town of Tyumen', a station on the Trans-Siberian railway, with rail-tank-car transport, by a 250 km. long, 30 in. diameter pipeline, which was the forerunner of several much longer and wider pipelines.

The longest and in many ways the most important of these pipelines will eventually be the planned extension of the Trans-Siberian trunk pipeline from its present terminal at Irkutsk to the Pacific port of Nakhodka, a project mooted for over a decade by Soviet sources. It was first mentioned as one of the Soviet-Japanese Siberian copartnership projects in the sixties, but owing to disagreement between Moscow and Tokyo on credit terms etc., discussions dragged on inconclusively until 1973, when agreement seemed likely. Meanwhile, Moscow decided on a much larger pipe covering the entire distance between the Tyumen' fields and Nakhodka *via* Irkutsk and which would run north round Lake Baykal and continue eastwards, some hundreds of kilometres north of the vulnerable Sino-Soviet frontier area, to Nakhodka. The Soviets are now building the western section of this 48 in. pipe between Aleksandrovskoye–Anzhero–Sudzhensk and Irkutsk alone and are reported to be making good progress. The probability is that they will soon be assisted technically on this construction from Anzhero–Sudzhensk by the Japanese.[1] and discussions have taken place between the two partners on the prices and credits etc., involved in this enterprise.

[1] This subject is further discussed in Chapter 13, and in the Postscript.

A trunk pipeline of this nature traversing geographical areas hitherto unserved by such transport is obviously an enterprise of considerable importance to the Soviet Union and not to Siberia alone. It should in the first place expedite the flow of oil for the domestic and industrial requirements of the Soviet Far Eastern Region and relieve the already overloaded Amur railway of oil tanker traffic, while also strengthening supply for the local armed forces (but see the Postscript). Production in Sakhalin is at present the main source of supply for the Soviet Far East, but output there is small and inadequate for the increasing fuel demands of the Region.

Another pipeline of considerable interest, and now completed, is the so-called 'Siberian Ring'. This Ring, consisting of an eastern and a western section, enables oil from the middle Ob' collecting station of Ust'-Balyk to be sent either south-west or south-east to join the Trans-Siberian pipeline. The first section to be completed was the western, linking Omsk (and its refinery) with Ust'-Balyk by a 650 km. long 40 in. diameter pipeline. The eastern section is formed by the above-mentioned Aleksandrovskoye–Anzhero–Sudzhensk pipeline about which some further details may be of interest. It is 818 km. long and was completed in 1972 having traversed the entire Tomsk oblast. The opening of this 48 in. pipe, the largest hitherto used in the Soviet Union, was celebrated as a great feat of Soviet construction by the Soviet press, the workers having had to cope with 50° of frost and other extremely harsh physical difficulties like the Vasyugan marshes and bogs. For the first time in Soviet practice 'polymer wrapping was used to insulate pipe on a large scale'.

The latest pipeline in west Siberia to be completed has attracted exceptional attention in Soviet sources (1973). This is the pipeline which will soon bring oil from the great Samotlor deposit to the collecting station at Al'met'yevsk in the Tatar A.S.S.R. Thence it will pass to the Volga plants and by the international *Druzhba* (Friendship) pipeline to the socialist countries of Europe. It is a 48 in. pipe and described as 'the longest pipeline in the world' by Soviet sources (1,836 km. from Ust'-Balyk to Al'met'yevsk, from Samotlor 2,119 km.). The actual laying of the pipe to Al'met'yevsk was completed in May 1973, but the flow-through was held up by various technical difficulties. Excavation and preparation of the pipeline was earlier beset by problems which threatened to delay construction but they were overcome by a rousing propaganda campaign urging the workers to 'victory on time'. This was a very difficult job, as means had to be devised to lay the pipe trenches across hundreds of kilometres of boggy ground, 200 rivers and many patches of hilly country in the Urals. It was not facilitated by the fact that in 1972–73 certain members of the management and other technical staff threw up their jobs and a general lack of coordination between the sectional construction teams caused many stoppages. These disturbances apparently took place in spite of a recent and much-needed reorganisation of the pipeline construction system, which established a 'unified' direction, putting all branches of the work on a sector of a pipeline under the control of one responsible manager.

Unlike the situation further north in the gas fields, none of these oil pipelines runs through a permafrost area. Permafrost has a constant temperature below the surface of 4° below freezing. Pipelines for natural gas can be drilled into it without undue difficulty but summer melting in the middle Ob' causes other major problems for oil pipelines which are outside the permafrost areas.

A number of pipelines are now also either operating, under construction, or planned, to bring the main flow of north Tyumen' natural gas to the western industrial centres of the Urals and European Russia, and also to Noril'sk. Two important pipelines radiate from the natural gas centre of Nadym both involving very difficult construction tasks through bogs and lakes and other natural obstacles on the way west. The *Siyaniye Severa* (Northern Lights) pipe from Nadym through Ukhta and Torzhok will eventually link up with the Moscow–Leningrad pipeline (a distance of 2,460 km. in all). The second pipe from Nadym will bring Medvezh'ye gas to Punga, which is already connected by trunk pipelines with the main Urals industrial towns and European Russia. It was reported in 1972 that gas from the Yamalo-Nenetskiy okrug was also being fed into the Medvezh'ye pipeline. Both the exploitation of the big Medvezh'ye field and the connecting pipeline with Nadym have been beset by design and equipment difficulties, so that the scheduled time-table for the completion of this pipeline had to be indefinitely postponed in 1970. The Ministry of the Gas Industry is held to be largely responsible for this break-down. The local newspaper *Tyumenskaya Pravda* found the situation so bad that it called for action against those whose irresponsibility and lack of discipline had held up work on this pipeline.

The first attempt to bring Messoyakha Polar gas to Dudinka and the thermal electric station and metallurgical plants of Noril'sk ended in failure. But at a second attempt a 270 km. long 'experimental' pipe was laid in 1970 beneath the deep waters of the Yenisey river, a considerable engineering feat. No gas pipeline had hitherto been laid in such high latitudes. A second string to this pipeline, 263 km. long, was completed between Messoyakha and Noril'sk, in 1973. The gas pipelines currently in use in the Tyumen' fields are 40 in. or 48 in. in diameter but trans-mission of gas is being hampered by the small diameter pipe. The technical assist-ance of German and Italian firms has been sought, so as to procure cold-resistant, large-diameter pipes, in bigger quantities than can be manufactured by Soviet plants without undue delays. Super-capacity pipes of 75 in. and 100 in. are also planned and the Germans are cooperating in the designing of suitable plant for this purpose. It is estimated that the use of these large diameter pipes will almost halve the transmission costs of this natural gas, compared to the costs of using 40 in. pipes. Apart from the need for wider pipe, compressor technology will have to be considerably developed to produce high pressures in this huge volume of gas to make its running economic. When these more powerful gas pipelines are in opera-tion, Tyumen' gas will be one of the most economical types of fuel in European Russia, according to Soviet estimates, and almost twice as cheap as Kuzbas or Donbas coals (which it may replace, to a large extent, eventually).

The progress of mechanisation is hampered by many equipment problems. Much research, for example, is still necessary to reduce capital costs and the excessive volume of metal in the equipment of the Tyumen' oil and gas fields. According to *Pravda*, a completely new modern technology must be evolved for giant units capable of producing 100 milliard cu.m. of gas annually, from 70–80 wells at

Medvezh'ye or Urengoy, compared to the 600 wells in the Komi A.S.S.R. or 1,500 wells in the Ukraine, required to produce the same amount.

In spite of the far-reaching advantages of Tyumen' natural gas for the Soviet fuel balance, a Soviet economist has warned that even when developed to its maximum (plus Central Asian gas), these supplies will not be sufficient to eliminate the fuel balance deficit in the European regions and the Urals, bearing in mind that owing to the lag in compressor technology, the carrying capacity of the super-diameter pipes can only be achieved some years after they are laid. Special long-distance pipelines to move gas from west Siberia to Central Russia in liquefied form would also be worth building, in the opinion of some Soviet scientists. This would mean liquefying large quantities at the gas fields and the liquefaction plant itself would be powered by gas.

In developing these huge new oil and gas reserves, the Soviet government was confronted with technological problems of great complexity and magnitude arising from the peculiarly harsh natural conditions of the area. Some of the more important problems seeking local solutions were and still are connected with the organisation of drilling work on swampy and flooded territories, collecting, preparing and transporting oil, as well as ways and means of industrial and civil construction in these conditions. The consensus of expert (and informed journalistic) Soviet opinion seems to be that the authorities concerned with these problems have been grossly incompetent and 'lagging' in handling them. Oil production has indeed risen rapidly since 1964 (when the first wells were commercially operated) but this is alleged to be essentially due to the high productivity of Siberian reserves. It could have been much higher if the responsible authorities had been more active and efficient in adjusting oil technology to Siberian conditions. In fact, a primary cause of great losses to the state, and disorder in the oil fields, originally came from the lack of technical preparation by the respective centralised ministries. Oil techniques and equipment developed for the entirely different conditions in the Baku and '2nd. Baku' (Volga-Urals) fields were originally transferred unaltered to the Tyumen' quagmire. This situation has been gradually improving, but too much excessively heavy equipment is still wastefully used on the sandy-boggy ground covering so much of these oil deposits.

Inadequate pipeline, tankage and collecting equipment to deal with the flow of mid-Ob' oil was also a problem criticised in Soviet sources. At one time, it even seemed unlikely that pipeline capacity would be large enough to meet the modest (for west Siberia) target of 120–125 million tons of oil in 1975. But the completion of the Anzhero–Sudzhensk pipeline in 1972 removed this threat, as far as can be foreseen, to the 1975 and 1980 plan targets for west Siberian oil.

Another cause for complaints is the delay in coping with the widespread electric power requirements throughout the oil fields. The Surgut G.R.E.S. (regional power station) one of the 'Komsomol construction schemes', specially designed to provide the necessary power is being built apparently 'intolerably slowly' and, until it is operating, local power demands 'hang on the thread of the Tyumen–Surgut L.E.P.' (electric power transmission line). Lack of power has also had repercussions on the already difficult housing situation in the oil-gas fields be-

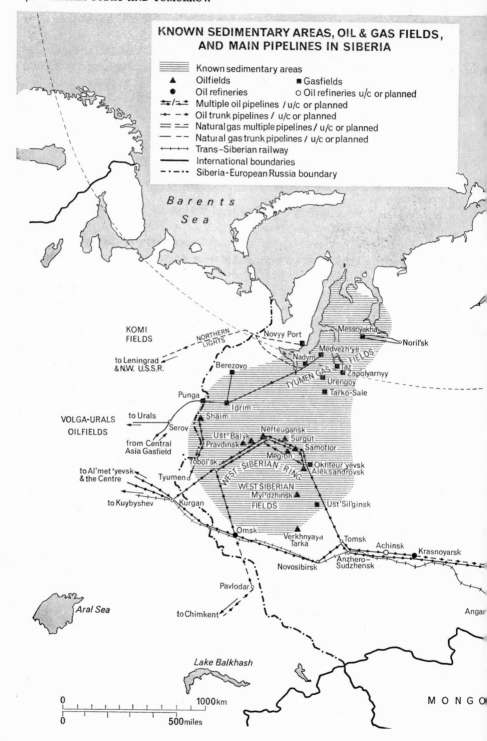

KNOWN SEDIMENTARY AREAS, OIL & GAS FIELDS, AND MAIN PIPELINES IN SIBERIA

- ≡≡≡ Known sedimentary areas
- ▲ Oilfields   ■ Gasfields
- ● Oil refineries   o Oil refineries u/c or planned
- ⇌/⇌ Multiple oil pipelines / u/c or planned
- - ―• Oil trunk pipelines / u/c or planned
- ≡ ═ Natural gas multiple pipelines / u/c or planned
- - - - Natural gas trunk pipelines / u/c or planned
- ┼┼┼┼ Trans–Siberian railway
- ──── International boundaries
- -·-·- Siberia-European Russia boundary

Barents Sea

KOMI FIELDS

NORTHERN LIGHTS

Novyy Port

Messoyakha

Noril'sk

to Leningrad & N.W. U.S.S.R.

Berezovo

Nadym

Medvezh'ye

GAS FIELDS

Taz

Zapolyarnyy

Urengoy

Punga

Igrim

Tarko-Sale

TYUMEN GAS

VOLGA-URALS OILFIELDS

to Urals

Shaim

Serov

from Central Asia Gasfield

Ust'Balyk

Pravdinsk

Nefteugansk

Surgut

Samotlor

to Al'met'yevsk & the Centre

Tobol'sk

Tyumen

Megion

WEST SIBERIAN RING

Okhteur'yevsk

Aleksandrovsk

to Kuybyshev

Kurgan

WEST SIBERIAN

Myl'dzhinsk

FIELDS

Ust'Sil'ginsk

Omsk

Verkhnyaya Tarka

Tomsk

Achinsk

Krasnoyarsk

Anzhero-Sudzhensk

Novosibirsk

Pavlodar

Aral Sea

to Chimkent

Angar

Lake Balkhash

0 ──────── 1000km

0 ──────── 500miles

M O N G O

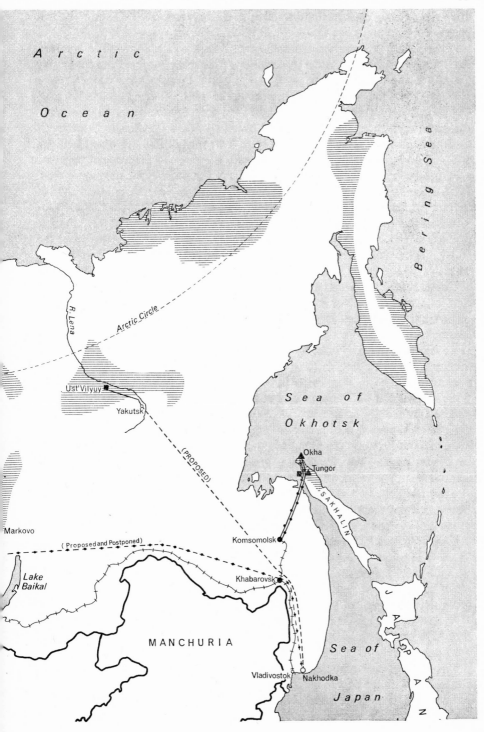

Arctic

Ocean

Bering Sea

R. Lena

Arctic Circle

Ust'Vilyuy

Yakutsk

(PROPOSED)

Markovo

(Proposed and Postponed)

Lake
Baikal

MANCHURIA

Sea of
Okhotsk

Okha

Tungor

SAKHALIN

Komsomolsk

Khabarovsk

Sea of

Vladivostok   Nakhodka

Japan

J
A
P
A
N

cause the housing construction combines could not operate satisfactorily without power. But by 1974, three sets of the G.R.E.S. were on load.

Major difficulties have also still to be overcome in connection with transport in the Tyumen' region. While the construction of the main Surgut–Tyumen' railway (scheduled for completion in 1971) was 'lagging' through 1972 and not completed by 1973, thus increasing difficulties in the transport of supplies to the mid-Ob' oil industry, other forms of transport have been developing much more satisfactorily. In spite of the difficulty and expense of road building in these boggy lands, 147.5 km. of all-weather roads were built in the Tyumen' oblast between 1965–70, 40 km. in the oil-bearing areas of the oblast and the planned target for 1971 was 80 km. of which 25 km. was to be in the region of the Samotlor field. Huge transport planes and helicopters which reportedly can carry large loads of heavy machinery for the construction workers in the roadless extreme north of Tyumen' and fly in almost any weather, are now operating satisfactorily. Further planned aims for transport in the current plan period are the expansion of the motor road network, airports and other means of communications. 1975 will see what this plan has actually achieved.

The west Siberian oil-gas experience goes to show that much of Soviet domestic equipment and technology is behind the latest developments in the U.S. and some other western industries. Deep drilling such as the Soviet oil men have been confronted with in west Siberia presents new technical problems for them. According to an American oil economist who has made a special study of the Soviet oil-gas industry, Soviet turbodrills (long favoured in the Soviet Union) have shown a poor performance in deep wells in the soft Siberian geological structure. The Soviets themselves have now stated that turbo-drilling has been unsuccessful in the middle Ob' and are using rotary drills whenever possible. 'Not only does their main disadvantage *vis-à-vis* rotary drilling, i.e. rapid wearing out of the bit, become more of a burden when the round trip to replace a bit takes so long, but also their main advantage – high mechanical speed – disappears because friction losses drastically cut power delivery to the bottom of the hole.' Soviet bits and strings are also not up to western standards, while the Soviet industry would certainly have benefited from earlier use of the kind of mobile equipment (used in rather similar conditions in Canada), which can be assembled or dismantled rapidly.

'Block construction' methods, by which heavy items of equipment are prepared in urban factories for assembly in the northern areas, are being extensively used, with a corresponding saving of labour and time in hauling such equipment over difficult terrain. The central organs and often *Gosstroy* are rebuked locally for not organising the supply of this equipment more effectively.

Against this background of technological problems, the Soviet invitation to the U.S.A. to participate in the west Siberian energy industry together with Japan is not surprising.

The basis of this proposed co-partnership deal would be that the American companies would be paid in natural gas for their technical assistance, which would presumably include installation of the latest western sophisticated equipment. With such assistance, the western Siberian industry might be expected to make a great leap forward in overcoming difficulties which might otherwise involve further wastage of time and money before finding a domestic solution.[3]

Moving away from these great oil-gas developments in west Siberia, to east Siberia and the Far East, the fuel position changes abruptly. In both these regions, with a few minor exceptions, the interest centres rather on the energy potential than on present exploitation and production of oil and natural gas. There is relatively little comment in Soviet sources on these fuel reserves of East Siberia and the Soviet Far East though their eventual economic and strategic-political importance is certainly considerable. Neither was mentioned in the Twenty-fourth Party Congress directives for immediate development, although east Siberia has been mentioned in earlier plans for oil development.

The latest geological investigation of the wild Bakhta river country and the basins of the Upper and Lower Tunguska rivers (tributaries of the Yenisey), yielded promising results for future oil development in this area of east Siberia, of which nothing was formerly known. Apparently new geological research methods were successfully used here in 1972, as traditional methods successful elsewhere were useless in the peculiar geological formation of this region. Interest in the deposits of top quality oil has been slow at Markovo, in the upper Lena basin (Irkutsk oblast), but drilling there is reported to be very expensive owing to the depth of the wells. Surveying work started some years ago in preparation for the construction of a Markovo–Irkutsk–Cheremkhovo pipeline, but nothing more is known abroad of its progress. Markovo also contains the largest deposit of wet gas in the Soviet Union. Once an important settlement on the old highroad to Yakutsk, Markovo may yet be destined for a new industrial life when, in the view of the Soviet government, it is opportune to invest in its development.

The most active area of exploitation and exploration of oil and natural gas in the Soviet Far east is on and around the island of Sakhalin. Here production is centred on the main oil deposits at Okha on the north-east coast and the newer wells at Neftegorsk. Annual output is estimated at about 3,000,000 t. but operations are far from easy in the appalling climate of the island. Sakhalin produced about 1,000 million cu.m. of natural gas in 1971. A trunk pipeline between Sakhalin and the mainland across the Tatar Strait was reported to be under construction in 1972 'so as to utilise this natural gas to better advantage'. Sakhalin oil is of high quality with a very low sulphur content. It supplies some 40% of the requirements of the Soviet Far Eastern region and is most useful as a convenient local reserve for fuelling the Far Eastern fishing fleet and domestic industry on the mainland. There is no refinery on the island. The crude oil is pumped from the Sakhalin port of Moskal'vo on the west coast to the refinery at Komsomol'sk through two underwater pipelines. A small percentage of this oil is also exported to Japan but the main Soviet oil exports to Japan are shipped from Black Sea ports. The idea of constructing a refinery on the island is now being discussed because of the high transport and distribution cost of this crude to the mainland.

On-shore reserves of oil are beginning to peter out in Sakhalin in spite of a few

[3] This subject of American and Japanese co-operation in the economic development of Siberia is discussed in detail in Chapter 12 below.

valuable new oil strikes which were reported in the Dagi taiga, in 1970–72. But there is the likelihood of considerable offshore deposits, and prospecting has begun there and on other parts of the Pacific littoral. Soviet sources are optimistic about the off-shore potential of the Soviet Far Eastern and Sakhalin coasts as being likely extensions of the oil deposits in the adjacent east China and Japan seas, but Soviet off-shore drilling equipment, derricks, etc., is known to be very inferior.

Production costs of Sakhalin oil are stated by Soviet sources to be much higher than the national average while productivity in the oil fields is relatively low. In view of the extremely harsh climate in the northern coastal region, great efforts are being made according to the Soviet press to retain the oil workers by providing better housing, food supplies, schools and kindergartens, especially in the new settlement of Neftegorsk.

The natural gas deposits of central Yakutiya are estimated to be very rich and to contain about 12% (13,000,000 million cu.m.) of the total Soviet reserves of natural gas. The explored reserves are put at 800 milliard cu.m. and the commercial reserves at about 220 milliard cu.m. but a complete scientific survey of these reserves has not apparently yet been made. They are situated in the remote Lena-Vilyuy area and were virtually untapped up to 1973. A small beginning was made, in 1966, to exploit the gas concentration at Tas-Tumus and a 250 km. long, 22 in. pipeline was constructed to Yakutsk-Pokrovsk, to supply fuel for domestic use and the Yakutsk gas turbine power station.

Japanese cooperation in the development of Yakutsk natural gas cropped up unexpectedly in the course of Soviet–Japanese discussions, in 1969–70, on the joint development of Sakhalin natural gas and the construction of a pipeline to bring the gas to the petro-chemical industries of the island of Hokkaido. Pleading that they had overestimated the extent of the Sakhalin gas reserves, the Soviet delegation switched the cooperation proposal to the much more complex and expensive development of the Yakutsk fields. The Japanese were annoyed at this change of policy and the negotiations were suspended.

Towards the end of 1972, there were indications that the Soviet government had at last decided to develop the Yakutsk natural gas deposits on a large scale. A special prospecting group was formed in Yakutsk 'with the task of handing over for industrial exploitation by the end of 1974 deposits with reserves of at least 800,000 million cu. m. of natural gas'. At the same time negotiations were renewed with the Japanese on the joint exploitation of these natural gas reserves and as it later transpired, discussions had also been proceeding about Soviet cooperation with the American Occidental Petroleum Corporation and its associates El Paso Natural Gas and Bechtel. It was then stated that the Japanese had agreed to U.S. participation in the project because of the very large credits, totalling between 2,500 and 3,000 million dollars (according to a Japanese source), required to develop this gas. The Occidental Petroleum group signed a letter of intent in June 1973 with Soviet officials for a $10-billion venture to develop Yakutsk gas and construct a 2,000-mile pipeline to a Soviet Pacific port and a liquefaction plant to liquefy this gas before transmission to the West Coast of the United States. Discussions with the Japanese and the Americans about this venture are continuing and much still remains to be settled about finance etc. and the track of this new pipeline. Two possible routes have been mentioned: one between Yakutsk and Ol'ga Bay (a port in the neighbourhood of Nakhodka) and another between Yakutsk and Hokkaido, presumably passing through Magadan before crossing the Sea of Okhotsk on the way to Sakhalin. The latter was the route proposed originally to the Japanese by Moscow in the abortive 1969–70 negotiations. Now that the Americans are to participate in a big way in this development, it is unlikely that the Magadan pipeline would suit their tankers destined for the West Coast of the United States. Construction of a pipeline by either route would be a lengthy and expensive undertaking and involve crossing some wild and difficult country. Shortly after the Soviet-American letter of intent regarding the development of Yakutsk gas was signed, Japanese involvement in this joint project was confirmed on the basis of a 'memorandum' (July 1973) under which the Soviet Union would receive U.S. and Japanese bank loans totalling $150 millions and supply 1.5 million tons of liquefied natural gas over 20 years to the United States and Japan. The terms of these loans had not been arranged at the time of writing and many other important details of this triangular deal remained to be agreed in later discussions.

The petroleum potential of Yakutiya is also believed to be very great (estimated at 'many milliards of tons'). The main fields are located a few hundred kilometres north of Yakutsk at Kangalassy and south-east of Yakutsk in the Aldan-Maya river basin. They are still completely undeveloped owing to the high capital outlay required to bring the wells into operation and to create the necessary infrastructure, while local industrial demand is at present lacking. As the Japanese have now become involved in the development of the Yakut gas reserves they may also be attracted eventually to the co-partnership possibilities of exploiting Yakut oil.[4]

Further east, Soviet geologists recently discovered a big 'gasser' in the Anadyr depression and there are now grounds for believing that the extreme north-east of the Soviet Union or Chukotka may become another national oil-gas region of some significance.

Statistical information about the volume of Soviet refining capacity is not published in the Soviet Union. So one is left at best with informed estimates. But on the score of refining capacity, Soviet sources leave no doubt that Siberian refining capacity has not yet caught up with the rapid rise in the output of west Siberian oil. The only refinery actually operating in west Siberia in 1972 was the old refinery at Omsk (probable annual capacity 22 million tons). It has now switched from its former Volga-Urals source of supply to Samotlor oil via the Ust'-Balyk pipeline. This refinery is being greatly expanded to cope with the flow of Tyumen' oil and is part of a big chemical complex scheduled to be fully operative in 1975.

West Siberian refinery capacity will be considerably increased when a number of new refining petro-chemical units, planned for construction in the near future, are completed. In west Siberia, these refineries will be at Tobol'sk, Tomsk and Niznevartovsk. The large petro-chemical plant scheduled for construction under the current F.Y.P. at Tobol'sk will produce a wide range of products, including ethylene and propylene and many types of plastic. In stressing the importance of

This subject is further discussed in Chapter 13.

accelerating completion of this plant so as to cut down expenditure on imports of chemical products, *Pravda* also stated that the present capacity of the Ob' oil extraction industry (1972) greatly exceeded the possibilities of processing this oil in Siberia, adding that almost all associated gas was still being flared off.

There were disquieting reports (1972) in the Soviet press in 1972 about the lack of coordination between the requirements of this Tobol'sk petro-chemical complex and the new Tobol'sk port being constructed to serve it, with warnings that if this situation was not put right in time it might be necessary to enlarge the port by the time it was completed.

Plants are also being constructed in east Siberia to process Tyumen' oil. A large refinery is being built at Achinsk, on the Trans-Siberian railway, west of Krasnoyarsk, but the Soviet press was critical of its rate of progress, in the early stages of construction, in 1972–73. The Angarsk refinery (operating since 1960–61) forms part of an important petro-chemical plant. Both are now being enlarged and modernised and when completed it is anticipated that the refinery capacity will be enlarged by 80% (present estimated annual capacity about 14 million tons).[5] The Angarsk refinery contains the largest plant for the production of petrol in the U.S.S.R.

According to some expert Soviet calculations, the location of oil refineries linked with petrochemical units in Siberia will provide savings of up to 8–10% in operating expenditure and 12–14% in capital investments, in comparison with the costs of producing equal quantities of similar products from Siberian oil in European Russia. These calculations are the more weighty in that they take account of the higher wage rates and costs of construction in Siberia.

In the Far Eastern region there are a few small refineries at Komsomol'sk, Khabarovsk and Vladivostok. All are to be enlarged during the current plan period and a second refinery is to be built at Komsomol'sk to deal with west Siberian oil when it arrives by the projected railway.

Electric Power. Siberia is very rich in both hydro and thermal sources of electric power. It far outstrips the other regions of the Soviet Union in this energy potential. Siberian hydropower originates in the great northern rivers, the Yenisey, the Angara, the Amur and the Lena and others of lesser force, while the large and widely distributed brown coal reserves can most economically be used for pit-head thermal power stations.

When more active development of this power potential was provisionally decided on in the late fifties and written into the sixth and subsequent plans, Siberian electrification was able to draw on the valuable experience of construction of large hydro and thermal plants in European Russia. In order to avoid costly pitfalls in planning, this European experience required primary adjustment to the very different climatic conditions of Siberia. The many special problems of construction and equipment of Siberian electrification schemes have therefore constantly engaged the attention of Soviet research institutions and individual specialists. There has also been some frank criticism by these experts of official Soviet energy policies, especially the failure to coordinate electrical output with demand. At

[5] This complex is further discussed in Chapter 7.

Bratsk for example, unknown quantities of electric power potential were wasted owing to delays in building the associated power consuming plants and even now some of the power has to be fed into the grid.

As a result of the operation of 'giant' new, reconstructed and expanded electric stations throughout Siberia, the production of electric power rapidly increased between 1958–69 and continues to expand. As is clear from the table below, expansion was greatest in Eastern Siberia where the largest volume of hydropower potential is concentrated.

Production of electric energy by economic regions (millions of kw. hours)

	1960	1970
RSFSR	196,988	470,211
of which:		
East Siberian region	16,157	74,040
West Siberian region	22,509	44,221
Far Eastern region	5,250	14,080

Source: Narkhoz RSFSR v 1970. p. 72.

Siberia's share of the production of electric power in the R.S.F.S.R. grew from 10.2% in 1940 to 28.11 in 1970 (in milliard kwh.) and its share of electric capacity in the same period from 11.9% to 32.3%. In all-Union terms the respective percentages in 1970 were 18% and 20%. The most powerful and economical electric power stations in the Soviet Union are operating in Siberia. Largely because of the great rivers located in these eastern regions of the R.S.F.S.R., the Soviet Union holds first place in the world of hydroelectric potential.

The elaborate publicity in the Soviet press, featuring the construction of 'giant' H.E.S. at Bratsk or Krasnoyarsk, with illustrations of 'heroic workers' triumphantly coping with the difficulties of such construction, should not be taken to mean that even with the rapid rise in production and its unchallenged energy potential, Siberia is yet the major producer of electric power in the Soviet Union. With its dominant industrial position, European Russia is still the major producer and consumer of electric power, both hydro and thermal. These 'giant' Siberian H.E.S. of 4–6 million kw. are still the exception in the Soviet energy system (though they are on the increase in Siberia). Over 70% of Soviet electric power is actually produced from thermal stations of about 100,000 kw. capacity distributed throughout the Soviet Union.

In Siberia, the conditions are, however, favourable for the development of big concentrations of electric power, round which 'industrial complexes' are, or will in future be, established, as is now the approved official policy. Moreover, Siberia is planned to play a large part eventually in supplying cheap electric power by superlong high tension transmission lines to energy-deficient European Russia. A unified grid has now been completed in Siberia similar to that earlier operating in European Russia. Work is also proceeding on a unified Far Eastern grid. Extension of the high voltage unified grid system will make it possible to take advantage of the great differences in the times zones, reaching many hours, between the Pacific areas and Moscow and the drops between maximum and minimum loads resulting in enormous savings of kWh. of energy. Soviet electrical engineers are now actively engaged in research on the technological problems which must be solved before Siberian energy can be transmitted from Siberia to European Russia. These distances are too great, at the present stage of technological development, for the establishment of one all-Union unified system. As the highest tension in the world is already in operation in the Soviet Union, the prospects are good for Soviet technologists eventually to solve these difficult problems. The chief Party organs attach great importance to the successful outcome of this research and its continuation is urged in the Directives of the Twenty-fourth Party Congress (1971). However, even at the voltages already achieved, transmission losses over the 2–3,000 kilometres concerned would be prohibitive and no final decision has yet been reached as to the best voltage to aim at or technology to use: transmission of this power in artificially refrigerated super-conducting lines has even been considered.

While recognising the use of high voltages and direct current transmission of electric power for reducing costs, the ranking Soviet economist A. Probst nevertheless had some reservations on the subject which are worth recording. 'It is quite obvious', he wrote, 'that neither progress in electric power transmission techniques, nor even the future improvement of the techniques and economy of pipeline and railroad transportation in general, will be able to equalise the cost of fuel and electric power in the regions of our enormous country. In the foreseeable future, technological progress can bring about only a certain reduction in the very substantial regional differences in the cost level of fuel and electric power.'

In spite of adverse natural conditions, the construction of hydroelectric stations in Siberia, according to Soviet expert calculations costs less than in European Russia. In particular, the generation of electric power at the big hydroelectric power stations of eastern Russia calls for capital outlays threefold or fourfold smaller, and amortisation of this capital investment several years earlier, than in the European part of the country, according to the same calculations. This favourable attitude is often criticised for not giving due weight to the admittedly high cost of creating an essential infrastructure for many of these power stations in the unindustrialised, uninhabited Siberian wilderness. The counter argument is that though the costs of transport and other necessary civil installations are relatively high for the service of individual, territorial isolated enterprises, such as the Noril'sk mining centre, for example, the capital outlay is considerably less if the infrastructure serves a 'complex' of industrial enterprises, or as it is sometimes called, an entire industrial node. The construction of such industrial complexes centred on electric power or energy bases is now Soviet policy and is currently being implemented, notably in the many-sided Sayan hydroelectric power complex, and the various industries being established on the basis of north Tyumen' oil and gas.

Such in broad outline are the aims and problems of the development of Siberian electrification. A lot of intrepid and expert work has clearly gone into the planning and construction of power stations in all kinds of difficult geological-climatic conditions, in spite of much ineptitude and delays in construction. The situation in individual areas of Siberia and the Soviet Far Eastern region will now be examined in greater detail.

In western Siberia, the opening up of the Tyumen' oil and gas fields in turn

top: Construction of the
Okha-Komsomol'sk oil pipeline
under the Nevelsky Strait
bottom: Samotlor-Almetyevsk
oil pipeline under construction

created heavy new demands for electric power which were entirely beyond the capacity of the existing small network of electric stations. A first, temporary, and wholly inadequate measure to supply power to the middle-Ob' oil fields was the construction of a 700 km. long high-voltage transmission line from the Tyumen' thermal station while a local T.E.Ts. (heat and power station) was put up at Surgut in 1970. But in order to provide more adequate supplies of power to the constantly expanding Ob' oil fields, construction was started in 1968 on a 2.4 million kw. G.R.E.S. in Surgut. After much delay, the first power unit was installed (200,000 kw. capacity) in 1972, and it should be fully operating according to the Directives of the Twenty-fourth Party Congress in 1975. Such at least is the planned timetable.

A labour force of 2,500 workers is now engaged in constructing this important station 'in a picturesque corner of the taiga'. Management, the Soviet press reports, have given unusual attention to providing comfortable living quarters and some essential services for the workers, no doubt to avoid the usual 'flight of labour' from such Siberian construction sites. Before tackling the main power station buildings, 50 km. of concrete roads, a river landing stage for supplies, repair workshops and stores were built. When completed, the new Surgut G.R.E.S. will be one of the most powerful stations fuelled by associated gas in the Soviet Union and its surplus power will be relayed to Tobol'sk, Tyumen' and the Urals. Various technical problems have arisen in the course of construction which were not apparently studied in advance. Apprehension was expressed in 1971 about the movement of the swampy ground on which the station was being erected, under the heavy weight of the powerful station structure. Experts from the Sverdlovsk and Krasnoyarsk Scientific Research Institutes were called in to advise on this urgent problem. At the same time, the supply situation was causing anxiety and the transport organs were accused by the Soviet press of obstructing the delivery of thousands of tons of materials required for this G.R.E.S. construction (and on which the swift increase in extraction rates of Tyumen' oil so largely depends). It is repeatedly stated that the development of this industry is being hampered by the lack of adequate power and the delays in improving the situation.

In the rest of the region, western Siberia obtains its power mainly from a number of thermal stations, large and small. Hydropower is only developed from the Ob' at Novosibirsk where there is a H.E.S. (capacity 400,000 kw.) completed in 1959 to supply this important industrial centre. For some time, there was a good deal of official steam behind a project to build a large H.E.S. (6–7 mil. kw.) on the Ob' estuary. The scheme finally foundered against the opposition of various scientific experts, stressing the damage it would inevitably do to the new local oil-gas industry, the fishing and timber concerns and the environment. The important industrial areas of Kemerovo and the Kuzbas basin are supplied with power from big thermal stations at Tomusa (capacity 1.3 mil. kw.), Belovo (1.2 mil. kw.) and many smaller units.

In adjacent east Siberia, as already mentioned, there is a long term project to develop one of the largest power complexes in the world, on the basis of the Kansk-Achinsk lignite deposits. The scheme included single mines producing 10 million

The construction site of the
Tuva cobolt plant

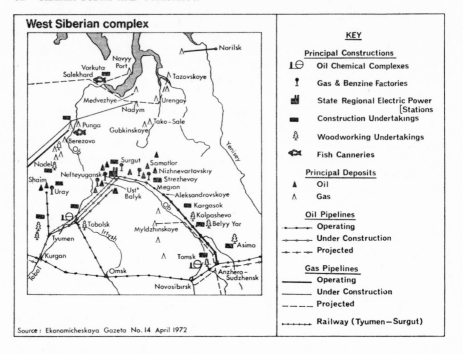

West Siberian complex

KEY

Principal Constructions

⦶ Oil Chemical Complexes

☗ Gas & Benzine Factories

State Regional Electric Power [Stations

Construction Undertakings

Woodworking Undertakings

Fish Canneries

Principal Deposits

▲ Oil

⋀ Gas

Oil Pipelines

Operating

Under Construction

Projected

Gas Pipelines

Operating

Under Construction

Projected

Railway (Tyumen–Surgut)

Source: Ekonomicheskaya Gazeta No. 14 April 1972

tons of brown coal a year, with huge power stations sited at the mines and transmitting the power to the western regions. It has been much delayed, though originally planned to start in the late 1970s, by the enormous capital costs involved and by the lack of any existing technology for the transmission of electric power over such vast distances without prohibitive losses. Nevertheless such a development is possible in future decades and would provide the cheapest power by far in the Soviet Union.

The development of east Siberia's unique hydropower has provided some of the most spectacular items of Soviet construction in post-war five-year plans. First, came the 'giant' Bratsk H.E.S. (4,700,000 kw. at full capacity) and in its time the most powerful hydro-station in the world. It was announced as the beginning of a series or 'cascade' of large-scale stations, to be built on the Angara river before its confluence with the Yenisey. The site of the Bratsk H.E.S., in a remote stretch of taiga in the depths of east Siberia, originally confronted the workers with many tough construction problems, while they simultaneously had to cope with the most primitive living conditions. The result was a considerable exodus of the weaker brethren and the prolongation of the construction some years beyond the scheduled commissioning date. This dragged on from 1954, when work started, until completion of the plant in 1967. It ran at low power and considerable financial loss in the early years, owing to the lag between the massive energy capacity of the station and the projected build-up of energy consuming industries. 70% of capacity was to be used by an aluminium plant, which has not yet reached full capacity. This uneconomic situation was revealed in N. S. Khrushchev's dramatic speech following his 1961 visit to Bratsk. By 1971, however, Bratsk was in full swing and was reported to have paid for itself three times over (though it is far from clear what the basis for this claim is). Most of this power is supplied to the important aluminium plant, but the new timber-processing, cellulose, paper, and other local industries also owe their existence to Bratsk power. It is transmitted by high voltage transmission lines to Krasnoyarsk and the new construction site at Ust'-Ilimsk hydroelectric power station.

On another stretch of the Angara river, in the 'virgin taiga', the Ust'-Ilimsk H.E.S. (capacity 4.5–5 mil. kw.) is being constructed, the first sets to go on load by 1974, according to the Twenty-fourth Party Congress Directives. This station is intended to be the centre of a new industrial area based on the large timber stocks surrounding[6] it and the three important iron deposits, Rudnogorsk, Neryunda and Kapayevo in the vicinity. Ust'-Ilimsk power will be used in the first place by the Rudnogorsk iron mines. This long-term project should entirely transform a former wilderness. Workers with experience of building the Bratsk dam in similarly inhospitable conditions have been transferred to Ust'-Ilimsk. Building materials, food and equipment can now reach this site either by the new branch line of the Trans-Siberian railway from Khrebtovaya to the new town of Ust'-Ilimsk, or along the trunk road (260 km.) from Bratsk. Photographs of the new town being built for the H.E.S. workers, published in the Soviet press, give a forbidding impression of bare gaunt buildings, devoid of trees or other greenery, in the recently cleared forest. The 'heroic' workers building this particularly difficult station through mid-winter frost and fog are frequently encouraged by flattering notices and photographs of them and their construction in the Soviet press. Ust'-Ilimsk is the third (after Irkutsk and Bratsk) in the 'Angara Cascade' construction programme, which originally had the ambitious aim of creating 16 stations with capacities up to 5–7 or even perhaps 10 million kw. But that will not be for at least another three to four five-year plan periods ahead. The proposal to build one of these 'Cascade' hydro-power stations at the confluence of the Angara and Yenisey was stopped by fears of resulting damage to timber combines and minerals.

After a short period of primacy, Bratsk has had to yield place to the Krasnoyarsk H.E.S. (capacity 5 million kw.) now the largest in the Soviet Union, and the world. This station is situated 20 km. up stream from Krasnoyarsk city, at the new town of Divnogorsk, on a central stretch of the Yenisey. The construction of the Kras-noyarsk H.E.S. dragged out some years beyond the official commissioning date and was ultimately completed in 1971. The event was celebrated by the installation on top of the station of a huge enamel plaque weighing about a ton 'crowned by an image of Lenin' whose centenary had occurred the previous year (when, according to schedule, the station should have been finished). It supplies essential power to the big new aluminium plant and the various metallurgical, timber-processing and other industries in Krasnoyarsk, and which is claimed to be several times cheaper than power from thermal stations.

Some 400 km. from the confluence of the Khantayka and Yenisey rivers, the Khantayka power station, the most northerly H.E.S. in the Soviet Union, is now being built in the desolate, permafrost area of the Taymyr peninsula. The Khantayka

[6] Further details of this Ust'-Ilimsk timber complex are given in Chapter 8 'Timber'.

river was dammed in 1970 when the first generating unit went on load. Its reservoir 'the man-made Taymyr sea' transformed the landscape for hundreds of miles but nothing further seems to have been revealed about this probably drastic transformation. Efforts are being made to complete this 441,000 kw station by 1975 and it has fallen badly behind the originally scheduled completion date of 1970. No. 7 set was 'put on idle run' in 1972. Construction started in 1963 entirely underground and the builders have had to cope with many complex problems. Owing to the remote site of this station, deliveries of heavy electrical equipment and other supplies are invariably uncertain. The big turbines can only reach Khantayka during the short summer Yenisey–Khantayka navigation season, shipped from the Krasnoyarsk base. Lighter goods can be dispatched much more expensively by air. A new town, Snezhnogorsk, was built in 1968 to house the construction workers and contained about 7,000 inhabitants in 1971–72. The main function of this Khantyaka H.E.S., situated as it is in a virtually uninhabited, undeveloped area, will be to improve power supplies at the Noril'sk mining-metallurgical complex now largely fuelled with Messoyakha gas.

To the south of Khantayka, on another tributary of the Yenisey, the Kureyka, also within the Arctic circle, preparatory technical research is now afoot for the construction of the Kureyka G.E.S. It is intended to have a capacity of 500,000 kw. and to supply Igarka, Turukhansk and parts of the Evenk national okrug with power. In the present state of development of these areas this would mean mainly the isolated but important timber enterprises exporting timber through Igarka, where efficiency is often hampered by lack of power.

The hydro-power position not only in east Siberia but throughout the Soviet Union is dominated during the current ninth five-year plan by the scheduled super-power Sayano-Shushenskoye H.E.S. With a projected capacity of 6.4 million kw. it will supplant the Krasnoyarsk H.E.S. as the largest station in the Soviet Union. The Sayan H.E.S. is being constructed some hundreds of kilometres south of Krasnoyarsk in a narrow gorge on the upper reaches of the Yenisey, near the old town of Mayna. 'Like a razor, boiling and foaming, Yenisey slices through the slope of the Sayan mountains, flowing down with a roar into the Minusinsk depression. Here it enters into the area of the Khakass people with a grotesque mixture of fertile steppes, verdant meadows and sleepy taiga.' In these words, Nedelya (13–19.12.1971) described the site of the new Sayan power station lying in what Lenin called 'Siberian Italy'. It is entirely different from the climatically bleak, inhospitable conditions in which the Khantayka and Ust'-Ilimsk H.E.S. are being constructed. Sayan is regarded as an extremely advantageous site for a power station. The width of the river bed at this point is only 300 m. and during the high water season 10,000–12,000 cu.m. of water per second pass through and even double that quantity some years. Everything about the Sayan station is massive. The dam will be 240 m. high and the shoulders of the 'concrete colossus' will rest on the rocky Sayan hills. Special equipment has had to be designed for the project and there is reported to be a 'high degree of mechanisation and automation in the construction'.

It is not surprising, in a scheme of this magnitude, that the engineers have been confronted with various new problems, in particular the question of the stability of

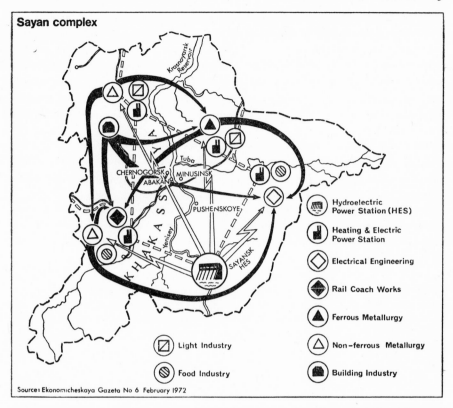

Sayan complex

CHERNOGORSK
ABAKAN
MINUSINSK
Tuba
PUSHENSKOYE
Yenisey
KHAKASSIYA
SAYANSK HES
Krasnoyarsk Reservoir

🏭 Hydroelectric Power Station (HES)

🏭 Heating & Electric Power Station

◇ Electrical Engineering

◆ Rail Coach Works

▲ Ferrous Metallurgy

△ Non-ferrous Metallurgy

▨ Light Industry

◎ Food Industry

▦ Building Industry

Source: Ekonomicheskaya Gazeta No 6 February 1972

the dam to withstand the great volume of water passing through. The volume of water passing per second through the huge turbines (original planned capacity 640,000 kw. each but may now reach the 'unprecedented capacity of 800,000 kw., from a height of 240 m.') is estimated to equal a river twice as big as the Angara. Some idea of the comparative force of this water power is shown by the fact that the most powerful waterfall in the world, the Victoria Falls, drops from a height of 120 m. The Sayan project has the advantage of being largely staffed by men with the experience of building the Krasnoyarsk H.E.S. behind them. The situation is very different from early days at Bratsk, when so many young people with no experience of hydropower station building were dumped on the raw site. Apart from the mild climate and skilled cadres, Sayan is fortunate in being in an area with relatively good communications, including some airline connections with European Russia, surfaced roads and the Abakan–Tayshet railway in the vicinity.

As Sayan is situated close to Shushenskoye where Lenin was exiled, it was inevitable that the Lenin myth should be exploited to the full in the construction of this H.E.S. All kinds of devices have been used to spur the workers on to intensive feats of labour productivity and unusual scenes of workers' enthusiasm have been reported from there, in honour of Lenin. The first concrete was poured by a 'specially honoured Brigade' dressed for the occasion in 'holiday attire' and silver roubles, watches, badges were piled into the concrete for luck. Quarrels apparently broke out among the drivers for the honour of carrying a twenty-ton marble slab to the foundations in the Yenisey river bed with the inscription: 'We are coming to you Yenisey.'

The Sayan H.E.S. is planned as the energy centre of a comprehensive 'Sayanskiy complex' embracing a wide range of new industries, mining sites, metallurgical and other enterprises. This industrial complex is also expected to provide certain industrial requirements for the northern regions. If this part of the ambitious Sayan programme succeeds, it might have far reaching results for these regions. The Sayan H.E.S. is thus from the outset planned on the 'territorial production' principle, being simultaneously linked with a large industrial complex to serve the needs of the surrounding country. This coordination of electric power and industrial-domestic production is an organised effort to avoid the costly 'disproportions' which occurred at Bratsk before industrial development was started. Sayan is an impressive project, but already some disconcerting discrepancies, apparently inseparable from the early days of all Soviet constructions, have cropped up there also.

The First Secretary of the Khakass *obkom* reported in 1971 that 'serious disorder' had been caused by the failure to prepare good design projects in time and that construction of the steel casting plant and the railway car complex were hampered by the delays in producing the necessary documentation. It was even stranger to learn, in view of the importance of this scheme, of 'the attempt of the planning organs and the supply ministries to carry over the financing of the key enterprises of the complex to the end of the five-year period.' This 'entirely unjustified policy' is deplored because 'it would create instability in the constructions' organisation and then lead to *shturmovshchina* (putting on a spurt), shoddy goods and other defects'. The First Secretary also found the attitude of the Ministry of Energy and Electrification of the U.S.S.R. 'especially incomprehensible' and accused it of keeping the Sayan H.E.S. constructors 'on very short financial reins'. It continued, this attitude could delay commissioning of the plant and threaten normal supplies of electric power to the enterprises of the complex. In order to eliminate the considerable losses being caused by the necessity of bringing prefabricated reinforced concrete from Novosibirsk, Bratsk and other remote places, it was also essential to establish a powerful construction industry on the spot and unless this was done, the situation, it was stressed, would become more acute as the complex developed.

The 'living problem', which has plagued Siberian construction sites for years had also emerged at Sayan in 1971. In the First Secretary's words: 'Questions of living-social-cultural construction arise with special acuteness in connection with the creation of the Sayan complex. The failure to provide living accommodation, children's institutions, shops, schools for a number of new enterprises has retarded the completion of production units and caused a great flight of labour.' The Ministry of Light Industry forced the construction of the Abakan knitwear factory and other light industries, but did not concern itself with the living accommodation and other domestic facilities for their workers. Now 'history is being repeated' as far as living quarters are concerned, in the Sayan H.E.S. workers' settlements.

Other disquieting aspects of the Sayan complex were stressed in an interview by

Academician Nekrasov, in 1971. 'It is necessary to admit', he stated, 'that there is still a lot of confusion [in the building of towns in the Sayan region]. Each agency is building at its own discretion. This threatens us with very unpleasant consequences. The question concerning a unified system of urban building within the entire complex must be resolved immediately. *Gosstroy* U.S.S.R. must certainly not have the last word with respect to this as well as to architectural supervision.' With luck, this well-deserved criticism of *Gosstroy* may have a beneficial influence on the planning of the new Sayan towns. The Sayan H.E.S. complex is undoubtedly a vast and imaginative project and when completed should transform Khakassia economically. It is a beautiful country and it is to be hoped that its natural beauty will not be destroyed by the tasteless industrialisation characteristic of Soviet development in Siberia (and all too familiar in the rest of the world).

Leaving the many hydroelectric-power schemes of eastern Siberia, the scene shifts to the Soviet Far East. Here there is a great hydropower potential in the powerful rivers, the Lena, the Yana, the Kolyma, the Amur, the Vilyuy . . . amounting to at least a fifth, it is estimated, of total Soviet hydropower. But this power is only beginning to be tapped, following urgent calls for increased energy from the rapidly expanding local mining industries.

The extremely harsh climate of many of these mining areas, the lack of infrastructure or ordinary amenities of civilised life, have also created peculiar technological problems and labour difficulties for the builders of thermal or hydro-power stations in the Far Eastern wilderness, where power was often most acutely needed. The first hydro-power station in the Far East was constructed in the permafrost at Chernyshevskiy in western Yakutiya. The place was most sparsely inhabited until a settlement for the workers was gradually established and the population reached 12,000 by 1968. Construction was protracted and difficult. In order to ensure an even temperature where winter frosts can reach as low as 70°C, the *Vilyuyges* (Vilyuy hydroelectric power station) had to be built underground. The kind of near catastrophic difficulties often faced by the builders of the station may be illustrated by the events of 1969. Then, the sluicegates which control the turbulent Vilyuy river were washed away by the spring floods and repairs had to be carried out by divers in the icy waters. Though originally planned for completion in 1966, the first set only went on load in 1970 and it was announced that the station would be completed by 1975 (capacity estimated at 312,000 kw.). *Vilyuyges* is primarily intended as the main source of power for the new Yakut diamond industry centred at Mirnyy (originally dependent for power on a small power plant at Lensk) and now being developed further north at Aykhal and Udachnyy. The completion of *Vilyuyges* is very important for the diamond industry for which it provides heat and power and for a growing number of other consumers in Yakutiya.

After some years of complicated discussion about the location of the site and the technical problems involved in harnessing the Kolyma river, a start was made in 1970 on the construction of the *Kolymages* (Kolyma hydroelectric power station), in the heart of the big Kolyma gold indsutry. It is now being built at Sinegor'ye a small village on the upper Kolyma. Lack of adequate power has long been a stumbling block in the development of the gold and other mining industries of this region. It is anticipated that the *Kolymages* will eventually provide large quantities of cheap power and ease the local energy deficit, the 'Achilles heel', according to Soviet commentators, of the gold industry. In particular, this power should make possible a much increased rate of automation and mechanisation of the productive processes. Meanwhile, the people working on this power station are up against daunting but familiar Siberian difficulties, as graphically described by a *Pravda* correspondent in 1971: 'Heavy frosts, strong stormy winds, permafrost, extensive summer flooding of the Kolyma river. There are no ready made facilities, everything has to be built up from scratch from roads to housing and supply stores. Unfortunately, the only road leading to the site is on the wrong side of the river so it was at first necessary to build a bridge. Then, the port installations at Nagayeva Bay had to be enlarged and improved so as to cope with the flow of freight brought in by sea.'

The main buildings, with the machine hall, are to be housed in a rock recess as a protection against this ferocious climate. Considerable assistance was rendered by the 'sister *Vilyuyges*' which sent a cavalcade of lorries with technicians and valuable equipment (tip-up lorries, powerful bulldozers, tractors) to help on the job, over a hazardous 3,500 km. journey from Chernyshevskiy. The first stage of the power station is scheduled for operation in 1975 but this may be premature, as the Twenty-fourth Party Congress directives only mention 'the start' of the construction. *Kolymages* is intended eventually to be connected with a large Kolyma grid and will be linked with the Arkagala G.R.E.S. (within the Susuman gold fields) and other local power stations.

Some hundreds of kilometres up stream at Cherskiy in the Kolyma estuary a power station of an unusual type is now moored. This is the 'Severnoye Siyaniye' (Northern Lights) coal-burning, floating power station (generating power 20,000 kw.), the first of its kind in the Soviet Union (though later another was to be built for the same design). It was constructed in the Tyumen' shipbuilding yards and towed through the precarious Arctic waters to start operating in Cherskiy in 1969. It was a remarkable feat, as such difficult ice conditions in the Kara Sea had not been experienced for at least half a century. This station provides industrial power for the gold mines round Bilibino. Though still an inadequate and temporary measure, it is very useful pending such time as it may be possible technically to bring high tension transmission power lines into Chukotka from more powerful stations. Pylons and power lines through the permafrost and tundra are also extremely costly to erect. In addition, more power for the local gold and tin mines of this area is to be provided by a small atomic power station, the only one so far in Siberia and for years now reported as 'under construction' at Bilibino with a generating capacity of 12,000 kw. Both Czechoslovakia and Hungary contributed equipment for the Bilibino power station and it had a long and difficult passage by rail and sea to the Yakut port of Zelenyy Mys and thence across 500 km. of frozen tundra to Bilibino. Workers from all over the Soviet Union were brought to Bilibino for this difficult job, especially those with previous experience of construction of atomic power stations. Pending a final solution of the region's energy problems, once it starts to operate, the Bilibino reactor will be welcomed for its effect on local industrial power, water and domestic heat and power supplies. The station produced the first power early in 1974.

The need for much more powerful sources of energy for the growing industries of the Magadan oblast, Chukotka, Kamchatka, the Primor'ye and the Amur basin is supported by the authoritative Director of the North-Eastern Complex Scientific Research Institute, Academician Shilo, who was also critical of the continual delays in getting the Bilibino atomic station started. 'A scientifically worked out plan of electrification of the Far East was necessary" he stated' 'so as not to have to have recourse to various kinds of "temporary expedients" which are not cheap for the government.' (*Pravda* 4.6.1971).

The Amur, the great southern river of the Soviet Far East, forming the boundary with China and some 2,690 miles long from its source to the delta, is an enormous potential source of hydro-electric power. The first hydro-scheme to get off the ground in this area is not directly concerned with tapping the resources of the Amur but rather its tributary, the Zeya. A hydroelectric power station is now being built on the turbulent, unpredictable Zeya river and planned generating capacity was raised from 1·20 mil. KW. to 1·5 mil. KW. in 1968. Construction of this station has been greatly delayed by the many difficulties created by the nature of the site. It is regarded as of key importance for the development of the southern areas of the Far Eastern economy, which is retarded by the present shortage of power. The Zeya river traverses a large area of excellent farm land, but crops and livestock are annually threatened by its spring floods. The aim of this project therefore is to curb this capricious river and prevent these annual disasters by the erection of a dam and reservoir. As the work progressed, it seems from a local press report (March 1972) that there was a good deal of anxiety among the workers to be re-settled after the reservoir flooding. No housing or domestic amenities had been created for them in the new places of settlement and an entirely irrational timetable threatened to destroy great stands of valuable timber. The whole resettlement operation seemed a combination of muddle and discreditable official negligence. Doubts have also arisen regarding the ecological effects of the proposed 300 km. long reservoir with a surface area of 2,500 sq. km. A team of experts from the Khabarovsk Research Institute of the Academy of Sciences were called in to advise on this situation in 1971–72. Their 'preliminary' findings were reassuring about the effect of the reservoir both on local flora and fauna. Various other difficulties have much delayed completion of this project beyond the original commissioning date set by the Twenty-third Party Congress. According to the directives of the Twenty-fourth Party Congress only the first sets are to be put on load by 1975. Greeted by 'local rejoicing', the Zeya was finally dammed in October 1972.

There is no immediate economic urgency to develop the vast latent hydro-power of the Amur river. Such a project would be on a par, if not greater in cost and difficulty, with anything yet attempted in this field in the Soviet Union. Nor is the present state of tension on the Sino-Soviet frontier conducive to peaceful construction of this nature. But it is interesting to recall that, as a result of the expert research conducted under the auspices of the joint Sino-Soviet Research and Development Project (while harmony still prevailed between Moscow and Peking), it was agreed in 1956 that the reserves of hydro-power of the Amur basin could best be developed under joint Sino-Soviet auspices. Accordingly, natural resources on both sides of the Amur frontier would be simultaneously developed with the aim of forming a great new industrial complex based on the Soviet iron and coal reserves and Chinese coal and other raw materials. Five hydro-stations, with an aggregate capacity of 5–6 million KW., to be situated on the upper Amur and two on the Argun rivers were initially proposed during these conversations (which ceased with the outbreak of Sino-Soviet hostility in 1968–69). If a scheme of this kind should be revived following a restoration of normal Sino-Soviet relations, it is believed that the Chinese, at any rate at the outset, would be by far the largest consumers of this power, transferred from the Amur stations to their relatively near local industries across the frontier.

Thermal power stations fed by the local lignite deposits dominate the energy picture in the rest of the southern Far Eastern region. The largest is the Primorsk G.R.E.S. (generating capacity 1.2 mil. kw.) now being built near the new town of Luchegorsk. This is a pithead station based on Bikin coal and of considerable local importance. Apart from providing heat and power for industry and local consumers, it is espected to promote the electrification of the Vladivostok–Khabarovsk section of the Trans-Siberian railway which runs through Luchegorsk. According to the Directives of the Twenty-fourth Party Congress it is to go on load during the current planned period (1970–75). The main centres in the Primor'ye, like Vladivostok or Suchan, have smaller thermal stations which provide power through the local grid to the mining and timber industries. But power supplies are far from adequate for the growing requirements of this kray. The situation is expected to improve to some extent with the completion of the Primorsk G.R.E.S.

In spite of the progress made in the last few decades, the electrification of the Siberian territory is far from complete. There is still a huge volume of untapped hydro and thermal power awaiting development, when the time is ripe, and work continues in the design institutes on projects for using it. Apart from hydro and thermal power, some less orthodox methods of generating power must be mentioned, in conclusion. For some years, experiments have been conducted to utilise the hot springs of Kamchatka. An experimental 5,000 kw. geothermal power station has been operating since 1965 at the Pauzhetka hot springs in south Kamchatka and others are apparently likely to be built in future. Preliminary work is also reported to be in progress on a tidal power station with a capacity of 10,000 Mw. at Tugur Bay, on the Sea of Okhotsk. According to Soviet estimates more energy could be generated by tidal power than by the present total capacity of Soviet hydro-electric stations once the techniques of utilising this energy are mastered.

chapter six

Mining and Metallurgy

Knowledge of Siberia's mineral wealth has been constantly expanding since the Russians fought their way across Siberia in the sixteenth–seventeenth centuries. They were early made aware of gold, silver and iron deposits by various groups of native peoples who were already working them in a primitive fashion, notably in Transbaykalia and the Altay. From these simple beginnings, the exploration of Siberia's minerals continued in a somewhat desultory way until the 1917 revolution. By this time, the Siberian gold fields, the Lena in particular, were famous, and Siberian silver and iron had begun to make their mark. But up to the end of the Tsarist regime, Russia was still heavily dependent on imported base metals.

A great spurt was given to geological exploration in Siberia by the forced industrialisation of the thirties, which required large quantities of metals and metallurgical supplies. Moscow was determined to reduce the heavy import bill as far as possible, by making the Soviet Union self-sufficient in various metals believed to exist in Siberia (and elsewhere in the country). Intensive geological research revealed many new reserves of ferrous and non-ferrous minerals. As a result, Siberia's contribution to Soviet mineral self-sufficiency has been specially valuable in regard to non-ferrous metals, in the first place tin, nickel, phlogopite-mica and rare metals like niobium and tantalum (found in relatively large quantities in the Evenk National Okrug). It was thus possible either to cut out imports of these metals altogether, or to reduce them to relatively small quantities. Siberian gold and diamonds also make large contributions to the Soviet treasury.

The Soviet government does not rigidly adhere to its policy of self-sufficiency in metals, but has adapted its policies to the practical requirements of industry. A case in point is bauxite, large quantities of which are imported from the U.S.A. and elsewhere, while the geologists actively continue the search for the mineral throughout Siberia. The ninth five-year plan Directives instructed geologists to concentrate their work on reserves and investigation of mineral raw material resources, 'primarily in regions of actual mining operations and also in regions most favourable for their industrial development'. This would seem to indicate an effort to cut down on the more expensive geological expeditions in the far north and remoter areas of Siberia and perhaps to concentrate more effectively on European Russia (as advocated by the U.S.S.R. Minister of Geology, Academician A. Siderenko), where less investment is required than in Siberia. But, judging from the number and variety of the current geological expeditions in Siberia, geologists still continue in great numbers to work in the wilds, with the active assistance of the many high-powered Siberian scientific research institutes.

The position of the geologist and the various measures officially taken to promote geological research in Siberia is a subject of some interest, in view of the great work done in this field in the last half-century in uncovering Siberia's mineral wealth, and the large areas still to be examined by the geologist's hammer. In a talk on Moscow radio (3.4.1971), the Minister of Geology recalled some of the geologists' major successes in the eastern regions in the 1965-71 period. The ore base of the Noril'sk mining-metallurgical combine was substantially strengthened by the rich nickel deposits discovered in the vicinity of the older mines. A new polymetallic ore is now emerging from geological prospecting in the northern Transbaykal area, where useful work has been completed on the Ozernoye zinc deposits. Geological prospecting in Yakutiya in recent years has yielded exceptional results, affirmed the Minister, new deposits of gold, tin, antimony and diamonds, *inter alia* having been discovered, and a very promising new gold and silver belt, stretching from Kamchatka to Okhotsk has also been found, he stated. Prospecting for mercury in Magadan oblast has led to the discovery of good commercial deposits.

Though geological exploration in the post-war period has added very considerably to the formerly known mineral resources of Siberia and the Far East, tasks of great economic importance still await solution by the geologist. Up to 1970, at least, no complete geological map of Siberia had been published, corresponding to those available for the European areas of the U.S.S.R. The searches for high quality bauxites 'on the Siberian platform' to supply the big Siberian aluminium plants, richer iron ores for the eastern metallurgical bases and 'agronomic ores' for the manufacture of Siberian fertilisers have high priority in the official geological programme in Siberia, but there has been little success after years of work.

Among the many measures instituted to promote and speed-up this geological research in Siberia and the Far East, the following may be mentioned. A computer was established in 1971 at the Far Eastern geological directorate to process data received from survey teams in the Amur basin, the Maritime kray, the Kolyma basin, Kamchatka and Chukotka. According to its plan, it would also compile geological maps and make forecasts of mineral deposits. This Centre thus has formidable assignments, but how far they will be fulfilled remains to be seen. Many-sided assistance is also given to geological investigations by the various institutes of the Siberian Department of the all-Union Academy of Sciences.

Simultaneously with this purely scientific work, some 150 geological teams were reported to be leaving for practical geological prospecting in the Far East in 1971, in search of new deposits of coal, tin, tungsten, mercury and gold. Earlier (1968), over fifty prospecting teams of the Far Eastern geological directorate were stated to be searching for deposits of gold, lead, tungsten and coal in the Maritime kray. Their tasks also included research in the Sea of Japan bed along the Soviet coast, for placer deposits of tin and gold. It was later stated that the costs of underwater mineral extraction in the Sea of Okhotsk were lower than for extraction on land.

Against this background, the training of geological experts is obviously of the greatest importance. For long, geological exploration in Siberia was conducted by experts from European Russia and this was so even after training facilities were established in Tomsk, Novosibirsk, Irkutsk, Vladivostok and other Siberian centres. Though the situation has basically changed in recent years, as a result of the establishment of these regional centres, it is still not entirely satisfactory. The experts of the Siberian Department of the Academy of Sciences undoubtedly attach great weight to securing local Siberians rather than trainees from European Russia or the Urals for this work. The sound practical reason behind this preference is that the latter group too frequently after a short stage in the field 'prefer to return to their native heath', thus causing great losses to the State, owing to the costs involved in transferring these trainees to Siberia. Moreover, in the opinion of the experts, the various centres of geological instruction from Tomsk to Yakutsk should concentrate more precisely on the problems of their respective areas. But the cadres available to carry out the big geological programme now under way in Siberia and the Far East are in fact far from adequate. Even this field of research has been hit by the 'flight of labour' scourge. As a result of the migration from east to west of the less adventurous geologists, Siberia continues to lose even some of its valuable professional cadres. The extent of this brain-drain is not known in the west.

The grievances of the engineering-construction specialists whose work is closely associated with the geologists and who may often work in their wake, were publicly voiced a few years ago, by the chief specialist of the Kemerovo group (and may also to a large extent apply to the geologists). Writing in *Pravda* (16.11.1968), he complained of the entire lack of physical training in the special schools provided for people who are to spend much of their time under the open sky, in wind and rain. There was also a lack of special equipment for drilling and digging and vehicles for tough going. Much more attention was necessary, he alleged, to providing moveable huts, comfortable clothing and footwear. There should, moreover, be an end to the pressure to accept old-fashioned wadded trousers and jackets, which nobody wanted, instead of the 'type of comfortable clothes manufactured for tourists and only a dream for us'. This Kemerovo specialist did not believe that the prevailing piece-work rates stimulated the quality of field research and urged that they should be raised. Above all, it was of primary importance to provide better living conditions and accommodation for his fellow specialists and workers. During the five years' existence of the Kemerovo trust, only three flats had been made available for 200 members of staff, while the position in regard to crèches was still worse, because 'there were none'. The result of all these discrepancies in Siberian life was that at a time when the need for engineering-prospective staff was growing annually, there was a movement to the 'homely regions' of the Soviet Union among these people, though many would not leave Siberia, he believed, if the supplementary, coefficient payments enjoyed by metallurgists and other categories of workers were applicable to them. These payments were apparently also made available later to the engineering-prospecting workers.

Geologists and workers in mining and metallurgy in Siberia often complain, as will be shown subsequently in the case of particular industries, that they are not being supplied 'with the tools of their trade'. The implication is that too often equipment is sent to Siberia which cannot withstand the extremely low temperatures of the country. Though this is a serious problem, and was too long neglected, scientists and metallurgists are now working to produce metals and equipment better suited to Siberian conditions. Ten years ago the life expectancy of a bulldozer in the permafrost region was one season. The winter cold caused the metal to freeze and crack and create another five tons of immovable scrap. There seems to have been little improvement yet, in spite of the research being conducted on this problem. The Yakutsk Institute for the Study of the Physical and Technical Problems of the North (est. 1970), for example, has been researching into a reliable method of electro-welding of metal in temperatures below $-50°$ and its work has now reached the stage when it plans to build a testing ground for trials of machines, mechanisms and structures, in low temperatures and permafrost conditions. This is only a first step in the inevitably long road leading to serial production of frost-resistant machines. But, at all events, it is a step in the right direction. Interesting work in this field is also reported from the Ukraine, where a group of engineers have produced drilling apparatus with a special nozzle, for work in permafrost, which within an hour can burn a 10 m. hole in the ground. A new type of cold-resistant steel was also developed in 1970 by a group of scientists at the Siberian Physical-Technical Institute attached to Tomsk University called 'Stal–Severyanka'. After long endurance tests, it was used in caterpillar tractors in Tomsk and other northern timber combines and worked without stoppages, but nothing is yet known of its life expectancy under the worst conditions. The basic problem for the metallurgists is how to overcome the huge additional expense incurred in the production of these special frost-resistant steels which require strengthening with various expensive alloys.

Ferrous Metallurgy. The oldest iron works in Siberia at Petrovsk, Abakan and Nikolaevskiy made a modest contribution to Russian iron production between 1885–1909, but no steel was made in Siberia before the 1917 Revolution. This situation was abruptly changed by Stalin's decision to create a Second Metallurgical Base at Stalinsk (now Novokuznetsk), to reinforce the First Metallurgical Base in the Ukraine, where the chief Soviet iron and steel plants were partly situated. It was rightly believed that this site in the heart of Siberia would be less vulnerable from attack from the west than the Ukrainian metallurgical base. This second base consisted of two centres, at Magnitogorsk in the Urals and Stalinsk, both equipped with large iron and steel plants. They operated on a shuttle system, with trains carrying coking coal from the Kuzbas to the Urals plants and iron ore from Magnitogorsk to the Stalinsk plants, separated by some 1,400 miles.[1] These plants were built with frenzied haste under most difficult conditions and the shuttle service

[1] A graphic first-hand account of this construction is given in John Scott's *Behind the Urals*. London, Secker and Warburg, 1942.

of raw materials was very costly. They paid off well when the Germans overran the Ukrainian base in 1941.

The original expensive dependence on iron ore from the Urals was considerably reduced by the post-war expansion of the local ore base to the Temir Tau, Tashtagol and other mines further south in the Khakass-Minusinsk area. According to Shabad's estimate by the mid-1950s, 80 % of the ore needs of the K.M.K. (Kuznetsk Iron and Steel Combine) were supplied locally, though the original smelting capacity had been expanded and it was still the only plant in Siberia with a full metallurgical cycle. None of these deposits were very extensive, and the geologists continued the hunt for richer local ore reserves, to meet with considerable success in the huge Sokolovka-Sarbay deposits of north-west Kazakhstan, also on the Magnitogorsk-Kuzbas railway system.

The decision taken on Khrushchev's initiative at the Twentieth Party Congress (1956) to create a Third Metallurgical Base in western Siberia represented a further important stage in the build-up of Siberian iron and steel production. The centre of the scheme was the much publicised *Zapsib* metallurgical works situated at Antonovskiy about 10 miles south-east of the original works at Novokuznetsk. It was planned to produce 15–20 mil. tons of pig iron within the following two to three five-year plans, 20–25 mil. tons of steel and 15–20 mil. tons of rolled finished products.

These targets were over-optimistic and in the light of the plant's record to date are unlikely to be achieved, if at all, until the late 1980s. Many technical hitches delayed the inauguration of steel production capacity until 1968 although the first blast furnace started up at the *Zapsib* works in 1964 and the second in 1967. The delays between the operation of these giant blast furnaces and the steel-making capacity resulted, for some years, in heavy and unnecessary expense involved in sending this pig-iron by rail to the Urals for conversion into steel ingots and slabs and then back to *Zapsib* for conversion into finished steel sheets. Throughout this period, the Soviet press carried alarming accounts of poor work-discipline, confused management and even serious mistakes in the original planning of a plant equipped 'with the most powerful and modern equipment'.

Zapsib was in fact the first Siberian plant to be entrusted with the production of oxygen converter steel. The metallurgical work force by all accounts seem to have been pretty green when the oxygen converter shop was at last inaugurated in 1968, though many had served a short apprenticeship at the Zhdanov and Krivoy Rog iron and steel works. Subsequently, *Zapsib* was further developed by the following measures: the most powerful blast furnace in the country (volume 3,000 cu.m.) was blown in 1971 with a great flourish of publicity in the Soviet press. 'It has no equal' declared *Pravda* 'for construction, the extent of automation and electrification. The productivity of the new unit is 7,000 t. of pig iron per 24 hours day'. This additional capacity is estimated by Shabad to mean that the total annual capacity of the K.M.K. and the *Zapsib* plant is about 9 million m.t. pig iron and 8 million m.t. of steel. Moreover, it was announced in 1971 that *Zapsib* is planned to have the largest coking battery (the 6th) in the country with an output of over 1,000,000 m.t. annually, by 1973, when it is scheduled for completion. The Czechs are also contributing to these developments at the *Zapsib* works, with equipment for a billet mill, as part of the large-scale Soviet-Czech exchanges of equipment in 1973. The result of these various measures at the *Zapsib* works should mean that by 1985 *Zapsib* should be producing 10,600,000 m.t. of pig iron, 14,500,000 m.t. of steel and 12,500,000 m.t. of rolled metal, according to Soviet official estimates.

While these major K.M.K. and *Zapsib* works can rely on adequate fuel supplies from the Kuzbas, the situation regarding iron ore is still not satisfactory. It has nevertheless been improved by supplies from the north-west Kazakh mines and by the exploitation since the sixties of the Korshunovo iron mines in the Irkutsk oblast. These mines form part of the great Angara-Ilimsk deposits, which remained unworkable in remote, inaccessible taiga, until traversed by the Tayshet–Ust'-Kut railway. Korshunovo or Korshunikha 'Iron Mountain' yields crude magnetic ore with a metal content of 30.9%. It is believed to be the largest iron mine yet opened up in Siberia, with iron ore reserves stated to be larger than the combined Ural Magnitnaya and Blagodat mines. A new town, Zheleznogorsk, has been built (since 1959) as the centre of this iron mining industry and contained 200,000 inhabitants in 1972. The mines were reported in 1972 to be producing 12 million m.t. of iron ore annually. An iron ore dressing combine started operations in Zheleznogorsk in 1965 and reached its full capacity of 5 million m.t. of concentrate (containing 62% iron) in 1967. The cost of transporting Kazakh and Korshunovo ores to the distant *Zapsib* works are high but necessary until better ore sources are discovered nearer the plant.

The future of the Tayshet metallurgical plant, originally mentioned as 'the third leg' of this Third Metallurgical Base, is still obscure but it would seem that at least for the present it has been quietly dropped. Should the project be revived, however, Korshunovo would provide a convenient iron ore base. These important new iron mines are still only found on the latest Soviet maps and apparently derive their name from Shostachko Korshunov, a Russian who was testing iron ore here three hundred years ago, according to local legend.

Two other metallurgical projects have been proposed in the vicinity of Korshunovo, at Rudnogorsk and Neryunda, both of which, like Korshunovo, would have the advantage of power from the Ust'-Ilimsk H.E.S. Neither is mentioned in the current five-year plan, nor is Siberia to be the site of any of the new iron and steel works to be constructed during this period. This seems to be a clear indication that further investment in these expensive plants would be unnecessary and uneconomic at the present time. The importance now given to the development of the Kursk Magnetic Anomaly probably to a large extent influenced this decision and means that, for the foreseeable future, European Russia will remain the all-Union centre of heavy metallurgy, with Siberia playing an increasingly useful supporting role by stemming the flow of heavy metal imports from Europe.

Proceeding east of Lake Baykal to the Soviet Far Eastern region, the untapped iron ore reserves are estimated to be very considerable. There are, for example, high quality iron ore mines in the Aldan district and in the upper Amur basin. Two of the largest of these deposits, at Garinsky (Amur oblast) and Kimkan in the Khabarovsk kray, are estimated by the all-Union Academy of Sciences experts to con-

Bilibino, site of the Far North
atomic power station

tain between them 1,000 million tons of ore. Garinskiy ore has an average iron content of 41.7% and can easily be concentrated; some of this ore has an even higher iron content of over 50%. Large hitherto unprospected iron reserves are also believed to exist in the wild mountainous region of the Uda river basin. So far, however, the northern areas of Yakutiya and Chukotka, so rich in non-ferrous and precious metals have not disclosed iron deposits of any significance.

The long-mooted establishment of a Far Eastern metallurgical base still awaits a final official 'all-clear'. Several expert Soviet conferences have approved the idea and recommended that it should be supplied by Chul'man coking coal (in south Yakutiya) and Khabarovsk iron ore. It now seems more likely that the recently discovered Iyengra iron ore deposits in the neighbourhood of Chul'man will be the ore base for this development of ferrous metallurgy in the Far East and that the project may soon go forward. It would be a great boon to the region, which is chronically short of heavy metal, a large proportion of which has to be imported from western Siberia and further west. This is very costly and adds greatly to the strain on the overloaded Amur railway, the only line serving the region. The Japanese have for some years expressed interest in these deposits of iron ore and coking coal, but neither can be worked commercially until connected either with the Amur railway or by a good road system linked to this railway – both lacking until recently. Now, a spur of the Amur railway is being built by the Soviets from Bam station towards the Chul'man mines which may be taken as an indication that it is intended to develop the important mining complex in this area with the cooperation of the Japanese.

At the present time, the only steel works in the entire Far Eastern region is *Amurstal*, built in the early thirties at Komsomol'sk, as part of the first five-year plan. It originally had no blast furnaces and worked on local scrap and some pig-iron imported from Manchuria. The works has subsequently been expanded and is now completely integrated. It contains a blast furnace, a continuous steel casting works and a large new shop was being constructed in 1971 to produce strong alloy steel. During the current plan period it is also intended to build a powerful electric smelting furnace at this works and 'to satisfy maximum local requirements for low alloy steel'.

The difficult problems involved in supplying the far-flung Soviet Far Eastern region with heavy metal might have found an efficient solution, if the rational scheme for joint operation of the iron and coal reserves on both sides of the Sino-Soviet Amur frontier, together with the development of Amur hydropower, had not been frozen by the border dispute. It is probable that when political relations improve between the Soviet Union and the Chinese Republic, this far-reaching economic scheme will be revived for the mutual benefit of both sides. But, in view of its complex strategic aspects, that day seems remote at present.

Since the conflict with China reduced former supplies of tungsten, such deposits have been more actively developed in the Soviet Far East. A large mining and concentrating combine was reported in 1971 to be under construction in the Ussuri taiga 'to exploit one of the richest deposits in the U.S.S.R.', near the river Tatibe. Another tungsten mine was under construction near Ulan Ude in the Buryat A.S.S.R.,

The wire shop at the Irkutsk
Aluminium Works

while in remote Chukotka, the important Iul'tin tin and tungsten mine has been operating since the late fifties.

Non-Ferrous Metallurgy. Siberia's position in the Soviet Union as a source of mineral supplies lies primarily in her strength as a producer of non-ferrous rather than ferrous metals. The big change which occurred in Russia's position as a minor producer of a few non-ferrous metals, gold and platinum, in the Tsarist period, to her present importance in the world of non-ferrous metals and gold, is largely due to post-revolutionary discoveries in Siberia and the Soviet Far East. In Tsarist Russia and until the end of World War II, non-ferrous metals headed the list of Russia's imports. They have now almost vanished from the country's imports. The Soviet government soon recognised the necessity to develop its domestic resources of these minerals, large quantities of which were required for the far-reaching industrialisation and electrification plans projected by Stalin in 1928. Hitherto, copper, lead and zinc were only mined in a primitive manner in small scattered deposits in Siberia and the Far East and many other minerals now known to exist had not yet been discovered.

From the onset of the Soviet industrialisation plans, geological research in Siberia was generously subsidised. Many old leads to undeveloped mineral reserves were successfully followed up, while a bewildering range of new discoveries continues to be made throughout Siberia and the Far East up to the present day. It is interesting to note that these non-ferrous minerals are heavily concentrated in east Siberia and the Far Eastern region, while west Siberia, so rich in natural gas and oil, seems to lack them all, according to the present state of geological research.

Statistics of reserves and production of non-ferrous metals and gold are not published in the Soviet Union and this information is classified by law as secret. The upward trend of the non-ferrous industry is nevertheless clear both from the decline of imports and the Soviet exports of some of these metals. It is also definitely reflected in the periodic ministerial reports on the industry. According to a recent report (1971) of the Minister of Non-Ferrous Metallurgy, Lomako, during the eighth five-year plan period, production of the non-ferrous industry had increased more than one and a half times, profits were double those of the previous period and productivity rose by 24%. More than 90% in the growth in production, he said, was the result of increased productivity of labour. The industry seemed in good shape in spite of many technical and other problems stressed in a number of expert reports. Lomako, however, did not hide his dissatisfaction with the present levels of mining machinery and equipment supplied to his industry and implied that it might have achieved better results if it had been provided with the right machines. 'The engineering industries', he complained, 'do not fulfil our orders accurately or supply up-to-date machines with spare parts.' Judging from letters and articles in the press, grouses about the type and quality of machines are common throughout all branches of the industry in Siberia and the Far East. If this important industry is to be better equipped technically, closer coordination is obviously necessary between the Ministry of Non-Ferrous Industry, the engineering ministries and *Gossnab*.

Large new capacities for the production of aluminium, alumina, nickel, copper, cobalt, lead, zinc, wolfram and molybdenum concentrates were brought into production in the Soviet Union, during the eighth five-year plan (1966–70), according to Lomako. He did not specifically mention Siberia in his roll-call of minerals, but owing to the region's predominant position in the production of most of these items, these new capacities must to a great extent have been situated in Siberia.

Nickel. At the present time, the only important copper producing unit in Siberia is the *Severonikel* (Northern Nickel) combine at Noril'sk in the far north of the Taymyr peninsula. Here copper is obtained as a by-product from the treatment of the rich nickel ores, together with cobalt, platinum and other valuable metals. In fact, Kazakhstan and the Caucasus are the chief known Soviet sources of copper supply, not Siberia. This situation should change significantly when the enormous Udokan copper mines in east Siberia go into production (further details of which are given below).

The Soviet Union is now the second largest producer of nickel in the world, after Canada, with an estimated annual production of about 100,000 t. Noril'sk is recognised as the main source of Soviet nickel and contains mines unequalled for their ore content and extent. The first Noril'sk mines were discovered almost by accident by Soviet geologists investigating local coal deposits for the lower Yenisey river craft, and ships plying in the Arctic Ocean, in the early twenties. The development of these mines starting from 1930, the construction of the metallurgical combine and the modern city of Noril'sk, under the extremely harsh natural conditions of climate, permafrost and isolation from inhabited centres, was a great feat of human endurance. It was all the greater because the labour force, from at least 1939–40 until Stalin's death, was almost entirely composed of concentration camp prisoners. The construction of the Noril'sk metallurgical combine was greatly assisted by the transfer of smelter equipment, from the then recently opened smelter and refinery at Monchegorsk in the Kola peninsula, after the outbreak of the Soviet-German war in 1941. In the sixties, the original Noril'sk mines were expanded by the even richer deposits at Talnakh discovered in 1961 and the Komsomol'skiy (1971) and Oktyabr'skoye mines, the latter scheduled to go into production in 1974.

One exuberant Soviet journalist carried away by the richness of the polymetallic ores concealed in the 'frozen vaults' (i.e. permafrost) of Talnakh, declared that the original Noril'sk mines seem 'almost dirt' in comparison, although in fact they proved not to be as extensive as originally thought. As a result of this expansion, the Noril'sk reserves of copper and nickel are now officially stated to be 300% greater than originally estimated.

From the most primitive beginnings some thirty years ago, in the Arctic wilderness, a great mining, metallurgical and industrial research complex has developed at Noril'sk. It now contains the largest nickel smelter in the Soviet Union and also the largest cobalt plant and operates an electrolytic copper smelter. The output of platinum from the underground Mayak mine is increasingly important. Opencast mining throughout the Noril'sk mining complex has now been largely replaced by underground mining. The modern city which has grown up round the mining-metallurgical complex (pop. 136,000) has greatly impressed the few foreign visitors, including Canadian officials familiar with similar climatic difficulties, permitted to visit it.

It is also used as a centre for the study of industrial plant and equipment and types of housing in conditions of severe cold. Noril'sk is certainly not the propaganda phantasy it is often supposed to be in the west. Technical improvements are constantly reported to be in train at the metallurgical combine. One of the latest additions was a nuclear resonance instrument to help to determine the presence of rare metals in the niccolite ore and which is a great improvement on the former more lengthy, less accurate, chemical analyses used at Noril'sk. Technical deficiencies have also been criticised at the Talnakh mines, side by side with a flow of success stories in the press. Angry complaints have been made about the danger of a sharp slowing down of driving speeds if the miners do not get a good electric motor. And there was dissatisfaction with the drilling done with manual perforators.

The head of the experimental research section of the combine expressed anxiety to *Pravda* (24.12.1970) about the staff position. Out of a total 325 workers and 160 engineering technicians, only 15 had university degrees and experienced staff were thus quite inadequate. Some were trying to leave for warmer climates, which would further complicate this situation. Though his aim was to create a first class 'training centre' at Noril'sk, he admitted that the laboratories and experimental equipment left much to be desired. There was no design office. There have been other references to the labour problem at Noril'sk and it was reflected in the combine's collective demand in 1970 for better living conditions for the workers. It was reported in 1971 that 800 demobilised soldiers had arrived in Noril'sk 'to work as volunteers in the Oktyabr'skoye mine' now in process of construction. How far they are to fill the places of 'fleeing workers', or are a normal addition to the labour force to work the new mine, is not clear.

In the hitherto unfamiliar conditions of the deep permafrost mines at Noril'sk, it is necessary to a large extent to proceed by trial and error, much of the way. Experience in one mine may or may not be useful in the one next opened up. Thus, it is planned to penetrate to a depth of 900–1,200 m. in the construction of the Oktyabr'skoye mine but nobody knows yet how things will go when this depth is reached. In spite of the exceptional difficulties in this region of the far north, no other mines in the Soviet Union, according to Soviet reports, were ever constructed as rapidly as the Talnakh complex, where the rate of driving exceeded the norm by 2–2.5 times.

Natural gas from the Messoyakha field, some 170 miles west of Noril'sk, is now brought by pipeline to the town and combine for heat and power. Electric power is extremely important for the many electrically based operations – electric furnaces and smelters – at the Noril'sk combine. The capacity of the original heat and power station is now to be reinforced by a new H.E.S. being constructed 170 km. away at Khantayka, which will be one of the most northerly hydro-electric power stations in the world. Another essential facility provided from early days (1937) in the roadless, railless area of Noril'sk, was the 70 miles long narrow-gauge railway to Dudinka on the Yenisey, converted to broad gauge in the fifties, thus providing an outlet for the metallurgical products of Noril'sk. Talnakh is also connected by a narrow-gauge railway with Noril'sk. The first train crossed the new rail and road bridge over the river Noril'ka in 1965 but the line was not completed until 1967. In spite of these efforts, communications between Noril'sk and European Russian centres remain precarious and expensive. Various ideas have been put forward to overcome these difficulties, in the first place the construction of a north-south spur of the Trans-Siberian railway following the course of the Yenisey river, to supplement the river barge and steamer traffic which is already considerable. But this proposal has not received much support in official quarters. The many problems inseparable from the establishment of a mining-metallurgical industry on the scale of Noril'sk in the Arctic have led to the conviction in some quarters that such industrial concentrations are not advisable, or economic, and that some of the finishing processes should be moved to the south. It will be interesting to see if this course is eventually followed, for example, in the case of the Udokan copper combine.

Though no precise statistics of output are available, Noril'sk is believed to produce about two-thirds of the Soviet 100,000 t. of nickel, annually. It must therefore contribute substantially to the Soviet exports of nickel which were running at about 11,000 t. in 1968. It declared a profit of some 380 million roubles in 1970.

Copper. Siberia's hitherto insignificant contribution to the Soviet Union's position as the second largest world copper producer may rise sharply when, as is now anticipated, the huge copper mines at Udokan in east Siberia, discovered in the late fifties, are opened up. On the basis of the published data, geologists of international status confirm the Soviet estimates of the unique character of this porphyry, both as regards the high metal content of the ore and the extent of mines. But the drawbacks to operation of Udokan copper are formidable. The mines are situated 500 miles from the nearest railway, in a roadless, uninhabited wilderness with a forbidding climate and very difficult physical conditions, including permafrost. But the rewards of overcoming these problems are also very attractive. Udokan is estimated to contain a couple of billions of tons of relatively high-grade ore (1.35–2% metal content) which places it in the same category as the great Chuquicamata (Chile) and Dzhezkazgan (Kazakhstan) mines. Provisional annual estimates of an output of some 400,000 t. are believed by western experts to be well founded. Should these forecasts eventually be realised, the Soviets would have a trump card to play on the world copper market.

Before news of the discovery of Udokan copper was disclosed to the outside world, in the mid-sixties, a good deal of necessary preparatory work prior to actual mining operations was carried out, in the form of tunnelling, geological analyses and a series of laboratory studies, the results of which were eventually published in the Soviet technical press in 1971. These investigations confirmed that unusually high capital investment would be required to develop Udokan copper and in the first place provide the complex infrastructure, variously estimated at 2 milliard dollars or £700 million.

The prospect of such a large capital investment coming at a time when Soviet capital funds were already heavily strained in more urgent schemes in Siberia, may have prompted the invitation to the Japanese in 1966 to participate in the development, on a co-partnership basis, of Udokan copper. According to Japanese sources, the Japanese were to receive Udokan copper concentrate equivalent to the sum of their investment in the scheme. Protracted negotiations ensued, but the Japanese apparently (at least for the moment) lost interest in the proposals, when it became clear that copper concentrate for smelting in Japan was not to be part of the Soviet bargain and financially the two sides were also fundamentally at variance.

At this stage, the Japanese had been keen to get a new source of copper concentrate for their copper-hungry industries and to process it in Japanese smelters. Above all, the Japanese business and banking companies concerned would only cooperate in the scheme if it proved to be commercially viable and showed possibilities of short-term profit and other advantages. The Soviets on the other hand seemed to expect the Japanese to bear perhaps half of the enormous capital investment required at Udokan. In the latest period, the Japanese attitude to copper imports has changed, with cut-backs in steel mills and non-ferrous smelters. This might in turn diminish interest in the remote and expensive Udokan project, except perhaps in partnership with an international consortium.

These abortive Soviet-Japanese bi-lateral negotiations were followed some years later by reports of Soviet proposals for western cooperation in the development of Udokan, either by individual countries (France, West Germany or Britain were mentioned) or an international consortium in which the Japanese might also participate. It seems generally agreed that the volume of investment required for the Udokan development is too large for any one country to undertake alone. The betting in 1971–72 was on the Rio Tinto Zinc group as a top favourite for this operation and this seemed to be reflected in the facilities granted to R.T.Z. engineers to visit Udokan for a preliminary survey in 1971 – an opportunity never granted to the Japanese in the course of their earlier negotiations.

It is not known at the time of writing how these Soviet-R.T.Z. negotiations stand or whether Moscow has come to any decision about the working of these mines. R.T.Z. was also believed to favour a consortium in which their primary function would be to organise the financing of the mining-metallurgical operations. Unlike the Japanese, they are not thought to be interested in obtaining or marketing Udokan copper concentrate.

Should a scheme of international co-partnership in the development of Udokan ultimately materialise, it is likely to follow the pattern established for other foreign capitalist firms working in the Soviet Union, e.g. the Fiat company constructing the big automobile plant at Togliatti or the giant nylon complex being built at Mogilev by the British Nylon Spinners. That would mean that the work and managerial force would be entirely composed of Soviet citizens while the engineering-design team would be mixed, i.e., Soviet citizens and representatives of the foreign firms concerned (see Postscript for later developments).

Tin. Most of primary Soviet tin is now produced in the Soviet Far East region. As a result of intensive prospecting, many rich deposits were discovered in northern Yakutiya and the Chukotskiy National Okrug before and after World War II. The discovery of tin deposits in the Far North came at a time when the old Chita tin mines, long the main domestic, but far from adequate, source of tin, were wearing thin and the Soviet need for a better domestic source had become acute. The former large imports of tin from China ceased in the mid-sixties and are now greatly reduced also from Malaya. In spite of the considerable quantities produced in the Far Eastern region, tin is the only base metal still on the Soviet import list because of a domestic shortage.

In northern Yakutiya, the richest ores are worked at Ese-Khaya and Deputatskiy in the Yana river basin. It is estimated that some 25% of the total Soviet tin output is produced in these mines, which are most difficult and expensive to operate owing to the harsh climatic conditions and supply difficulties. A concentrator was built in 1958 at Batagay, at lightning speed, because tin from Ese-Khaya was an urgently needed strategic metal.

Batagay has become the new capital of the great tin ore industry of Verkhoyan'ye – formerly a preserve of the notorious *Dal'stroy* organisation and worked by its victims. It is also the headquarters of the regional Soviet and Party organisations. Batagay was entirely unknown until the development of the tin industry. According to a Soviet author who visited it in 1967 'it was a pleasant surprise. An entire townlet had been built in the taiga on the banks of the river Yana, with roads, small houses, a concentration plant and a landing stage. At the foot of the famous flattened cone of the Ese-Khaya (Bear mountain), lay the mining settlement, the surface installations of the pits and the barracks of the former inmates of the prison camp. There also were the derricks of the drills used to penetrate the depths of this unique tin mine.' It has recently been suggested that the Ese-Khaya mine is nearing exhaustion and that the last and deepest ore levels, at a depth of 400 m. have been reached. Even if this is so, it will scarcely affect the position of Batagay as the tin centre of a region with several other rich tin deposits in the vicinity.

Further east between the Indigirka and the Verkhoyansk mountain range, one of the great tin belts of the world is being worked. Centred on Deputatskiy, it continues some 1000 km. eastwards, across the Kolyma mountains, to Chukotka. The first stage of a mining and concentration combine was completed at Deputatskiy in 1970. Its placer is reported to yield the cheapest tin in the country and a rich lode mine is also in process of coming into production. Deputatskiy is popularly known in the Soviet Union as the 'Pearl of the tin world,' as the metal content of its ore is particularly high. It is estimated that its tin output will increase Yakut output by 100% in 1975. Apparently, a great deal is being done to make it worthy of being a leading enterprise of the Soviet Union. If Soviet reports are reliable, 'Deputatsky houses will be of silicate, concrete and glass with all communal facilities including schools, sports-halls, crèches, connected with the concentration combine by covered galleries'. All these precautions are being taken to protect the inhabitants of Deputatskiy against the ferocious winter weather. It is to be 'the undying centre of a big ore plexus on the cold pole'. For, in fact, Deputatskiy has now been found not only to be a great source of tin, but promising gold placers have also been discovered in the neighbourhood as well as polymetallic ores.

The eastern extremity of this tin belt runs through north-east Chukotka to Chaun

Bay, where the first known local deposits were worked at Vakumey, south of the new mining port of Pevek. In south-east Chukotka, there is an important tin and tungsten mine and a concentrator at Iul'tin. Prospecting in the Chaun area has now extended to the sea bed. Cassiterite was discovered 70 m. off shore in 1968 and other mineral deposits later. Prospecting is also continuing in the area of Cape Billinga, where at least one tin deposit has been located. Local geologists working here believe that 'almost the whole coast of Chukotka holds promise', though so far no major finds seem to have been reported. In spite of these varied activities in the northern tin industry, much more could be done in the opinion of Academician N. Shilo, Director of the Complex Scientific Research Institute, in Magadan, who stated in 1971 that, owing to incomplete engineering-geological preparatory work, some tin deposits in Chukotka and Yakutiya were not being industrially developed. This is perhaps because all these northern mines are so extremely difficult and expensive to operate and organise. Moreover, working seasons on the many placers are short, which means relatively low production. The Magadan oblast, which includes Chukotka, is estimated to produce about 30% of Soviet tin.

Tin is also produced in the southern area of the Far Eastern region: the Khabarovsk and Primor'ye krays, where conditions for mining are far less arduous than in the north. In the Khabarovsk kray, tin is mined at Solnechnyy, 20 miles north-west of Komsomol'sk. There is a mining-concentrator complex at Gornyy (a new mining town near Solnechnyy) and a second concentrator was opened in 1969 at Solnechnyy, to process low-grade ore from the nearby Molodezhnyy mine, the largest in the complex.

There has also been a considerable post-war development of tin mining in the Sikhote-Alin area of the Primor'ye. The main centres of this industry are at Khrustal'nyy and Krasnorechensk where there are rich, but thin-veined, deposits. Extensive reconstruction of the Khrustal'nyy mining and dressing complex was completed in 1971, a rod mill and other sets of integrated machinery were reported to have been installed. It is interesting to note that there is (or was, certainly until a few years ago) a great deal of 'private enterprise' in tin production in the Southern areas of the Far East with small free-lance teams panning the streams where deposits are too small to warrant industrial development and making a comfortable living by selling their product to the State. Off-shore prospecting for tin is also in progress along the Primorsk coast. At a rough guess, foreign experts estimated the total tin (concentrate) production in the Soviet Union to be between 23–25,000 metric tons in 1970, distributed as follows: Magadan oblast, 7,000 metric tons, Yakutiya 6,000 m.t., Khabarovsk kray 6,000 m.t., Chita oblast 2–5,000 m.t. These crude tin concentrates are sent for processing to the Novosibirsk, Ryazan' and Podolsk smelters with high transport costs increasing the already high cost of production.

Aluminium. The Soviet Union has made enormous strides in the production of aluminium since launching the first five-year industrialisation plan, when none was produced. Less than 1,000 tons were produced in 1932 but post-war output rose to more than an estimated 1,000,000 tons in 1969. In the post-war period, the massive development of hydropower first brought Siberia significantly into aluminium production with the advantage that the Soviet Union had already accumulated considerable experience in this industry. It is now a major producer of Soviet aluminium from the chief plants at Shelekhov (near Irkutsk), Bratsk and Krasnoyarsk (in that chronological order of construction). There is also a big aluminium plant at Novokuznetsk which pioneered this industry in Siberia when equipment was evacuated there in 1943 from the old Volkov works in Leningrad.

The large Shelekhov plant, stretching eight miles along the river Angara southwest of Irkutsk, was in its day (1962) the 'first-born' of the east Siberian aluminium plants. It followed some years after the construction of the Irkutsk hydro-electric station provided the necessary power for the aluminium reduction plant. The lack of local bauxites originally necessitated imports of alumina from the Urals, later supplemented by alumina from the Pavlodar and Achinsk plants. A new town has rapidly grown up outside the aluminium works, named, like the plant, after G. I. Shelekhov, the rapacious nineteenth-century Russian explorer of Alaska. His brutal strongarm tactics in Alaska seem to have been overlooked by a recent Soviet author who wrote that 'after a hundred years, his grateful descendants, related to him by indomitable spirit and drive would give his name to the new town of "big aluminium" in east Siberia'. Soviet sources do not conceal the great hardships endured (willy-nilly) by the hundreds of young Komsomols from European Russia who responded to the Party's call to construct this town and plant in 1956. They lived in tents in the 'desert-like site'. According to one Soviet account, they endured all the construction hardships 'with boundless enthusiasm' and were rewarded by seeing a great works arise where a few years previously there was nothing but uninhabited taiga.

The Shelekhov plant has been considerably enlarged since the original construction and has an estimated capacity of 200,000 tons annually. It was reported to be a profitable concern until, in 1969, a short-fall of 'thousands of tons of metal' was disclosed. This was apparently due to the gradual wearing out of equipment and bad management. Machinery had been run to death and some never repaired in 5–7 years. This resulted in losses of millions of roubles and 'lessened the workers' sense of responsibility and interest in the well-being of the plant'. This was by no means the end of the disorders revealed at Shelekhov at this time. The Party Committee was in the dock because it took no notice of the complaints about worn-out machinery and other business-like suggestions made at factory meetings. Raw materials were distributed uneconomically and alumina was scattered around the shop. The workers were equally disorganised. Absentees were protected by their bosses and even appeared among lists of those at work, while some workers left an hour or two before the end of the shift. The workers' postings were also erratic. Some communists with engineers' or metallurgists' technical diplomas were to be found among the ordinary workers. Others functioning as brigadiers or erection leaders, had diplomas as agronomists or veterinary specialists: no steps had been taken to train or build up staff properly. On the other hand, no encouragement was given to the excellent workers who achieved good production results in spite of the difficult conditions in the plant. The final criticism was that neither the director, nor the Party Secretary, nor the Chief Engineer, ever went the rounds of the plant. History does not relate how this deplorable lack of 'communist discipline' ended at Shelekhov, nor what happened to the plant 'Brigadier' from whose reports these details are taken. Against this background, it is interesting to note that a special industrial base was established in Irkutsk in 1968, where prototypes of equipment for the aluminium industry were to be made, tested and perfected. Its services were obviously not yet called on to improve the situation at Shelekhov in 1970.

Construction on the 'giant' aluminium plant at Bratsk, also in east Siberia, was begun some years after Shelekhov, in 1961. After many delays, production started in 1966 with a reputed output of 80,000 t. and increased to 360,000 t. in 1970, but output will largely depend on the availability of alumina. The planned capacity of 480,000 t. was reached in the same year. An electrolysis shop was finished in 1971 and is the largest in the Soviet Union. Almost unlimited quantities of aluminium could be made at Bratsk if required from the huge amount of cheap energy available from the big local H.E.S.: But in spite of Soviet claims the position regarding alumina is not so satisfactory. Soviet sources describe the enthusiasm of foreign experts for the high quality of aluminium produced at Bratsk and the special processes used to produce it. Some delegates sent from the U.S.A., Canada and Japan to get first-hand experience of the plant allegedly wanted to 'buy the patent'. The Soviet success in overcoming the lack of domestic bauxites, by substituting alumina based on Siberian nephelines, was also of international interest, according to Soviet sources, while they added 'the Americans maintain a whole commercial fleet to import bauxites from Jamaica, Australia and Guyana'.

This boast is somewhat hollow, as it is known that the large alumina plants at Achinsk and Pavlodar, the main suppliers of the Siberian aluminium industry, can barely cover the increasing supply requirements of the industry, nor has the use of the nephelines been an unqualified success, while imports of American bauxites continue at a high rate and the Russians are on the constant look-out for new sources, particularly in Africa. The first cargo of alumina (about 120 t.) was reported to have been imported from Japan *via* the Far Eastern port of Vanino in 1971. These Japanese imports, presumably for the east Siberian aluminium plants, would have to travel thousands of kilometres before reaching their destination, in contrast to the favourable position for imports enjoyed by the American plants situated near east coast ports. The need for high-grade bauxite is thus acute in Siberia, where none has yet come to light. The Twenty-fourth Party Congress therefore urgently directed the geologists to intensify their Union-wide searches for domestic sources of high quality bauxites.

After Bratsk, another 'giant' aluminium plant was erected outside the city of Krasnoyarsk. It was equipped with 'the latest machinery and technology' and its planned capacity when completed was 400,000 t. After prolonged delays, it went into operation in 1969 and was reported to have been held up by delays in the local Dvinogorsk H.E.S. from which it derives its power. Like the Shelekhovo plant it was originally supplied with alumina from the Urals, but it is now supplied by the Achinsk alumina works. There have been many complaints about the state of affairs at the Krasnoyarsk plant. According to the director in 1970, 'only one-third of its capacity had been built in nine years, the construction trust in charge had not fulfilled the plan and the auxiliary economy of the plant was being slowly developed.' He bluntly listed all the specialised machines required for the powerful electrolytic equipment to be employed . . . all of which was lacking. At its own risk, the collective tried to solve some of the technical problems created by the lack of equipment. 'But, is it possible to feed a giant with handicraft tools?' asked the director. As a result of the lack of mechanisation, about 2,000 additional workers were employed, though mechanisation was originally boosted as the best means of reducing the plant's need for scarce labour. Negligence at the Ministry of Non-Ferrous Metallurgy seems to have been at the root of the plant's unsatisfactory progress in getting the new electrolysis complex on its feet and other difficulties.

Still another big aluminium plant is planned for Siberia, in connection with the industrial complex to be created round the new Sayan H.E.S., south of Krasnoyarsk. It is so far only at the 'drawing board' stage, but a site for the works was chosen in 1971. In a study of the aluminium industry, a hint was given by an expert of the Siberian Department of the all-Union Academy of Sciences that excessive concentration of aluminium production in Bratsk could lead to infringement of Soviet sanitary regulations and result in a transfer of capacity to the Sayansk region. As the Soviet government is showing increasing sensitivity to environmental pollution problems, this may well be a consideration behind the projected Sayan aluminium plant.

The post-war development of the aluminium industry in Siberia, even to the extent it has already taken place, has important national strategic implications, apart altogether from its many industrial applications. It is common knowledge that owing to the lack of domestic aluminium, the Soviet aircraft industry was badly hampered during World War II and had to a large extent to rely on imports of aluminium from its Western allies. Clearly, the Soviet government is determined that this situation should not recur. But if they have to rely indefinitely on imported bauxite, they will not be much better off.

In spite of the various discrepancies in the organisation and performance of the Siberian aluminium and alumina plants, the need for greater mechanisation to cut down on the labour force and the many operations still done in 'the old-fashioned manual fashion' even in the new Achinsk alumina plant (where powerful suction pumps to remove dust were lacking in 1970), the availability of such quantities of cheap energy gives Siberia a unique advantage for the location of aluminium metallurgy. Using this cheap energy, Soviet experts estimate that the disadvantages of the higher costs of capital construction, scarcity and high costs of labour, are fully compensated for by the favourable energy position. Accordingly, they reckon that economies of 75.6 roubles per ton of aluminium can be achieved in the production of aluminium in the east of the country. Their conclusion is that 'in future it will be advisable to develop aluminium metallurgy chiefly through establishing new capacity in the eastern regions, especially in eastern Siberia. Looking ahead, the proportion of the eastern regions in the production of aluminium could reach approximately 80%.'

Asbestos. Since the incorporation of the Tuva's Peoples Republic in the U.S.S.R. in 1944, Soviet geologists have been searching the steppes and forests for useful natural resources which were hitherto either unknown to the Tuvinese, or not worked by them. Exciting reports of large deposits of asbestos, cobalt and polymetallic ores as well as of gold and silver began to appear in Soviet sources with a tantalising lack of precise information. These reports have now been positively confirmed and the mining of asbestos and cobalt, *inter alia,* has been established on a commercial basis by Soviet mining engineers. One of the most important discoveries to date was the large Ak-Dovurak asbestos deposit, where production started in 1964. Though surpassed in volume by the major Urals asbestos deposits, Tuva asbestos is the finest in quality in the Soviet Union. Its discovery helped to put the Soviet Union ahead of Canada as the world's leading producer of asbestos.

The fibre-bearing rock is processed at the *Tuvaasbest* combine, where production was reported in 1968 to have reached 26,000 tons of fine quality asbestos, though according to the then First Party Secretary, the late S. Toka, the plan only demanded 15,000 tons (the capacity of the first section of this combine has been stated to be 30,000 tons). The combine seems to be forging ahead, as it was set a target of 180,000 tons by the plan for 1970. Nevertheless, there is still a long way to go to approach the 1,507,000 tons output of the older Urals plant in 1969. But any comparison of the situation in these two plants should stress the difficulties which must be encountered in establishing a modern industry in a country like Tuva where the native people have had no previous industrial experience, while the Urals is among the most highly industrialised regions of the U.S.S.R.

Cobalt. The second major discovery of Soviet geologists in the Tuva A.S.S.R. was the big cobalt mine at Khovu-Aksu (about 50 miles southwest of the capital Kyzyl). The adjacent *Tuvakobalt* combine went into operation in 1970. Cobalt obtained elsewhere in Siberia, as at Noril'sk, is a by-product of nickel. But the *Tuvakobalt* combine obtains its metal from a rich cobalite deposit. So far there is no concentrator in Tuva. The concentrate has to be sent thousands of miles westwards to the nickel-cobalt smelter at Nizhniy Ufaley in the Urals. Soviet sources stress the up-to-date technology installed at *Tuvakobalt* which, coming so late into the Soviet industrialisation system, is not burdened with obsolete plant. It is not surprising, however, in the still relatively primitive Tuva A.S.S.R. that there were complaints in 1968 about the delays and unsatisfactory methods used in installing this machinery. As a result, a lot of harm was done and the enterprise was slow in getting on its feet. The Krasnoyarsk board (*Glavk*), responsible for the work at Khovu-Aksu, was blamed for not satisfying the construction's urgent needs. Things were also far from well on the staff side of the enterprise, according to *Pravda*'s special correspondent, in 1969. 'There are no specialists even in such main sectors of construction management as production and economic planning', he reported. 'The great mass of equipment, apparatus and instruments for installing automatic processes is to be found many hundreds of kilometres away from the construction site in the Abakan depots. Transport is lacking. The site is situated more than 500 km. from the railway while the available motor transport is overloaded with bricks and ferro-concrete, coal for the thermal power station, foodstuffs and other goods. Skilled workers, including concrete mixers and carpenters, as well as machine installation specialists, are reluctant to settle here because of the unsatisfactory housing. Funds for building are not lacking but no building is taking place.'

The situation as thus depicted by *Pravda* seems to have changed completely in just a year (or had it?) according to Mr. Owen Lattimore's personal impressions reported in *The Times* (23.11.1970). Mr. Lattimore, not himself admittedly a technical expert, is one of the very few foreigners permitted to visit Tuva and its cobalt combine since the establishment of the autonomous republic. His impressions are therefore worth recalling. 'The Tuvinians claimed', he stated, 'that this cobalt-copper-nickel mine and refinery were the most sophisticated in the Soviet Union'. The top manager is a Ukrainian and most of the departments are headed by Tuvinians, he continued. In section after section of silent, highly-automated machinery, the sole employee watching dials and adjusting controls was most often a Tuvinese and as often a woman as a man. Thus, within a year nothing of the disorganisation bordering on chaos reported by *Pravda*'s correspondent was observed by Mr. Lattimore. Could it have been a case of a 'Potemkin transformation'? If his report reflects the actual situation in *Tuvakobalt* and other enterprises in the country, then the native Tuvinians are already participating in industrialisation to a greater extent than most of the northern Siberian peoples, except the Yakuts.

Though the Tuva A.S.S.R. is not yet linked with the rest of the Soviet Union by rail, the new motor highway connecting Kyzyl with the Abakan rail junction provides an outlet for its asbestos, cobalt and other products, if it is not overloaded.

Lead and Zinc. The Soviet Union is the second world producer of lead and zinc, but Central Asia and the Caucasus, not Siberia or the Soviet Far East, are the main Soviet sources of these minerals. Production in Siberia is heavily concentrated in the rich but relatively small mines at Tetyukhe, in the old Sikhota-Alin' mining area of the Primor'ye (Far East). The former source of lead and zinc at Salair in the Kuzbas is now virtually exhausted. But the Belovo plant originally founded to refine Salair ores is still used to refine ore from other parts of Siberia.

The Tetyukhe mines were discovered by the Chinese in 1840–41 and transferred as a concession to a British corporation in 1924, preceding expropriation by the Soviet government in 1932. They were then reorganised as the *Sikhalikombinat* and as a result of subsequent modernisation and expansion, this is now a large mining-metallurgical enterprise producing lead and zinc concentrates. Tetyukhe is only some 20 miles from Tetyukhe Bay, a port with which it is connected by a narrow-gauge railway. Zinc concentrate is shipped thence for refining to the remote smelters at Konstantinovka (Donbas), Ordzhonikidze (north Caucasus) and Belovo (Kuzbas).

Siberia's position as a lead-zinc producer is expected to be greatly strengthened by the discovery in the late 1960s of lead-zinc deposits at Gorev (Krasnoyarsk kray), under the lower Angara river bed. It is described by a Soviet source as 'the richest in the country'. Trial bores were sunk in 1969 near the new town of Novo-Angarsk, which is being built for some 200,000 mining workers. It is planned to divert the lower reaches of the Angara which is nearly 2 km. wide at this point, so as to facilitate 'the construction of an open pit on the deposit', according to Shabad. This would obviously be a major and very complex operation and at the time of writing it is impossible to predict when the mining of Gorev lead-zinc will be practicable.

The Yakut A.S.S.R. is an important producer of phlogopite mica, a useful material for electrical insulating. With an estimated output of 9,000 tons in 1964, it was then believed to be the largest Soviet producer and much more important than the former major sources of supply at Slyudyanka near Lake Baykal. Both mines are now eclipsed by the big Kovor reserves of mica in Murmansk oblast, which are, incidentally, much more conveniently situated for development and shipment to industrial enterprises using this material in European Russia, than the Far Eastern mines. The muscovite type of mica has long been mined in the Mama area of east Siberia and was originally used in place of glass in windows. When it was replaced by glass in the eighteenth century, these mines ceased to be worked, but the mining was revived here in this century when sheet mica was required by the electrical industry.

Gold. World attention has been increasingly drawn since World War II to the Arctic and sub-Arctic areas of the Soviet Far East, by the exciting discoveries made year by year of great and varied mineral wealth. Gold both in lode and placer deposits is lavishly distributed throughout the region, but most heavily concentrated in the Kolyma river basin, in north-west and southern Yakutiya (Aldan) and in the extreme north-eastern regions of Chukotka. Intensive prospecting for gold in the last forty years, often following up dedicated pre-Revolutionary geologists' lone expeditions and hunches, has resulted in an enormous increase in total Soviet gold production, which is now estimated to be only second in the world to that of South Africa.

The utmost secrecy is maintained officially regarding Soviet gold production statistics, which are withheld from publication as being classified information. In default of official information, informed guesses from experts in this field, bullion merchants, bankers and other specialists, are not lacking, though there is no means under present circumstances of checking their accuracy. An apparently well founded gold production estimate for 1971 puts Soviet output at 212 tons, an increase of only 4 tons over 1970. Sales in the West were variously forecast at between 20–30 tons, while an additional 32 tons of Soviet gold is believed to have been sold by the G.D.R. In 1972, these sales were greatly increased by the big Soviet purchases of Canadian and American grain (recalling Khruschev's run-down on gold stocks for the same purpose in the 1960s). But output again rose in 1973–74.

Recent Soviet sources indicate that some 95% of the Soviet Union's gold comes from the eastern regions; 60–65% probably from the Magadan oblast, which contains the major Kolyma and Chukotsk fields, although a very large new deposit in Central Asia (at Muruntau in the Kyzylkum Desert) may be reducing these shares. As a result of the rapid rise in Far Eastern gold extraction, since the opening up of these large producing areas, the one-time famous Lena-Vitim goldfields, though still operating and much better mechanised than most newer enterprises, have been overtaken by the latter as a producing area. But far from being abandoned, they still make a valuable contribution, it appears, to Soviet gold stocks. There, one new dredger alone covers as much ground and produces as much gold as all the 20 dredgers that had been working in the Lena fields before.

It is extremely difficult to keep up with the flow of news items in the Soviet press and broadcasts about the new deposits of gold and other precious metals, diamonds, tin, tungsten, etc., which have been regular occurrences in recent years in the Soviet Far East. All credit must go for these discoveries to the persistence of a generation of Russian geologists, in the most daunting conditions of climate and terrain. Many of these finds flash into the news from places not yet even on Soviet maps, only to disappear, maybe for years, before reappearing as the site of a new mining complex or combine complete with a settlement, sometimes of hundreds of working people. In the case of important established gold industries like the 'Golden Kolyma', articles and bulletins appear relatively frequently but the information on production and conditions is usually tantalisingly meagre.

Production of Kolyma gold was officially reported to have increased 86% between 1963–68 and these mines are now generally regarded as the biggest producer in the Region. Between 1959–68, production of gold in the entire Magadan oblast (containing most of the Kolyma and all the Chukotsk fields) almost doubled. Pressure from Moscow to increase production had been strong and obviously successful. The greatly improved working conditions and wage levels, since the abolition of the infamous concentration camp methods by which Kolyma was first worked, must also have contributed to the reported rise in production, during the eighth five-year plan period.

A well-known expert on the Canadian north, Farley Mowat, one of the very few foreign visitors even allowed to fly over 'Golden Kolyma', reported in 1969: 'We transected the region called Golden Kolyma, which may be the richest gold-bearing area on earth. There is hardly a sand bar or a gravel bench in any of its innumerable mountain valleys which is not filled with placer gold – nuggets and dust. And, as if this were not enough, the area is now yielding gold in abundance from dozens of hard-rock mines. No official figures about production are available but an estimate given to me in Magadan suggests that annual production from the Kolyma region is now over a thousand tons of gold a year. Whatever the truth may be, the gargantuan effort being put into placer and hard-rock gold mining in this area is obviously producing handsome returns.'[2]

The Aldan gold-fields in southern Yakutiya were opened up by concentration camp labour about the same time as 'Golden Kolyma'. They contain some of the main placer mines in the Soviet Union. Before gold was discovered in the twenties, the Aldan region was wild and uninhabited. Now the town of Aldan (530 km. south of Yakutsk) has become an important centre as the headquarters of the Yakut Gold-

[2] cf. *Sibir* by Farley Mowat, p. 277. This estimate of Siberian gold production is either a slip or a gross exaggeration. It cannot be taken seriously.

Mining Trust and the Advanced Mining Institute. Aldan is connected by a highway linking it north to Yakutsk and south with Bolshoy Never on the Trans-Siberian railway. It is thus much better placed for supplies than the remote and isolated northern gold-mining towns.

In the rigorous conditions of the extreme north of the Region a great new belt of gold, tin, mercury and tungsten became the scene of a most promising expansion of the Kolyma and Aldan reserves in the fifties and thus for the most part escaped *Dal'stroy*'s monstrous regime (abolished in 1956–57). This was the fabulously rich 'Golden Crescent', which stretches from the challenging but little-known Kular mountains in north-western Yakutia along the Arctic coast and the Chaun Bay area to the bleak forbidding wilderness of north-eastern Chukotka. The Malyy Anyuy river basin was found to be rich in placer gold deposits and the industry developed round the new mining town of Bilibino as well as in several other centres further east. A fascinating travelogue published in the Yakut writers' journal *Polyarnaya Zvezda* (no. 3–4, 1967) described the geologists' tough experiences in exploring the hitherto almost inaccessible Kular range, formerly as little known as 'the mountains of the moon', in their quest for more and more gold.

The gold-bearing possibilities of Chukotka were predicted years ago by a Russian geologist, K. I. Bogdanovich, who wandered along the shores of the Sea of Okhotsk in 1895 with a geologist's hammer and saw in the Chukotsk extremity of the 'Golden Crescent' a continuation of the north Alaska goldfields. Later many of his trails were successfully followed up by the Soviet geologists Y. A. Bilibin (after whom Bilibino is named) and S. V. Obruchev, who extended the range of their prospecting from the Kolyma wilds to the remoter Yana-Indigirka region (containing the Kular deposits). The great physical difficulties involved in Kular mining operations are described by a Kular engineer as follows: 'Kular gold is not easy to extract. Ninety per cent of the very rich gold-bearing sands are concealed deep beneath the earth in ancient river beds, buried under sedimentation. The buried rivers do not correspond to those at present on the surface. Here on the map is the gold-bearing riffle of the ancient channel, to the right of the present-day Burgat river and covered by a 30-metre thick terrace. The length of the buried placer is several kilometres and the depth of the gold-bearing sands is thrice the height of a man. There is much more gold in them than in the legendary sands of the Indigirka . . . The depth of permafrost here is 500 m. The 4 m. layer of gold-bearing sands is located at a depth of 30 m. on the ancient bed of the river. A conveyor machine is used to transport the sand to the surface . . . We can extract Kular gold only with powerful machines. Machines and spare parts are as necessary to us as air. We are increasing the metal annually by 19–20% . . .' This report relates to 1966–67.

Though production statistics are withheld about all sectors of the Soviet gold industry, a great deal of information about the ups and downs of its operational side is published in the Soviet Union. It is difficult to decide whether the stream of complaints, often from local Party officials, about 'lagging enterprises' in the Soviet Far Eastern gold industry, represents a state of affairs marked by extraordinary negligence, mismanagement and lack of coordination, or whether perhaps the charges are somewhat exaggerated in order to prod workers and management to greater

The meteorological station at the
Oymyakan, the Pole of Cold

efforts. Some of these local reports do however suggest that the direction of the mines leaves much to be desired.

Susuman is a key centre of the Kolyma gold-fields. Owing to its importance in this industry, the goings-on reported at a meeting of the Susuman *raykom*, in 1971, deserve notice. This meeting was attended by the directors and chief engineers of the Susuman placer mines who admitted that 'an alarming situation had developed at the complex's placer mines because some supervisors' sense of responsibility for the fulfilment of annual plans had become 'blunted'. Moreover, the complex was 8% behind its schedule for the year (1971) as a result of extensive stoppages of excavating and mining equipment at placer mines.

In spite of various discoveries of new deposits and indications of ore in the Okhotsk-Chukotka belt, the responsible north-eastern territorial Geological Directorate was subjected to severe criticism by the Magadan *obkom* bureau, also in 1971. Prospecting for gold, it was alleged, was not receiving due attention, the more promising deposits were not surveyed satisfactorily and proper weight had not been given to progressive methods in organising mining and sinking operations. Finally, grave errors were said to have been committed in planning and carrying out main forms of research which precede detailed surveying. But the *obkom*, on the other hand, admitted that the prospecting parties (which it had been criticising) 'do not have sufficient modern prospecting and power equipment and means of transport.' Not surprisingly under these circumstances, in the same year *Severovostok* (north-eastern) gold output declined and it was reported to have failed badly in achieving its annual production plan. The indications are that output fluctuates considerably from year to year in this industry.

Such revelations of inefficiency and negligence in a high-priority sector of the Far Eastern gold industry must be viewed against the exceptional climatic-supply difficulties with which mining in this part of the world has to cope. Chukotka, forming the extreme north-eastern frontier region of Soviet Asia, is one of the most bleak, yet promising, of the new mining areas. Its natural riches are hidden in a tundra wilderness where ferocious blizzards, permafrost and exceptionally low temperatures are part of the seasonal hazards. So far, only placers have been found in Chukotka but the hunt is on for lode gold sources. It is believed by the Russians that these lodes may paradoxically be found offshore. If they are found, Chukotka may prove even more important as a source of gold than at present.

The state of affairs reflected by the bitter complaints made year after year by Far Eastern mining groups of the lack of specialised machinery to withstand Arctic conditions is less easy to understand or justify. The failure to supply this machinery has caused great financial losses to the Soviet state, estimated by some Soviet experts at the huge figure of 400 million r. annually. A graphic picture of this situation as it was in 1968, was given at a Conference of the Development Problems of Magadan oblast in 1968 (cf. *Problemy Ekonomiki* no. 10, 1968). 'Mass produced, standard, non-northern equipment cannot be efficiently used in the low temperature, permafrost conditions of the north-east', declared the rapporteur. 'Here we need specialised, powerful, reliable, highly-productive, transportable and easily repaired machines with an increased margin of safety ... At the present time the

The Arctic city of Noril'sk

north-east has virtually no "northern equipment", although it has been discussed for many years. This costs the economy dear. For example, the basic machine in the Kolyma gold fields is the bulldozer, constructed on the lines of a low-powered tractor which is specifically designed for agricultural work. According to expert opinion is has proved unsuitable for use in mining operations owing to its low power, frequent breakdowns, long stoppages, and an average life of one season. With such machines the planned fourfold increase in mining work in the north-east is hardly possible . . . This description of bulldozers applies in their several ways also to the majority of other types of earth-moving, mining and transport machines.' *Gossnab* and the relevant engineering industries have taken a long time to rectify the inappropriate types of machinery supplied to the Arctic and sub-Arctic regions and yet, from the oil and gas industries of Tyumen', oblast to the Far Eastern gold fields, there are the same complaints of their wasteful inefficiency. But no major improvement can be expected in this situation until an adequate supply of at present expensive low alloy steels is available for the manufacture of more suitable equipment.

These complaints were not confined to the Kolyma gold-fields. Further south, in the Aldan fields, productivity was reported in 1968 to have been reduced by one-third in winter, because the metals used in the dredges could not withstand the cold. 'Cold resistant metal must be used in northern equipment as in Finland, Sweden and Canada' demanded one Soviet critic.

Yet, in spite of all these problems, production of gold in the Kolyma and Chukotka areas was a record, according to Soviet sources in 1970.

All Soviet gold (including Far Eastern gold) is sent to the central gold refinery at Novosibirsk for refining. This seems surprising when, under similar climatic conditions, Yakut diamonds are processed in a special new plant at Mirnyy and that there are tin concentrating plants in the remote towns of Batagay and Deputatskiy. A gold extraction works, to treat up to 100,000 cu.m. of ore annually, was constructed at Nizhniy Kuranakh in the Aldan area of southern Yakutiya in the late sixties, but the administrative centre of the Far Eastern gold industry remains at Ust'Nera on the upper Indigirka, nearly 10,000 km. from Moscow. A report from Yakutsk, in 1972, was critical of the way the plan for gold extraction and the reconstruction of the gold extraction works at Kuranakh was progressing. 'Serious shortcomings' were found in the supervisory work and in the enterprise's failure to meet its reconstruction plan. Administratively, the Siberian gold-fields are divided into a number of trusts, all subordinate to the all-Union Ministry of Non-Ferrous Metallurgy. They were named as follows in 1971:

a Severovostokzoloto (Northeastgold, containing the Kolyma and Chukotsk group of mines);

b Yakutzoloto (Yakutgold);

c Lenzoloto (Lenagold);

d Amurzoloto (Amurgold);

e Zabaikalzoloto (Zabaykalgold);

f Primorzoloto (Primor'yegold);

Diamonds. There were no known domestic sources of diamonds of any significance in the Soviet Union until 1954, when a rich kimberlite pipe was discovered in the 'untrodden' depths of the western Yakut taiga. This was indeed a major discovery both for the Soviet Treasury and Soviet industry, as future developments showed. During World War II, the Soviet Union's need for industrial diamonds was so acute that diamonds to the value of £1,425,000 were imported from the U.K. alone. The government realised the seriousness of this deficiency and Soviet geologists got the message.

Following up some local legends of 'fire stones' and the discovery of a few alluvial diamonds, the hunt was on for diamond deposits in the Vilyuy river basin. After some false trails in this wilderness and the exciting efforts of a couple of women geologists, luck was on the side of young Yuri Khabardin, who hit the now famous Mirnyy pipe in 1954. Mirnyy turned out on investigation to be one of the richest diamond reserves in the world, comparable to the old Kimberley blue-earth of South Africa. Unfortunately, in the subsequent scramble to extend this diamond field, the surrounding taiga was burned to the ground leaving Mirnyy in the midst of a scene of ghastly black destruction.

Having surmounted the early strenuous living conditions in tents and log huts, resulting in a considerable 'drift-away' of the less dedicated workers, Mirnyy has now been built up as a modern if aesthetically unattractive town, according to the few foreigners who have visited it recently. There are large blocks of flats 'with all amenities' for the near 40,000 people of many Soviet nationalities mainly occupied in the diamond industry.

The centre of activity in Mirnyy is the diamond processing plant, claimed by the Soviets to be the largest in the world. It runs night and day in spite of the exceptionally harsh climate and is entirely automated. It is built of special materials and is supplied with insulation which, according to a Soviet report, cannot be penetrated even by the formidable Yakut frosts. Having been processed at Mirnyy, the diamonds are dispatched by air to Moscow, to be dealt with by the Ministry of Finance. For its good work in fulfilling the tasks allotted to it under the eighth five-year plan, Mirnyy was awarded the accolade of the Red Banner of Labour order in 1971. Thus, though no precise statistics accompanied the award, it would appear that Mirnyy diamonds were produced in gratifying quantities during that period (1966–71).

Four years after opening up the Mirnyy pipe, the Yakut diamond industry was extended north to still richer pipes at Aykhal and later to Udachnyy, 600 km. north-east of Mirnyy. Udachnyy is to have its own diamond-separation plant which has been under construction since 1970. It seems from a *Pravda* (5.7.1971) report that the authorities were jogged into expediting the development of Udachnyy by an 'old Siberian hand' who had also been active in producing 'central heating, sewage and piped water' in Aykhal 'where nothing previously existed' . . . 'His temperamental interventions at enterprise meetings and Party conferences' produced the desired result and the necessary finance and materials were forthcoming to work the Udachnyy pipe and to build a 280 km. road to Aykhal, in hard frost.

It was estimated by foreign experts that the Yakut diamond industry produced about 7.8 million carats of diamonds in 1968, of which up to a million carats were gems, the main products being industrial diamonds or bort. Claims are frequently made in the Soviet media of finds of diamonds of 'unique' size and value. In 1969, for example, a giant diamond extracted by *Yakutalmaz* weighing 315 carats was reported, but nothing was said about either the quality or type of this stone.

The expansion of diamond production in the remote areas of western Yakutiya, where all the pipes so far known are located, depends to a large extent on the growth of power facilities. Though there are no exact statistics to prove it, there is little doubt that production must have been greatly assisted by the construction of the Vilyuy hydroelectric power station which went on stream in 1967–68 and was expressly planned to provide much needed power for the diamond industry.

In the early years of the Yakut diamond enterprise, there was no experience of diamond processing techniques and little of modern diamond prospecting methods in the Soviet Union. But Soviet scientists, geologists and technologists soon made good these deficiencies and no foreign technical aid was commissioned to help out in developing the Yakut industry, which is reliably believed to be technically on a par with the highest world standards. However, foreign technical progress in regard to the diamond industry was no doubt studied from the pages of the international technical press, imported in large quantities into the Soviet Union.

The increasing need of industrial diamonds in a wide range of Soviet industries where all kinds of abrasive tools are in demand, has led to the establishment of a Soviet synthetic diamond industry which is now the next largest world producer of these diamonds after the U.S.A. The chief producer of Soviet synthetic diamonds is the Ukraine. According to expert foreign estimates, synthetic diamonds are now used in about 95% of diamond abrasive tools in the Soviet Union. But it is generally recognised that the quality of Soviet diamond tipped bits, for the oil industry and other equipment using these diamonds, is far below the best world standards and foreign-made bits are therefore largely imported to replace the inferior domestic product, either on loan or bought.

Soviet diamonds are not only useful at home, they are also sold abroad. Very soon after the first Yakut diamonds were processed, a contract was concluded in 1959 with the international diamond firm de Beers to market Soviet diamonds, but as a result of the Soviet boycott of trade with South Africa this contract was not renewed in 1963. Soviet diamonds continued, however, to reach the international diamond market, handled it is believed by a subsidiary of de Beers. It was announced in the English press in 1973 that the Soviet Union had arranged to market part of its diamond putput through a newly formed company, the Association of Belgian and Soviet Diamond Dealers. The possible turnover, in default of any official figures, was estimated at 1 million carats a year of polished stones. One of the Belgian partners to this deal added that the Soviets have three centres for polishing stones each employing from 2,000 to 3,000 people, in Moscow, Smolensk and Kiev. (*The Financial Times* (17.7.1973).)

The Soviet government hopes to expand the known diamond wealth of the country by further discoveries in the Far East and elsewhere in Siberia. Ground geological prospecting for this purpose is now being reinforced by aerial-prospecting in the Far East. The reason behind this development is that it is believed that kimberlite pipes are of above average sensibility and instruments, installed in these prospecting aircraft, register the slightest deviations in the strength of the magnetic field in the areas under survey. As a result of these aerial investigations, it was reported in 1966 that over 100 deposits containing kimberlite pipes and other minerals associated with diamonds had been discovered in the Yakut A.S.S.R. This report was followed up by the sensational news a few years later (1968), that among the 'colossal' reserves of the still primitive Evenk National Okrug, the diamonds might be expected eventually to compete with those of the Yakut A.S.S.R. No further information seems to have been released about these Evenk diamonds.

This survey of Siberia's great mineral wealth would be incomplete without a cautionary word about the dangers arising from the poor conservation practices which have accompanied the working of its near inexhaustible natural resources.[3] Expert observers of the Soviet mining scene, both Soviet and foreign, are at one in deploring the often wanton use of many valuable reserves and the generally indifferent attitude to conservation. Decisions of the economic planners have in the past for the most part ignored these problems, especially when any conflict of interest arose between conservation and their primary production-development objectives. Recent legislation should work towards a better state of affairs but it will be no easy matter at once to overcome the vested interests involved and old, wide-spread, ingrained attitudes on this subject, with which the western world is also too familiar.

Machine Building (Engineering) Industries. These Siberian industries amounted for the most part to little more than repair shops for machinery imported from European Russia and the Urals before World War II. This situation was entirely changed by the evacuation of many sophisticated machine building engineering plants and their skilled workers to Siberia during World War II. The impact of this war-time evacuation on production in the eastern regions was rapid and dramatic, between 1941–45. Thus, in western Siberia the gross output of this branch was 23 times larger in 1956 than in 1940 and much higher than the national average increase. In considering the disparity in these levels of increase, the low starting point of the Siberian industry in 1941 and the disastrous effect of the war on the European industry, must be taken into account. In the later post-war years, the impetus given to machine-building in Siberia by the war was not sustained. As the major plants in the Ukraine and European Russia were reconstructed, the share of Siberia in all-Union production fell. Few new plants were built in Siberia for some decades and any growth in capacity came from expansion of existing plants.

At the present time, this industry is a specialised branch mainly in west Siberia, where its gross output and labour force exceed average Union indices and constitutes about 3% of industrial production. In east Siberia and the Soviet Far East it is much less important or developed, though it has considerably expanded in both regions, in recent years. In west Siberia, the industry can rely on a strong metallurgical base and has developed many new branches some of which contribute significantly to all-Union production. These are the energy, electro-technical,

[3] cf. Philip R. Pryde, *Conservation in the Soviet Union*. Cambridge University Press, p. 102.

tractor and agricultural machinery branches. Agricultural machinery is made in large plants in Novosibirsk and Krasnoyarsk and also in Irkutsk in east Siberia. Tomsk and Tyumen' specialise in the production of electrical machinery, much of which is shipped to other parts of the U.S.S.R. In particular, west Siberia holds an important place in the production of steam boilers of large capacity (above 50% of Union output) tractor ploughs (45% of Union output) and tractor disc harrows (100% of Union output), direct current electric machines (50% of Union output). West Siberian engineering plants centred in Novosibirsk are for the most part large specialised enterprises fulfilling specific all-Union requirements.

This export capacity of the west Siberian industry does not imply that all is well with its branch structure. In fact, the position is far from satisfactory. While West Siberia distributes many engineering products throughout the Soviet Union, the local engineering industry only satisfies some of the region's engineering requirements by 20–25%, though engineering costs in west Siberia are estimated to be 20% lower than elsewhere in the country. This results in expensive imports of such essential items as bulldozers and lorries, excavators, rolling mills, pumps, electrical and steam turbines which are almost entirely supplied by European Russia. The lack of coordination between domestic production and requirements in this industry also extends to the manufacture of rolled metal. A limited range of rolled metal is produced in Siberia but it does not correspond to the region's engineering requirements. The domestic product is therefore exported and replaced by more suitable rolled metal from the Urals.

These anomalies in the structure of the Siberian machine-building industry and its products in relation to local requirements can, to some extent, be traced back to the many plants evacuated from European Russia during the war and which have not meanwhile been reorganised to produce machines designed to meet Siberian conditions. Unwanted or unusable in Siberia, these goods swell the exports to western Europe. The post-war development of the Siberian mining industries has intensified the demand for mining machinery but the range of equipment produced locally is far below demand. In particular, there is a constantly underfulfilled demand for drilling equipment of high quality, suitable for the important oil and gas industry of west Siberia. Soviet critics complain about the present concentration of repair facilities for overhauling oil and gas equipment in Tyumen' and urge that they should be located to a larger extent in the Ob'-Irtysh oil-gas complex area and supplemented by repair shops at Tobol'sk, which is closer to the oil-gas development area. Such a move should be much easier now that the railway has reached Tobol'sk. Tyumen' however is likely to be the site of the new west Siberian oil equipment industry now under consideration, owing to its old established industrial links, good communications with European Russia and experienced labour force.

Though Siberia is to a large extent supplied with machines and equipment from other parts of the Soviet Union, there are constant complaints that these items also are unsatisfactory and are neither designed, nor built, to suit harsh Siberian conditions. The northern regions are particularly badly off in this respect. In the north of Krasnoyarsk kray, in Yakutiya and the Tuvinskaya A.S.S.R. where large areas are solid with permafrost, 'the usual construction machines do not resist, but are smashed to bits in winter'. And various other types of equipment are similarly affected because they are not made of special cold-resistant steel. This is all the more serious because of the present expansion of mining and other industries in the north. Writing in *Pravda* (9.4.1969), a high official of the Krasnoyarsk construction department stressed the gravity of the problem: 'We desperately need highly productive machines and equipment', he wrote, 'to work permafrost ground. What we now have and use in local conditions is entirely inadequate for the extent of the work, or the need for a rapid rise in labour productivity in construction. In Siberian conditions, bulldozers with engines of 100 h.p. are required for earth work, and for permafrost ground engines of 250 h.p. But the actual machine-work is relying on bulldozers manufactured on the lines of the standard agricultural tractors of 55–75 h.p. We have no machines for moving earth frozen to a great depth.'

Another Soviet commentator expressed himself even more strongly on the subject: 'Machines for the north practically do not exist. The most necessary type of equipment in construction is tower cranes and excavators. They are designed to work at not lower than minus 35°–40°C and at a wind velocity of not more than 14 metres a second. But in Noril'sk, the annual average number of days with a temperature lower than − 40°C is 37–42! And the wind velocity is 14–16 m. a second, for 55 to 58 days. Thus, it is impossible to use this equipment a quarter of the year.' These unsuitable machines are causing the Soviet state enormous financial and output losses in the mining industries of northern Siberia. According to data published in 1969 by the Institute of Economics of the Siberian Department of the all-Union Academy of Sciences, 'the damage caused from the use of equipment unsuitable for Siberian conditions in the last two years in the Noril'sk mining-metallurgical combinat alone amounted to about 15 million roubles. In Yakutiya, the costs of operating and repairing only one bulldozer is 12,000 roubles a year, which is almost twice as much as its cost price.' Two years later, the First Secretary of the Yakut *obkom* was again complaining about these unserviceable bulldozers (about which and other equipment supplied to Yakutiya, local reactions continue to be bitterly critical).

Much of the blame for this state of affairs must it seems be laid at the door of the leading scientific design-research institutes in this field, which are criticised by Soviet sources for producing many models of machines, totally unsuitable for Siberian conditions, with which they vie with each other to 'gain kudos' in competitions. The only machine suitably designed which passed all the tests was never mass produced and only one reached Krasnoyarsk, because of the technical confusion at the Chelyabinsk factory which produced it.

The need for more and better equipment is intensified by the demands both of the developing Siberian economy and also of the mechanisation programme designed to make good the shortage of labour in Siberian industry and agriculture.

Soviet experts considering the pros and cons of the production of this equipment in European Russia or Siberia, have expressed widely different views on the extent to which Siberia could efficiently and economically participate in such production plans. An authoritative investigation of this problem was published under the joint auspices of the Academy of Sciences and *Gosplan* in 1971. It concluded that estimates of costs showed that the lowest costs of construction of engineering enter-prises were found to be in the Central, Central Black Earth and Volga-Vyatsk regions of European Russia, owing to much more favourable climatic conditions than in Siberia, together with an available construction base, adequate raw material reserves and a highly qualified labour force, adding that costs alone should not be the deciding factor in regard to this location problem. While conditions in north and east Siberia were admittedly wholly unsuitable for this industry (with the exception of some locally necessary repair shops) and only branches supplying specific local needs or contributing to trade with Pacific countries should be considered for the Far Eastern region, there were serious grounds for the establishment of a new engineering base in west Siberia to reinforce, *inter alia*, the electro-technical and energy, tractor-agricultural branches already operating there.

A new base on these lines, it was pointed out, was required to promote the de-velopment of the eastern regions as a whole, so as to increase the supply of energy, chemical, construction, transport equipment and other branches of the metal-intensive engineering industries. Finally, the investigation concluded, 'the rational-ity of the development of the engineering industry in this region must be deter-mined by a whole complex of economic, social and political factors, not by costs alone . . .' Moscow apparently did not regard the establishment of such a base as a matter of any urgency, because there was no provision for it in the current five-year plan. On the other hand, many of the existing plants are to be expanded during this period. It may well be that in the course of the simultaneous process of modern-isation and mechanisation, now in train, the former imbalance in the structure of the west Siberian machine building and engineering industries will be rectified, though no specific information on this point has been noticed.

Turning from west to east Siberia, the main centres of the regional engineering industry are located along the Trans-Siberian railway at Krasnoyarsk, Irkutsk and Ulan-Ude. About 20% of this region's industrial workers are employed in engineer-ing enterprises. But east Siberia only produced some 25% of its domestic engineer-ing requirements in 1966. Production in this region tends to specialise, either in the manufacture of mining, wood-working or transport equipment. The old city of Ulan-Ude, an important junction on the Trans-Siberian railway, has the largest plant east of the Urals for building and repairing diesel locomotives and rail cars. It was built in the thirties under the auspices of Commissar Lazar Kaganovich, and has latterly been modernised and expanded. An engineering plant in Chita, of which little is generally heard, is now manufacturing refrigerating plant and exported a consignment of it in 1971 for installation in passenger liners, tankers and timber carriers, to shipyards in the G.D.R., Poland and Hungary. Moreover, the east Siberian industry has also made a start in the production of electrical equip-ment for every-day general use, but the great electro-generators for the big east Siberian hydropower and thermal electric stations and the equipment for the high voltage transmission systems, have all been produced in the old industrial centres of Leningrad and Khar'kov. Most of the wood-chemical and paper machinery in-stalled at Bratsk was imported from foreign countries like Sweden.

As in west Siberia, there is no domestic outlet for a considerable proportion of the engineering production of east Siberia, which is either exported to other parts of the Soviet Union or abroad. Among such products are mining-extraction, metallurgical and cement-making equipment. The engineering industry of east Siberia should assume an entirely new importance once the complex of electrical engineering enterprises known as the 'Elektrograd' now being constructed near Minusinsk (in Krasnoyarsk kray), as part of the Sayan H.E.S. scheme, is operating. According to a Moscow report, for the first time in the history of the Soviet engineering industry 12 large enterprises will be located on a common site. They will produce turbo-generators, electric motors, transformers, high-voltage equipment and electrical insulating materials. 'The turbo- and hydro-generators will include giants, the power of each of which will be equal to two contemporary *Dneproges* (Dnieper hydropower stations)'. Thus, if all goes according to plan with this big *Elektrograd* project, it will be able in time to supply the various projected Siberian electric power stations with machinery, formerly imported over long distances and at great expense from European Russia or abroad. The largest railway wagon works in the country is also being built as part of the Sayan project, at Abakan, with a planned annual production of 40,000 rail freight cars and a 300,000-ton capacity foundry.

East Siberia's engineering capacity will be further increased by the long deferred decision, in 1971, to go ahead with the construction of the Chita truck assembly works, the first east of the Urals. Further east, engineering, properly speaking, only started in the Far Eastern region with the construction of the *Dal'dizel* plant which evolved in the thirties from the old rather primitive engineering-munitions shop, 'Arsenal', set up to make guns etc., in preparation for the Russo-Japanese war (1905). As a result of the various new branches established before and since World War II, engineering has become an important sector of Far Eastern industry. The plants are unevenly distributed throughout this vast territory except in the Far North, where engineering is restricted to repair shops for the mining or other local industries. More than half of the engineering production of the Soviet Far East originates in the Khabarovsk kray, which contains the most important plants. *Dal'dizel* was re-equipped after the last war with up-to-date machinery and complex automation. It now produces diesels and diesel-generators, claimed by Soviet sources to be 'on a level with the best world models' and fifth in capacity in the Soviet Union. 'There is not a river or a sea in the U.S.S.R., nor an ocean, where Khabarovsk diesels are not working on the ships of different countries', boasted *Pravda* (20.10.1972). Other engineering works in Khabarovsk which have made their mark nationally are *Energomash* (electric power machinery works), which is the sole manufacturer of 3,000-kw. gas turbines and centrifugal compressors and produces machinery for the chemical industry, and *Amurkabel* (the Amur cable works), which manufactures 50 different types of cable for industry, ship-building and urban communications, etc.

Amurlitmash (Amur foundry) is one of the most successful engineering enterprises in the Far East. It is situated in the rapidly growing industrial town of Komsomol'sk-na-Amure and produces mining, crushing-grinding, transport and casting equipment: 33% of the total Union output of casting machinery is produced at this plant. It exports equipment, mainly shot-blasting machines for castings, to

India and other foreign countries including eastern Germany and Bulgaria. It was reported (in 1966) to be the only Soviet enterprise manufacturing different types of metallurgical cleaning machines and to be designing automatic equipment for cleaning steel rods to be used at the Izhevsk and Cherepovets metallurgical works, in European Russia. The lifting equipment works at Komsomol'sk also has a leading place in Soviet industry for the production of cranes, which are exported both to other parts of the Soviet Union and abroad. It exported a 10-ton electric bridge crane in 1973 and other hoisting mechanisms in 1972 to Iskenderun (Turkey) where a metallurgical complex is being constructed with Soviet assistance.

Dal'sel'khozmash in Birobidzhan (capital of the Jewish autonomous oblast) has taken over the name and function belonging to *Dal'dizel*, for a time in the fifties. It manufactures agricultural machinery and achieved some recent publicity with the reported export of some of its new rice combine-harvesters to Cuba, Iran, Iraq and other countries.

In the Primor'ye, there is a big engineering works in Ussuriysk which produces woodworking machines for the local timber industry and foreign markets. According to Soviet sources, some of these machines were exported in 1967 to Bulgaria, Mongolia, Canada, North Vietnam, and Pakistan, with what success is unknown. The plant is reported to be producing a model specially designed for African countries and the tropics.

Ship building and ship repairs are traditional – if rather primitive – industries in the chief ports along the Soviet Pacific coast. Vladivostok has a floating dock. The standard of ship repairs in these ports is often criticised by units of the Soviet fishing fleet based there, but latterly Soviet reports tend to stress the improvements and modernisation of port equipment in the Soviet Far East, which should produce an improvement also in standards of ship repairs.

Though the Soviet Far Eastern engineering industry has developed considerably since World War II, both in the number of plants operating and the diversity of items produced, a large number of machines still have to be imported, e.g. tractors and bulldozers, to satisfy domestic needs, while about 80% of domestic production, according to Soviet sources, is exported. It seems that there is a definite long-term government policy to increase exports of Far Eastern engineering products, as far as they are acceptable, to the countries of the Pacific basin and beyond, where engineering industries are still in their infancy or non-existent. In view of the remoteness of the Soviet Far East from the main Soviet engineering production supply centres and the heavy cost of rail transport to the Far East, it seems curious that more has not been done to gear the region's engineering industry to domestic needs. There is, however, no lack of comment on the subject in Soviet journals and some Soviet experts are of the opinion that it would be 'rational' for the Soviet Far Eastern region to have its own, better-balanced, engineering industry producing equipment for heavy industry, and manufacturing electro-technical, construction and road-making, agricultural and automobile machinery. This seems an over-ambitious programme. But, even if it were substantially reduced, a preliminary requirement would be the establishment of the long-discussed Far Eastern Metallurgical Base, which could supply these new engineering plants with the essential metal. This has now to be imported to a large extent and expensively, and is a main cause of the high production costs of Far Eastern engineering goods, in some cases 20–30% higher than in European Russia. Costs are also increased by high wages and construction costs.

In attempting to come to any conclusions regarding the present position of the Siberian engineering industry, the words of the First Secretary of the Kemerovo oblast' Party committee, A. F. Estokin, at the Twenty-fourth Party Congress, may be usefully quoted: 'In Siberia, the engineering industry is entirely inadequately developed for the mining-metallurgical complex and therefore we cannot create the necessary technical base for the mining extraction industry. West Siberia markedly lags behind other regions for the production of progressive types of prefabricated, reinforced concrete, although in Siberia, with its long winter, "monolithic' (i.e. solid blocks) reinforced concrete is more efficiently replaced by pre-fabricated concrete structures.' Novosibirsk experts seem more optimistic about the future of west Siberia's machine-building-engineering industries. Forecasting a marked increase in the region's ferrous metallurgy and a share in all-Union production of iron and steel by the year 2000, in comparison with 1970, they were of the opinion that the prospects of the engineering sectors which produce metal intensive and relatively non-labour intensive products, e.g. large electrical machinery, boilers, mining-metallurgical and chemical equipment, should be more promising than formerly.

chapter seven

Chemical Industries

The Siberian chemical industry is of relatively recent date and significance, in spite of the abundance of the local raw materials and the large sources of energy available for its development. The small Siberian industry reflected the poor state of the Soviet industry as a whole in the post-war period, with run-down plants and out-of-date techniques. It was dramatically changed by Khrushchev's 'Big Chemical' campaign launched in 1959 and the large financial allocations made available by the seventh five-year plan programme. At this time, few chemical enterprises of all-Union significance existed in Siberia. The year 1959 may, therefore, be regarded as a turning point in the chemical industry of the Soviet Union and of Siberia in particular. The simultaneous discovery of the huge Tyumen' oil and gas deposits in west Siberia created a new local base for the Siberian petro-chemical industry, while the chemical processing of the brown coals of the Kansk-Achinsk basin and sulphur from these coals could be used to produce sulphuric acid, which is scarce in Siberia.

As man-power had already become an increasingly acute problem for Siberian industry, it was one of the decisive factors in determining the location of new industries. The Soviet centralised planning and economic organs were therefore inclined to discourage the establishment of labour-intensive branches of the chemical industries (among others) in Siberia. As a result, a limitation has been imposed on the production of the labour-intensive synthetic polymers and nitrogen fertilisers in trans-Urals areas. Higher wage rates in Siberia led to increased labour-production costs, with the result that only energy-intensive and highly automated branches of the chemical industry are thought suitable officially for location in Siberia, though in practice this ruling is not exactly observed.

The costs of rail or other transport of raw materials and the finished chemical products are also a brake on the sale of Siberian chemical products in European Russia, in view of the enormous distances from Siberia, and tend to limit some products to local markets and to exclude them from those more remote. The concentration of the manufacture of man-made fibres, fertilisers, plastics, resins and rubber goods may be expected to continue, as at present in European Russia.

On the other hand, the coke-chemical industry, with coal derived feed-stocks from the local coke ovens, was the earliest important chemical industry in Siberia and still leads (in spite of many-sided new developments in the Siberian chemical industry). It is centred in and around the two towns of Kemerovo and Novokuznetsk in the Kuzbas. However, the former situation there in which coke-chemical stocks far outpassed the Siberian supply of petro-chemicals, is now changing rapidly, with the intensive development of Siberian petro-chemicals, which produce nitrogen fertilisers, paints and some phenol-'Bakelite'-type resins.

There should be 7 plants for synthetic rubber, artificial fibres, plastics and some new chemical products in Siberia and the Far East by 1976, if the scheduled programme is completed on time. An expert Soviet analysis of the distribution of gross chemical output between west and east Siberia in 1968 (now probably somewhat out of date) put west Siberia in 6th place and east Siberia in 7th in the all-Union table. The Siberian proportion in all-Union production of some basic chemical products was at this time estimated as follows:

Sulphuric acid production in Siberia	4%	
Soda ash production in Siberia	1%.	
Methanol production in Siberia	3.5%	
Nitrogen fertiliser production in Siberia	13%	
Ammonia production in Siberia	14%	
Chemical fibres in west Siberia	10%	of Union output
Chemical fibres in east Siberia	6%	
Plastics and synthetic resins in east Siberia	18%	
Phenol-based resins in west Siberia	44%	
Carbamide resins in east Siberia	9%	
PVC resins in Siberia	24%	

Surveying the present situation of the chemical industry in west and east Siberia, there appears to be a general process of expansion of older plants and the establishment of a number of new enterprises, often to make products not hitherto manufactured in Siberia. In west Siberia the main petro-chemical centres are Omsk, Tobol'sk and Tomsk. Omsk, the site of an old refinery, is planned to have an entire chemical complex in operation by 1975. The sulphuric acid plant at the oil refinery began operations in 1966. Its tyre plant, which had a rather unsatisfactory start in 1959, produced an estimated 3.4 million tyres of the Union total of 34.6 million tyres in 1970. A synthetic rubber plant was opened in 1963 to supply raw material for this tyre factory. There were soon complaints of shortage of such raw materials as butene and propylene, although the synthetic rubber plant was close to the refinery and for some time it was necessary to supplement supplies by expensive imports of petro-chemicals from Bashkiriya, Sumgait and Baku. The shortages were eventually traced to an inefficient gas-separation plant at the refinery.

Stereoregular rubber (polyisoprene and polybutadiene rubbers), the closest replicas to natural rubber so far made, are also to be produced in Tobol'sk and Tomsk in the mid-1970s. The old Siberian town of Barnaul in the Altay is yet another Siberian chemical centre of growing importance. Its tyre plant (part of a manufacturing complex under construction since 1960) reached its full capacity in 1971. The range of production there includes tyre cord, viscose rayon staple fibre and carbon black.

According to the directions of the ninth five-year plan, major petro-chemical complexes are to be built in the vicinity of Tobol'sk and Tomsk, to process crude oil and associated gas. This is a logical development as both towns are closely connected with the west Siberian oil fields. The Tomsk petro-chemical complex is to be built by the Leningrad *Plastpolymer* and three other research and design organisations. The first section of this plant is planned to have a capacity of 300,000 tons of ethylene a year. It will also be highly mechanised and automated in line with the current official aim of adjusting Siberian industrial development to the acute manpower situation.

In the Altay, a new coke-chemical works is scheduled for commissioning in 1975, according to the Plan. It will eventually be the biggest of its type in the U.S.S.R.

In east Siberia, the chemical industry is being most actively developed in or around Krasnoyarsk, Irkutsk, Bratsk, Usol'ye Sibirskoye and Angarsk.

The Krasnoyarsk kray contains the following chemical capacities:

1 A wood chemical complex with a synthetic fibre plant;
2 A synthetic rubber plant;
3 A tyre plant.

The Irkutsk oblast contains petro-electro and coal-chemical units producing ammonia, nitrogen fertilisers, sulphuric acid, caustic soda, phenol, benzine and butyl alcohol. Poor coordination of the available technological processes and servicing throughout these areas has, Soviet sources allege, resulted in shortages of sulphuric acid and caustic soda. Apart from the wood-chemical complex (which will be described separately below), synthetic rubber and tyres are made in Krasnoyarsk. The tyre plant produced 2.5 million tyres in 1970, or a good deal less than the Omsk production in the same year. Krasnoyarsk also produces a wide range of other chemicals facilitated by the great electrical power resources of the new Dvinogorsk H.E.S. station near by. Among other products are viscose fibres, ethylalcohol and feed stocks for other processes. There is also a Dacron monomer plant. As a result of these activities, Krasnoyarsk is becoming an increasingly important centre of the Siberian chemical industry.

Irkutsk oblast is also of major interest in this industry with its expanding plants at Angarsk, Usol'ye Sibirskoye and Bratsk among the most significant. The Angarsk petroleum refinery and its associated petro-chemical complex extends for 4 km. along the Angara river bank and is powered by the Irkutsk H.E.S. It is a major enterprise with plants producing lubricants and various chemicals. Its plastics production capacity was greatly enlarged by the commissioning of two additional automated plants (for objects of mass consumption) in 1971. A new plant is also under construction at Angarsk refinery, which should greatly increase productivity by the use, for the first time in Siberia, of the ELOUAVT process of solvent extraction. Angarsk synthetic rubber is among the cheapest produced in Siberia.

Angarsk refinery gases supply the big Usol'ye-Sibirskoye chemical complex at Zima, with which the refinery is closely associated. The complex is based on the huge rock salt deposits situated along the Trans-Siberian railway for hundreds of kilometres, between Talunda and Zima. A new electric-chemical complex is now being constructed at the new town of Zima which will contain, apart from the additional chemical shops, engineering and repair plants and a power station. Chlorine and caustic soda, p.v.c., organosilicon, varnishes and other products are also manufactured from this salt.

The wood chemical industry is being belatedly developed in Siberia. In view of the enormous stocks of timber in the taiga extending from northern Tyumen' oblast to the shores of the Pacific and the accessible power resources, this industry should have very bright prospects and is now rapidly expanding, in the first place in east Siberia. It was virtually neglected until Khrushchev's chemical programme launched in 1959. Anticipating this development, the first large wood chemical plant was opened in Krasnoyarsk in 1956 based on the hydrolysis of wood cellulose (capacity 200,000 t.). Some years later, one of the largest wood-chemical industries in the world was initiated at Bratsk, utilising the abundant timber and power locally available. The cardboard section started work in 1967 and when the Bratsk timber complex becomes fully operational with the completion of new works, output of cellulose, it is anticipated, will double to an output of 1,000,000 tons a year. But it was reported in the Soviet journal *Sotsialisticheskaya Industriya* in 1971 that, 'there had been serious negligence in the building of the complex'. It was originally equipped with the most up-to-date machinery from Finland and Sweden. A Scandinavian engineer who had visited the works in 1964 told me that plan-obsessed workers were running the machinery so hard that expensive break-downs and stoppages were not uncommon. At this time, at least, there was a lack of properly trained workers to run this equipment. At Bratsk, lumber is converted into sulphate, cellulose and newsprint, paper rosin and industrial yeast. The Bratsk rosin works is the largest in the U.S.S.R.

Another big wood chemical enterprise, specialising in the production of sulphate pulp, has been under construction since 1966, at Baykal'sk on the south-eastern shore of Lake Baykal. A big row blew up later about the siting of this plant, following the public realisation that its effluents were seriously polluting the crystalline waters of Lake Baykal.[1] The assurances of action to stop this pollution by the management were found to be completely inadequate and efforts continued to ensure that the Ministry of the Cellulose-Paper Industry more strictly supervised the installation of purification works by the negligent Baykal'sk cellulose plant.

The Soviet Far Eastern region with its big unexploited stretches of virgin forest, has also been slow to develop a local chemical industry. As in east Siberia, unprocessed logs until the last decade or so dominated the timber industry. The establishment of a wood chemical industry is possibly the most promising method employed by the Soviet government to put the timber industry on a more up-to-date, less wasteful, profitable footing. The first wood chemical complex in this Region (apart from the well-organised cellulose-paper factories taken over from the Japanese after the war in Karafuto), started partial production in 1967, at Amursk (the new town near Komsomol'sk). This first section of the Amursk plant had an annual capacity of 75,000 tons and the second, alleged to have double this capacity, went into production in 1968. Apparently with the unfortunate example of Baykal'sk in mind, it was boasted in 1971 by TASS that 'the Amur remains clean despite the fact that

[1] This pollution problem is discussed more fully in Chapter 1 on the Environment.

about 800,000 cu. m. of waste water a day is discharged into it from Komsomol'sk pulp and cardboard works . . . Purified industrial effluent is kept in aerated ponds for several months.'

Another big wood chemical plant has been built in the Ussuri taiga, at Novo-mikhailovka, with Polish technical assistance. It is equipped to produce more than 20 different products from timber waste. The Japanese have supplied the equipment for the first chip-board factory in the Soviet Far East which is under construction at Nakhodka port. When these various plants are in full production and over their teething troubles, this formerly stagnant industry should contribute substantially to the economic development of the Soviet Far East. Meanwhile, the first-class cellulose-paper industry inherited from the Japanese in south Sakhalin (Karafuto) remains the main source of paper and cellulose produced and exported from the Soviet Far East region. The primitive state of transport, in vast, still roadless areas in the Khabarovsk and Primorsk taiga, greatly complicates the removal of logs for processing and in turn acts as a brake on the more rapid development of the wood chemical industry. Latterly, however, some progress is being made with narrow gauge railways and forest tracks to overcome this problem.

Up to the present the development of the chemical industry in Siberia (as throughout the Soviet Union) has been substantially assisted by the imports of more sophisticated and efficient machinery from the west than Soviet equipment. Great Britain, West Germany, Sweden, Finland, the Netherlands have all supplied chemical machinery to Siberian plants in the last two decades. The equipment at the Bratsk works, for example, was imported from Finland and Sweden, while Omsk received synthetic rubber drying and packaging plant and lubricating oil additives plant from the U.K.

It was decided in 1971 to make good the serious shortage of phosphorous fertiliser in west Siberian agriculture, by working a number of phosphate deposits in the south of the Krasnoyarsk kray and the construction of a fertiliser plant (annual capacity 240,000 tons annually) possibly associated with the Sayan hydroelectric power scheme. Technical problems connected with the processing of these phosphates seem to be still unsolved, so it is not clear at the moment what the fate of the fertiliser plant will be. It may be significant that it was not mentioned among the Twenty-fourth Party Congress directives regarding the Sayan scheme. In view of the big chemical fertiliser deal negotiated in 1973 between the Soviet Union and Dr. Hammer's American firm, in which super-phosphoric acid is to be imported in large quantities, these Krasnoyarsk phosphates may not have the same importance as formerly.

Reviewing the critical comments in Soviet sources regarding the development of the Siberian chemical industry, it is difficult to decide how far the specific defects alleged in the sixties still exist, or have been eradicated. In the first place, serious errors were found in the structure of the industry. Then, the time taken to construct some of the most important plants, like Bratsk, was stated to be excessive. Perhaps more serious, was the disproportion alleged between basic production and requirements. The disparity between the specialisation of the

Siberian chemical industry and local demand for its products was also severely criticised. As a result of the inadequate utilisation of some local raw materials, common salt, sulphuric acid, liquid chlorine, industrial alcohol and many semi-finished goods have to be imported, while a large proportion of the chemical items produced locally have to be exported to other regions because of restricted local demand.

chapter eight

Land and Water

Agriculture. From the earliest days of the Russian conquest of Siberia to the present time, the provision of food crops has been a constant preoccupation of the central Russian government. Originally, it was the Cossacks, the fur-seekers and the small nuclei of administration that had to be fed. And now in the twentieth century, the settlers and workers developing Siberian natural resources also require bread and meat.

When the Russians first reached south-west Siberia at the end of the sixteenth century, after traversing the boggy northern wilderness of the Khanty-Mansi plain, where no food crops were known, they found themselves among the Tatar-Bukharan settlements, where grain was grown. These peoples' methods of cultivation were probably not inferior to those of the invading Russians (though Soviet propaganda often suggests that the Russians taught all the Siberians agriculture). The west Siberian lands, between the Urals and the Altay, were thus the nucleus of Siberian agriculture and are still the most fertile of the whole Siberian land mass. In the vast expanse of Siberia many different types of soil and environment more or less favourable to agriculture are to be found. Thus, the fertile west Siberian plain tails off, agriculturally, into the less favoured area of central-east Siberia, while agriculture thrives to some extent again in the Amur oblast and the Primor'ye of the Soviet Far East. Here, in the upper reaches of the Amur basin, conditions are suitable for arable farming and the production of grain crops is the second largest in Siberia. Nevertheless, the enormous Far Eastern region remains a grain-deficient area, requiring large and expensive imports of grain, as well as meat and other foodstuffs, including even milk.

Great efforts have been made to extend the areas under the plough in Siberia. And there is much discussion about the possibilities of agricultural expansion. Many large-scale amelioration and irrigation schemes are under consideration, for the Altay and the Primor'ye in particular. But elsewhere there are definite territorial limits set by soil and climate to the raising of crops in this region. Experiments will no doubt continue with new varieties of grain, especially frost and drought resistant strains, adapted to Siberia's harsh climate. It is not, however, to be expected that the area of the Far North will ever produce agricultural supplies on a large scale, or do more than provide vegetables under cover for small groups of workers in the Polar regions. But stock breeding is successfully maintained as far north as Oymyakon, in central Yakutiya.

Before the Bolshevik revolution, Siberian industry was poorly developed, while agriculture flourished in the hands of generations of industrious peasant settlers. But the policy pendulum swung sharply in the opposite direction after the revolution. Siberian industrialisation was then promoted by the Bolsheviks at the expense of agriculture, which was neglected and misdirected in accordance with Marxist industrial orientated ideology, and the drive for industrial power. The more successful farmers, dubbed *kulaks* in Siberia as throughout the Soviet Union, were driven from their farms while a series of ill-conceived agricultural policies, culminating in forced collectivisation, wrought havoc in the once-prosperous Siberian countryside, which had formerly produced abundant and cheap supplies of grain, meat and butter. The large pre-revolution exports of agricultural produce to European Russia and western countries, including Great Britain, ceased and have not been renewed to date. It is only in recent years that Siberian agriculture is beginning to recover from the effects of years of Soviet mismanagement and bad cultivation.

In spite of its decline as a producer of foodstuffs, Siberia is the second 'breadbasket' of the Soviet Union and occupies an overall important place in the country's agricultural resources. Some 15% of the U.S.S.R. grain, 11% of its meat, and more than 20% of its wool, originates in Siberia. And Siberia produces many items at lower cost than the Union's average prices while productivity of labour in its state farms is reported to be about 10% and, on collective farms, 20% higher than the Union average.

After years of neglect under Stalin, Khrushchev's 'Virgin Lands' policy of 1954 was a dramatic move to expand grain production and improve agriculture, mainly in Siberia and northern Kazakhstan. Millions of acres of fallow meadow land and steppe were ploughed up and sown to grain in the southern areas of west Siberia and some excellent harvests were produced before disaster in the form of serious soil erosion, low yields and infertility, hit the grain fields. This critical state of affairs was largely caused by the obscurantist attitude of bureaucrats throughout the virgin lands to expert advice about the correct cultivation methods to be used, and their persistence in wrong methods. The lessons of this costly bureaucratic stupidity were eventually learnt and west Siberian yields gradually improved, but continued to show considerable fluctuations between 1960–69. There has not, to date, been the

Sown areas all under grain crops (in all categories of farms, th. ha.)

	1960	1969	1970	1971
West Siberia	13,598	12,496	11,786	11,464
of which:				
Altayskiy kray	5,788	4,960	4,679	4,624
Kemerovskaya oblast	953	970	950	940
Novosibirskaya oblast	2,734	2,587	2,439	2,313
Omskaya oblast	2,780	2,541	2,547	2,270
Tomskaya oblast	307	338	340	351
Tyumenskaya oblast	1,036	1,100	921	956
East Siberia	4,891	4,958	4,969	4,912
Far Eastern region	1,009	1,143	1,142	1,132

steady increases in the sown areas or in production anticipated in Party plans and propaganda.

Gross grain crop (In th. tons)

	1960	1969	1970	1971
West Siberia	14,458	10,803	15,252	17,199
East Siberia	4,562	3,998	5,685	6,477
Far Eastern region	704	1,358	1,161	1,189

Grain deliveries (In th. tons)

	1960	1969	1970	1971
West Siberia	7,014	3,750	6,541	7,488
East Siberia	1,661	960	1,859	2,129
Far Eastern region	192	379	269	336

Source of the three tables above: Narodnoye Khozyaystvo RSFSR v 1971g.

Grain yields in west and east Siberia were equally unsatisfactory during this period (1960–69). In west Siberia, the average grain yield fell from 10.6 centners[1] per ha. to 8.6 centners per ha. and in east Siberia from 9.3 to 8.1 centners per ha. Yields subsequently began to rise as appears from the table below.

Gross grain yields (tons per hectare bunker yield)

	1960	1969	1970	1971
West Siberia	1.06	0.86	1.30	1.50
East Siberia	0.93	0.80	1.14	1.32
Far Eastern region	0.70	1.19	1.02	1.05

based on source of three tables above.

By a stroke of good fortune and good weather, in 1972, when the best grain lands of European Russia had a disastrous harvest, the harvest in west Siberia was exceptionally good and earned warm praise from Brezhnev. Speaking of the harvesting, he said: 'A real battle for bread grain was unleashed. Siberians, people of the Urals and the working people of Kazakhstan did not fall behind. They justified the hopes and confidence of the country'. In fact, the bread grain growers of Siberia and the Urals delivered to State granaries almost 17,000,000 tons of grain and the Altay alone over 5,000,000 tons, according to Brezhnev.

Bad husbandry and inadequate fodder supplies were obstacles to achieving the increases in Siberian livestock anticipated by the pre-1970 plans. The failure to reach production targets was particularly noticeable in regard to large horned cattle. Since 1970, the situation has been improving.

Large horned cattle (in th. head)

	1961	1967	1970	1971	1972
West Siberia	5,535	7,178	6,958	7,215	7,442
East Siberia	2,607	3,289	3,162	3,238	3,371
Far Eastern region	1,159	1,415	1,368	1,403	1,429

Source: Narodnoye Khozyaystvo RSFSR v 1971g.

The poor state of Siberian livestock production has long roots. Some grim facts have been released by the Soviet authorities regarding the losses suffered, as a result of Stalinist policies, by producers of Siberian livestock and livestock-products and

[1] One centner equals one quintal or one-tenth of a ton.

the miserable state of the cattle. Throughout Siberia, owing to high costs of production and low procurement prices, milk was profitable only in the Tyumen' oblast. Pig breeding did not pay anywhere in Siberia (though the State nevertheless demanded regular deliveries from the farmers at starvation rates) and the only people profiting from the sale of wool were the collective farmers of the Altay. In a number of areas, the livestock numbers increased only because the collective and state farms bought livestock from the privately owned stock of the people. Reproduction was virtually at a standstill in the state and collective herds. The poverty-stricken condition of the Siberian farms was further aggravated by the severe limits long imposed on private holdings of livestock. Against this background, reports that Siberian (and other Soviet) farmers have been careless in their use of farm property like tractors, combines, etc., and were lethargic about work plans and failed to respond to the Party's call for increased production, are not surprising.

In Siberia, as throughout the Soviet Union, various improvements in agricultural conditions were introduced by the Brezhnev reforms of 1965. Procurement prices for agricultural produce were greatly increased and Siberian farmers received new wage increments. But these measures have so far had little or no effect in checking the exodus of the Siberian rural population, either to the towns or to other parts of the Soviet Union. In discussing this problem, the consensus of opinion among the Novosibirsk experts of the Siberian Department of the all-Union Academy is that it may be largely caused by the failure to adjust even the increased wage scales to the levels of the local cost of living, or to improve amenities in the remoter countryside. The impact of this rural exodus on Siberian agriculture is regarded as extremely serious. Some 800,000 farm hands were reported to have left Siberia during the seven-year period 1959–65. And in the decade 1960–70, the rural population of Siberia as a whole declined by 30% and of west Siberia by 17%. This rate of exodus from the countryside is exceptionally high when compared with the all-Union average rural population decline of 3% in the same period. A large number of these departures were of able-bodied young men and women, skilled tractor and combine drivers. According to the Siberian Department of the Academy of Sciences, under the improved wage system less than 15% of these farm workers throw up their jobs 'for financial reasons' (*Pravda* 17.2.1971). The main reason was stated to be the still unsatisfactory domestic-living-cultural and trade-supply conditions, while the much higher rate of departures from the more isolated settlements was attributed to 'roadlessness'. The construction of roads in these areas is therefore regarded as a major problem locally. Against this background, it is not surprising to learn from Soviet sources that Siberian youth has 'a negative attitude to the land and village life'.

The exodus of labour from rural districts of Siberia is to some extent offset during the harvesting period by the 'rallies' regularly held in European Russia, the Ukraine and the Caucasus, to recruit 'mechanised cadres'. It is thus hoped to ensure that the harvest is saved in the more important grain growing areas of west Siberia. The need for this supplementary labour and harvesting equipment is all the more crucial in Siberia because the harvesting of the different crops, grass, grain, silage and vegetables, has to be simultaneously completed in the short 40–45 days Siberian harvesting period, with no breathing space between harvesting operations as in

But, old chap, a machine would do a better job.
I can't help it, comrade Harvest, mine is still being repaired. (*Pravda* XI. 7. 1972)

other areas of the Soviet Union. In practice, however, these stop-gap harvesting arrangements are frequently disrupted by inefficient organisation and other hitches. For example, not one of the 1,700 harvesting machines promised by the U.S.S.R. Ministry of Agriculture to the Omsk oblast had arrived by August 1971, though 320 were reported by the Soviet press 'to be on their way'. Nothing was reported about the rest of the promised vehicles.

Another serious problem threatening large areas of the grain growing zone of west Siberia is erosion. Its magnitude is reflected in an official statement in 1971 that 'after completion of anti-erosion measures millions of hectares of land will be brought under cultivation'. Utter ruin from erosion, as a result of inimical methods of cultivation, threatened the newly ploughed uplands in the fertile Kalunda steppes. There, former thriving settlements were deserted in the sixties as thousands of the inhabitants fled, in three years, including a fifth of its mechanised cadres 'unwilling to remain on scorched fields' (*Pravda* 14.10.1971). After belated but efficient intervention, this erosion has been halted and fertility apparently restored in parts of Kalunda. Other areas of west Siberia and Transbaykalia are still threatened by erosion, often arising from the persistent use of 'obsolete' unsuitable cultivation methods, like mould-board ploughing on light soils in Buratiya and in the Altay. There is certainly no lack of expert advice on these matters but it is often disregarded by wrong-headed, or indifferent, local authorities and farmers.

The mechanisation of agricultural operations is now an acute problem in Siberia owing to the labour shortage. *Sel'khoztekhnika* (the distribution agency for farm equipment) and the Ministry of Agricultural Construction have been subjected to much caustic Soviet criticism for their slow and unsatisfactory handling of Siberian requirements for farm machinery. It is time, declared one indignant Soviet Party Secretary, to leave defective and expensive machines in the store-rooms of *Sel'khoztekhnika* (*Pravda* 15.3.1970) ... The supply of machines, he continued, is frequently erratic. 'A milking parlour is supplied but you get no spare parts, or if you get a conveyer then the loading-unloading and other mechanisms may be lacking. That is why on farms where the milking is mechanised, a third of the work is still done by hand. At present, 400 milking parlours in the Altay are not working because of the lack of spare parts.' The same writer also bitterly criticised the state of cattle transport as a result of which cattle in fine condition on setting out, have to be driven long distances to delivery points and lose heavily in weight on their way. He attributed the good harvest in the Altay in 1971 to the thousands of skilled cadres and the good supplies of agricultural machines 'including the wonderful *Sibiryak* combine, available. But the *Sibiryak* did not contain a cab for the often cold, rainy days at the end of harvesting. Later, when it could be bought as a separate item, 'industry would only give one cab for three machines' (*Pravda* 27.5.1973).

Soviet economists reckon that agricultural conditions in Siberia, on the whole, require a level of mechanisation 20–25% higher than the R.S.F.S.R. average. In fact, the load on the Siberian farmer is estimated to be much heavier than the all-Union average. The special types of machines required for Siberian farms are frequently not provided, while the types suitable for European Russia when sent to Siberia can be a near or total loss to the recipient. There is a constant stream of complaints in the Soviet press about the unsuitable types of tractors and combine-harvesters provided for the farms and the frustrating delays in the supply of badly needed transport. The mechanisation of stockbreeding also poses an acute problem. Labour costs in this field are relatively high, but the labour required is not available at present. At the same time the large expansion of production demanded by the ninth five-year plan (1971–75) requires more labour if it is to be achieved. Mechanisation is the only solution to this dilemma, but this in turn requires a radical improvement in the machine supply situation. Some useful measures were initiated during the seven-year plan period (1959–65) to raise the numbers and efficiency of skilled cadres in Siberia. The number of engineers and other technicians in western Siberia rose from 2% to 15% of the work force, but this was still too low to ensure farm efficiency. All aspects of farming were affected by the low level of skilled workers: mechanisation, electrification, organisation of production and even book-keeping. Owing to the lack of properly trained staff in the latter field, 'unsolved problems', closely affecting the workers, pile up on the farms, relating to pensions, payments of subsidies for temporary disablement, length of vacations, etc.

The disparities in the supply of machines throughout Siberia were well illustrated by an angry letter to *Pravda* (15.2.1969), from the manager of a State farm in the Khanty-Mansiyskiy rayon of the Tyumen' oblast, complaining of the R.S.F.S.R. Ministry of Agriculture's neglect of local farms. Writing from the vast boggy expanse of northern Tyumen', he headed his letter, 'We do not live on asphalt' . . . 'This particular farm exists to supply the food needs of the oil workers of the neighbourhood, i.e. meat, milk, potatoes and other vegetables,' he wrote. 'Its production plans were based on an expansion of the farm's machinery, but the vehicles supplied were frequently unsuitable for the local terrain. Heavy tractors are badly needed, but only MTZ–50 type were received, which went out of action in 3–4 months. The automobiles supplied to the farm were suitable for hard surfaces, but not for work in marshes and heavy snow such as are found there.' This farmer was specially irked because all this happened not through lack of the right type of vehicle or carelessness. 'The Kyanty-Mansi Seismographic Group', he continued, 'has six powerful tractors and other suitable machines' . . . 'The geologists can travel wherever they wish, anytime, while we, a large farming unit, cannot stir 5–10 km. beyond our village. Then the Pravdinsk oil research expedition working on the farm's own land is supplied with a lot of excellent machinery and we see wonderful machines passing along the Tyumen'–Surgut road (which also traverses our land). we wonder why none of these machines are destined for us ?'

Shortcomings in the use of agricultural machinery on Siberian collective and State farms were deplored in a special resolution of the Presidium of the R.S.F.S.R. Council of Ministers in March 1973, which outlined specific measures to improve the situation and for the overhaul of the entire machinery and tractor pool in Siberia for the beginning of the spring field work. But the resolution made no mention of the many serious shortcomings in the supply of agricultural machinery.

Since the eruption of the Sino-Soviet conflict, exceptional attention is given by the Soviet press and radio to the agricultural supply position in the Far Eastern region. Even the remote agricultural wilderness of Sakhalin (now strategically important to Moscow) is frequently featured in the news for its efforts to produce more potatoes, or livestock, in the extremely difficult local soil and climatic conditions. The best arable land in this vast region lies in the strategically vulnerable border areas of the Amur oblast' and the Primor'ye. It was therefore to be expected that great efforts would be made to increase the production of agricultural products in this Region, so notably deficient in the growth of local foodstuffs, and where Moscow sees a constant threat from hostile forces across the frontier. Among other measures reflecting Moscow's concern about the local food supply situation, a Party-Government decree of 1967 urging that the Far Eastern region should be able to supply its own grain and livestock requirements, may be mentioned. However desirable such self-sufficiency may be locally and nationally, it certainly will not be achieved according to the present rate of progress in the near future, But some improvement has been achieved in the food supply position since 1967.

Agricultural possibilities and production differ greatly between the main areas of the Soviet Far East. About 67% of its grain crop is produced in the Amur oblast, 25% in the Primor'ye kray and the remaining 8% between the Khabarovsk kray and the small pockets of arable land in central Yakutiya. No grain is apparently produced in Sakhalin but great efforts have been made in recent years to increase the main potato and vegetable crops. Most foodstuffs (except soya beans) have to be imported at considerable cost to make up deficit local supplies. Since the sixties, grain (not only for local distribution) has occasionally been imported from Canada and Australia to Far Eastern ports and this is a much more rational means of supply than relying on long hauls of grain by rail, from western Siberia or Kazakhstan.

The Amur-Zeya basin is the granary of the Soviet Far East and grows wheat, rye and oats. Since the early fifties, official policy has aimed at expanding the land under cultivation and the livestock herds. These efforts have often been frustrated by the spring floods of the turbulent Zeya river. Now that the dam is completed on the new Zeya power station presently under construction, flooding is expected to be curbed and agricultural expansion should no longer be in jeopardy in this area. Meanwhile, in spite of these difficulties, the grain crop has considerably increased in the Amur oblast since 1959, rising from 400,000 in 1960 to 814,100 tons in 1699. The important wheat crop, in particular, did well during this period. The number of large horned cattle also rose, but sheep and goat herds declined. Pig breeding has improved and expanded in the new special state pig farms which were established.

Though the Far Eastern region, and notably the Amur area, is the most highly mechanised sector of the R.S.F.S.R. for ploughing and grain cultivation, yields of all agricultural products are generally low and the overall grain yield is the lowest in the U.S.S.R. The *per caput* livestock production is also below the Soviet average. This unsatisfactory situation is the result not only of adverse natural conditions – the monsoon climate, winter frosts and heavy rains during the harvesting season – but also of years of bad husbandry and the often locally unsuitable machinery.

In the Far East, as throughout Siberia, lack of farm-hands hampers production. Migrants partly fill many vacancies on the farms, but they are costly to bring in from distant European Russia and the Ukraine, while many leave the region after a short stay. In fact, in the end result, immigration virtually adds little or nothing to the labour force in the Far East. Mechanisation is seen by the local authorities, after years of frustrating experience of immigrants, as the only practical solution to this acute labour problem.

Writing in *Dal'niy Vostok* (no. 3, 1971) the First Secretary of the Amur oblast' stated that all production of grain and soya was mechanised, but the machines supplied were under-powered and otherwise unsuited to 'our Amur conditions'. Much more horse-power is required in the Amur oblast than elsewhere in Siberia. But owing to the unsuitable machinery supplied to the farms, the development of new lands was relatively slow. According to this report, no powerful tractors had yet been supplied, though badly needed in the Amur area.

At least this Party secretary had no illusions about the causes of the flight of agricultural workers from the region and the remedy. Create proper living conditions and offer wages equal to urban employment (such as he describes as existing on one State farm) and there will be no problem, he declared. 'But,' he added, 'when dairy maids have to work from 5 a.m. till late afternoon, do not be surprised that school-leavers are not keen on taking on the job.'

Further east in the Primor'ye, there is specialised, large-scale cultivation of soya beans, rice and sugar beet. A call for more intensive production of rice and soya was issued by the Twenty-fourth Party Congress Directives. Dairy-farming and stock-breeding for local consumption are also being actively encouraged. The soya crop is highly valued in the Soviet Union because of the multifarious industrial uses of the bean, apart from its value as a nutritious foodstuff. More than a third of the arable land in the Far Eastern region is planted with soya and considerable expansion is planned. There has however been recent local criticism of 'a mistaken Ministerial policy of narrow specialisation' in terms of bean production, but it is too early to say how far this criticism will find a favourable response in Moscow.

The attempt to build up 'a food base' in the Primor'ye border area was reflected in the increases in livestock and meat deliveries under the eighth five-year plan and much larger targets for meat, milk and eggs set for the ninth plan period, with a big expansion in irrigated lands. Various amelioration schemes are already under way to drain marshlands and clear hayfields of weeds with a view to improving and extending cultivation. Much still remains to be done through such schemes, in a large area with only 220,000 ha. of arable land under cultivation.

The cis-Ussuri plain by Lake Khanka is an area where rice cultivation is well established. The Koreans grew it successfully there until they were deported to Soviet Central Asia in the late thirties and now Russians and other settlers from European Russia continue this work. The area under rice is to be greatly expanded by the provisions of the ninth plan when ten new rice farms are to be established near Lake Khanka. Several Far Eastern scientific research institutes are now actively engaged in promoting rice cultivation in the Primor'ye by soil and plant research work. Among these bodies are the Far Eastern Scientific Research Institute of Hydrotechnics and Melioration in Vladivostok, the all-Union Far Eastern Rice Research Institute and the Chief Far Eastern Water Economy Construction Institute. With their cooperation steps have apparently been taken to install automatic regulation of the water economy. Work on the further mechanisation of the rice paddies in the Primor'ye was declared an all-Union Komsomol' 'shock construction' in 1969. 'But', commented the local Party secretary, 'many heads of the Komsomol' organisations failed to take this task seriously. As a result of their negligence, only 32 of the 150 Komsomols promised by the Georgian Komsomol' organisation arrived to work, and of these only 6 remained on the job.' Equally disappointing results were produced by the Vladimirskiy Komsomol'. Instead of the 150 young volunteers expected, only 70 were sent, almost all of whom lacked any special training for this work.

Statistics of the annual rice harvest are not regularly published in the Soviet Union so it is difficult to determine the exact levels of production over the years. It would appear that good results were achieved in 1968. According to published information, yields of more than 30 centners per ha. were achieved in the specialised rice sovkhozy, which sold 26,000 tons to the State. Bad weather caused a fall in the crop and yields in the following year. It is officially claimed that all rice sovkhozy are profitable and that capital invested in amelioration schemes is quickly repaid. According to a Conference on Land Improvement in the Primor'ye held in Vladivostok in 1971, the local rice crop could be extended to a total area of 250,000 ha., where soil and climatic conditions are favourable. This is obviously an optimum target for the distant future.

Though all concerned are agreed on the importance of intensifying rice cultivation in the Soviet Far East, a difference of opinion seems to have arisen between the local Party organisation and the central Ministry of Melioration and Water Economy, on the wisdom of excessive specialisation (as in the above-mentioned case of the soya bean). The Party deplores a too-narrow specialisation and wants dairy farming and stockbreeding to be encouraged as well, so that the work force may be occupied in winter and a good food balance maintained. The top-level Party-State instructions regarding agriculture in the Far East since 1967 undoubtedly endorse this broader food policy, if they have not in fact inspired it.

Like rice, the Far Eastern sugar crop was originally concentrated in the Khanka plain. The situation regarding the region's sugar industry has however become obscure, since production statistics have recently ceased to appear in Soviet sources. But in the fifties and sixties when they were available, there were big fluctuations in this crop. It fell, for example, from 88,000 tons in 1958 to 42,000 tons in 1963, rising in the following year to 84,000 tons. Subsequently, the large imports of Cuban sugar through Far Eastern ports must have had a significant influence on this industry with possibly a big reduction of the domestic crop. Even during the best production period, the region was far from able to supply its own sugar requirements and 145,000 tons were imported in 1966.

Further north, the most favourable zones of soil and climate for agriculture in Yakutiya are the central districts of Olekminsk, Vilyuy and Yakutsk, where grain and potato growing has long been practised by old Russian settlers and their example followed by the native inhabitants. Olekminsk is famous locally for its potatoes and throughout these areas fair sized crops of wheat, oats and barley as well as potatoes and fodder are produced. More land is continually being brought into cultivation in these arable areas of Yakutiya, but soil and climate impose severe limitations on the expansion of agriculture in Arctic Yakutiya. Livestock farming thrives, however, in the 'pole of cold' area of Oymyakon in northern Yakutiya.[2] It forms part of a state farm employing 600 workers and containing 2,000 cows (in barns during the winter), 10,000 reindeer, a fox farm and many horses which remain outside the year round in the extremely low temperatures of this place.

The tundra of Arctic Yakutiya and the entire Far North of the Soviet Far Eastern region, though unsuitable for arable farming, is the home of great herds of reindeer. After the tragic mishandling of the native reindeer breeders and their herds in the period of forced collectivisation, resulting in heavy losses of human and animal lives, the Soviet government gradually recognised the folly of these harsh collectivisation policies. General denomadisation was dropped in favour of a more rational policy of partial nomadisation and settlement of the herders adjusted at once to the needs of reindeer herding and to the advance of the herdsmen and their families to a less primitive existence through the provision of schools, housing and other amenities of modern living.

The reindeer is the basis of the northern native peoples' economy, providing essential supplies of meat, milk, fur and hides for their food and clothing. Since the development of the big mining industries in the far north, this invaluable animal

[2] This information was kindly supplied to me in a personal communication from Dr. T. Armstrong following his visit to Yakutiya in 1973.

has acquired a new economic importance. It is often the only source of food for the mining workers and the reindeer herders do well as a result of the high prices paid for reindeer meat and the relatively low costs of production.

There were nearly 2½ million head of reindeer in the northern areas of the R.S.F.S.R., in 1972, most of them in the Far Eastern region (1,335,800).

Agricultural Scientific Research in Siberia and the Far East. The basic agricultural problems peculiar to Siberia and the Far East are now being studied by an increasing number of scientific research bodies, established between Omsk and Vladivostok. If efficient coordination were established between the Party-Soviet authorities, the farms, and these expert establishments, their co-operation should go far towards solving many of Siberia's agricultural problems, but this is still far from being the case.

The decision, in 1969, to establish a Siberian branch of the all-Union Academy of Agricultural Sciences was an important step forward in this work. Construction of this establishment started on a site near Novosibirsk in 1970. It will eventually consist of a number of research Institutes concerned with animal husbandry, technological design, mechanisation and electrification, use of chemicals, agricultural economics and fodder. This grouping on the analogy of the now famous *Akademgorodok* (Siberian Department of the all-Union Academy of Sciences) is planned to form a self-contained 'townlet'. The building site covers 200 ha., and contains a large area of experimental fields.

Apart from the various scientific institutes forming part of this new scientific centre in Novosibirsk, a number of other scientific bodies will operate under its direction throughout Siberia and the Soviet Far East, e.g. the Siberian Scientific Research Institute in Omsk; the all-Russian Soya Research Institute in the Amur oblast; the Agricultural Research Institute of the Far North in Noril'sk. The important new Far Eastern Scientific Centre of the U.S.S.R. Academy of Sciences, established in Vladivostok in 1970, contains a Soil Research Institute among the many bodies set up to study the development of the productive forces of the Far East up to the year 2000 and beyond.

Good seed selection is obviously crucial to Siberia's progress as a major grain producing area of the Soviet Union. But the present situation is far from satisfactory and many problems still await solution by the scientific research institutions. These bodies were criticised by *Pravda* (8.2.1971) for their poor work in providing highly productive types of spring wheat suitable for local soil and climatic conditions. In particular, the all-Union Scientific Research Institute on Grain and Leguminous Plants was criticised in 1971 for its inefficient coordination of the activities of zonal experimental stations, during its eight years of existence.

In view of Siberia's need for special seeds, it is astonishing that there were no seed selection centres in Siberia, up to 1971. 'Each experimental station "fashions" varieties in its own way! As a result, the grain economy is based entirely on Saratov (oblast) selection. And in general there are no highly productive varieties for the eastern region of the Altay.' So wrote the first secretary of the Altay *kraykom* in March 1971, when making the case for the establishment of a modern seed selection centre in the Altay to produce the kind of highly productive and quick-ripening varieties of spring wheat locally required. It was reported some months later that major seed selection centries were being established at Omsk, Barnaul (capital of the Altay *kraykom*), Krasnoyarsk and the Soviet Far East.

Among other measures to improve agricultural productivity in Siberia, apart from seed selection centres, the first Soviet agrochemical organisation set up in Tyumen' in 1971 should be mentioned. It was established on an experimental basis and its tasks included the protection of plants and animals from pests and disease, the improvement of land by chemicals, the construction of stores for agricultural chemicals, and the application of fertilisers by contractual agreements with farms. It would be interesting to learn how this complicated programme is progressing, but so far nothing further seems to have been reported about its implementation.

Stockbreeding is another important branch of Siberian agriculture on which more scientific advice is needed than is presently available. Stressing the need for more assistance from the central and planning organs to raise the production of Siberian livestock, the first secretary of the Altay *kraykom* (the same mentioned above) also complained that the scientific institutions paid little attention to stockbreeding. 'At present many Siberian farms cannot get advice on questions of the mechanisation of labour-intensive processes and more importantly, acquire the necessary machines. It is therefore often necessary to "devise a bicycle" or go to the ends of the earth to see how others do these things.' (*Pravda* 15.3.1970)

Clearly, major practical and scientific problems must be more firmly tackled if the better balance between industry and agriculture, now official policy for Siberia, is to be achieved, and agricultural production increased to the levels required, to feed the industrial population at the oil-gas sites, power stations, metallurgical and other enterprises throughout Siberia.

The Timber Industries. The largest forest cover in the world is in the Soviet Union, and about 75% of it lies in Siberia and the Soviet Far East. Timber logging and woodworking are among their oldest traditional industries. Throughout Siberia, from the Tyumen' oblast to the Far Eastern region, many different types of tree are found reflecting the varieties in climate: conifers, aspens (used for match sticks), birch and large stands of the valuable larch which provides good hard timber for telegraph poles and railway sleepers and grows further north than any other Siberian tree,[3] even flourishing in the bleak permafrost soil of Yakutiya. A unique product of the Southern area of the Amur is the cork oak tree. More than 1,000,000 ha. of the Ussuri tagai is reported to be stocked by this tree and the Union's only factory producing cork, which is in great demand, is in Khabarovsk. This corkwood is a good substitute for the classic Algerian cork tree and Brazilian oak and is also used instead of other insulating material in ships, aircraft, refrigerators.

The Siberian timber industry (and in particular the Far Eastern industry) has long

[3] A more detailed description of the Siberian forests may be found in James Gregory's *Russian Land and Soviet People*, George Harrap. 1968. I have also found the careful analysis of the Siberian-Far East timber industry in Paul Dibb's *Siberia and the Pacific* op. cit. most useful.

lagged behind the enormous production potential of its huge timber stands. The areas of active timber working, though expanding, are still relatively very small in comparison to the untapped reserves. It was, for example, estimated that less than 1% of the permissible cut of the Siberian and Far Eastern forests was actually felled in 1966. Moreover, it was only in the post-war II period, that some attention was given to developing a sophisticated wood-processing industry in Siberia and the Far Eastern region.[4] In general, progress in this industry is handicapped by the situation of so much of the forested area in remote areas, which are either inaccessible or virtually inaccessible owing to the lack of roads or other forms of transport. Other adverse factors are the lack of electric power, a bitterly harsh climate, the quick turnover and shortage of labour, all creating considerable difficulties for the logging and removal of timber, in the wooded terrain. But there is also a large volume of relatively accessible timber in the Krasnoyarsk and Irkutsk areas where the timber industry is heavily concentrated. In view of the great potential economic wealth in these forests the Soviet Government's efforts to promote the industry, by building roads and narrow-gauge railway tracks and special equipment, must be regarded as having been only perfunctory, for many years. The backwardness of the timber industry was indeed recognised as long ago as the Eighteenth Party Congress (1939) but there was little improvement in Siberia until the state of the industry was examined again in the late fifties.

Under Stalin's government, most of the lumberjacks in the Siberian northern forests, whose miserable physical condition was reflected in correspondingly low output rates, were provided by forced labour from the concentration camps. But when this labour was withdrawn after Stalin's death, production fell heavily in some camp areas.

The older sawmills in Siberia, mostly dating from pre-war, were situated along the Trans-Siberian railway at Omsk, Novosibirsk, Krasnoyarsk, Kansk, Irkutsk, Chita and Khabarovsk. Under the seventh, eighth and ninth plans, many new mills were opened, and gradually re-equipped and expanded. The most important of these enterprises was the big industrial-timber complex at Bratsk. The decision to establish a new industrial complex based on the west Siberian oil and gas industry also awakened interest in the virgin forests of the area and a target output of 7 million cu.m. was set for 1971. In general, the timber industry of west Siberia produces less than half that of east Siberia and is about on a par with that of the Far East. But production is steadily if slowly rising.

Within the eastern regions of the R.S.F.S.R., the most developed timber industries and the cheapest costs of production are in eastern Siberia. But the major producing areas, though dwindling, remain in the north-west areas of European Russia, where the industry is better organised, and transport and living conditions are much better. Though the exports of timber have for years been larger from the Irkutsk oblast than from Krasnoyarsk kray, the two major timber producing areas of east Siberia, the Irkutsk forests are now apparently threatened with exhaustion from overfelling. There are still very large unexploited timber stands in

[4] The wood-chemical industry is discussed separately in Chapter 7 on 'The Chemical Industry'.

the Krasnoyarsk kray where development prospects, given some basic improvements in organisation etc., are better. Some 20% of the Soviet Union's timber stands are located there.

Owing to the all-Union significance of the Krasnoyarsk timber industry, which includes the important Maklakovsk-Yeniseysk timber enterprises, the current state of affairs in this industry is worth noting. Fortunately, Soviet sources provide some illuminating information on this subject.

The then first Party secretary of the Krasnoyarsk kray *obkom*, V. I. Dolgikh (promoted to full membership of the *Politburo* in 1973), reported at the Twenty-fourth Party Congress (1971), that the backwardness in the kray's timber production and woodworking industry in recent years had 'assumed a chronic character and compared very unfavourably with the increased output in other industrial branches such as electric power or non-ferrous metals.' The organisation of work and the living conditions of the workers needed to be put on a more satisfactory 'principled' basis, he said. He attacked the existing system of small settlements set up further and further from the felling sites, and where it is impossible to establish the necessary conditions for the rest and service of the workers and the childrens' education, and the timber fellers have to be daily transported for 100–120 km. over roadless taiga. All these factors, he urged, were an increasing brake on the development of the local timber industry.

Instead of these small settlements, urban-type bases uniting a number of timber enterprises should be established, which would provide much better living conditions and also raise productivity. The urgent question of roads, according to V. I. Dolgikh, was not being given sufficient attention by the Ministry of Timber and Woodworking Industry of the U.S.S.R. This led to the paradoxical situation that the industry was being supplied with powerful equipment, including transport, but it was impossible to use it in the roadless state of the region. He drove his point home by stressing that in the first quarter of the year, when there is firm frozen ground, 8–9 million cu.m. of timber is procured but in the second quarter only 3 million cu.m. Like so many other commentators on the Siberian timber industry, Dolgikh criticised the large 'disproportions' between the development of the logging and woodworking sides of the industry. The capacity of the timber-felling enterprises manifestly outstrips the capacity of the wood-working side, which leads to selective cutting of timber, leaving aside the poorer qualities, with a lowering of labour productivity and excessive transport of round timber. The failure to develop enterprises for the chemical processing of poorer grades of wood and wood wastes was also criticised as causing great losses to the national economy. V. I. Dolgikh's colleague from the Primor'ye also expressed concern about 'the slow development of timber production and woodworking industries in his kray at the Twenty-fourth Party Congress, and the lowering of the productivity of labour in this industry as a whole.

A year after Dolgikh's speech, a *Pravda* (28.3.1972) correspondent toured the big Bogochany forests, also belonging to the Krasnoyarsk timber industry, and painted a grim picture of the living conditions he found there. Winter clothing such as heavy coats, fur boots and hats was generally lacking in the forestry settlement shops, where there were also no kitchen tables, chairs or cupboards. In fact no useful furniture was to be found in the shops either, he reported. There was also a great shortage of refrigerators to keep meat, milk, etc., fresh in summer and also of proper storage for fruit and vegetables (delivered in small quantities by plane), so that in remote places the workers were badly supplied with these foods. More important was the acute housing and public services problem as a result of which thousands of workers leave the forests. 'And those who come do not settle.' *Pravda*'s local contacts held out no hope of improvement in this situation as long as the Ministry of Timber and Woodworking 'contributed only miserable sums for housing etc.'

Letters from workers in other Siberian timber settlements confirmed that housing there was also unsatisfactory. Some alleged that the housing allocations made by the Ministry of the Pulp and Paper Industry were far below the amounts required to house the numbers of workers sent into the forests. At the big Novoyeniseysk timber combine, for example, only a thousand sq.m. of living space was constructed for 4,500 workers. These workers ventured to invoke the Ministerial order of 1970, calling for measures to improve living-cultural conditions for the workers of the Maklakovsk-Yeniseysk timber enterprises, thus leaving no doubt about the discrepancies they resented, between official principles and practice, in regard to housing and other public services.

These social problems in the Siberian timber industry leading in turn to a shortage of labour have been stressed because, together with the failure to create adequate sawmill capacity, they are so many impediments blocking the way to realisation of the great latent potential of this industry. They will no doubt be overcome in time, but at present the performance of the timber and woodworking industries of Siberia is on the whole unsatisfactory and timber badly needed for housing and industrial production, including mining, is in short supply; according to Soviet calculations more than 250 mil. cu.m. of Siberian timber are 'underexploited'.

Against this background, the resolution of the Central Committee of the C.P.S.U. and the U.S.S.R. Council of Ministers in 1972 on 'additional measures to improve the living conditions, retail trade and everyday consumer services of workers and employees employed in forestry' seemed long overdue. Explicit instructions were issued to the relevant authorities 'to allot foodstuffs and industrial goods in amounts which satisfy more fully forestry workers' requirements'. But how far all these essential measures have actually been implemented in Siberia, it is impossible to say at the time of writing. However, the wording of the resolution at least shows that the government is fully aware of the forestry workers' grievances throughout the country (though Siberia is not specifically mentioned, the resolution is, of course, applicable there).

Apart from these social problems, the structure and management of the Siberian timber industry have come in for a good deal of criticism. According to Mr. Dibb's precise calculations,[5] about four-fifths of the timber shipped out of eastern Siberia is in the form of round logs, though some export-grade timber is also shipped down the Yenisey to European ports through Igarka and the Northern Sea route. Largely owing to under-exploitation of the huge timber stands, east Siberia as a

[5] cf. Dibb, op. cit. p. 104.

timber producer still ranks only second to north-western European Russia, still the leading Union producer, though of declining importance. If things go well with the large new timber complexes being planned on the model of the Bratsk and Krasnoyarsk plants, the position could change in the foreseeable future in east Siberia's favour. Among these planned developments, the important new timber and woodworking complex now being established in the midst of a huge area of virgin taiga as part of the Ust'-Ilimsk hydroelectric power scheme, may be noted. An unusual feature of this project is the 'multi-national pulp (cellulose) works' to be built jointly by Bulgaria, the G.D.R., Hungary, Poland, Romania and the U.S.S.R., with France providing Frs. 260 million worth of equipment. It is primarily intended to supply the C.M.E.A. countries with raw material for the production of paper and cardboard (though there is a perennial shortage of both products in the U.S.S.R. itself). Preparatory work on this pulp works apparently started in 1973. When completed, the wood-working complex is planned to contain a sawmill with an annual capacity of 1,200,000 cu.m. of sawn timber and a large quantity of railway sleepers, as well as factories for the production of wood-fibre board and fodder yeast. It is an ambitious project in a very inhospitable area, but Ust'-Ilimsk is planned to become a new major industrial zone by the end of this decade.

The timber industry of the Soviet Far East is in many ways similar, and yet dissimilar, to that of east Siberia. It is beset by many of the same problems as exist in east Siberia, but it possesses a much greater variety of tree species than are found in neighbouring east Siberia. It is specially fortunate in species suitable for the new pulp and paper industries now being established there. And a high percentage of the hardwood used in the R.S.F.S.R. originates in the Far East. The main forests are in the Khabarovsk kray. Costs of timber production differ widely throughout the huge area of the Soviet Far East but they are generally much higher than the Soviet average, mainly due to high wage differentials.

Astronomical figures for the Far Eastern timber stand are frequently given in Soviet sources, but no exact survey of the timber forests' wealth has ever been made and indeed some of the more inaccessible cover has not even been properly explored. A recent Soviet survey allocated one-sixth of the country's timber resources to the Far East. In view of the large, treeless tundra area in the north of the region, some of the more generous statistics of timber reserves – large though they undoubtedly are – are thus probably exaggerated. Until transport and power are more efficiently developed, a considerable part of these woodlands will remain unexploited.

After years of neglect, the measures to develop the Far Eastern timber industry on a more economic basis and to expand it and build up a wood-chemical industry, initiated by the seven-year plan (1959–1965), promised a brighter future for all branches of the industry. Accordingly, new timber centres were established in the Khabarovsk and Maritime krays, the Amur oblast and in Sakhalin.

Since about 1966, there have been various indications of greater efficiency and better management in this formerly very badly run industry. The percentage of wastage in total timber production is being reduced, it seems, by cutting the excessive level of unprocessed logs in the total timber production, as well as the proportion of sawn timber in exports. In spite of these improvements, the most productive and efficient timber industry in the Soviet Far East remains the prosperous South Sakhalin (formerly Karafuto) enterprise, seized in 1945 by the Soviet Union as part of the spoils of World War II from the Japanese.

Sakhalin is now being further built up as a major timber production centre. A big timber-industrial complex was under construction in 1971 in Poronaysk, in east Sakhalin, based on logging operations in the nearby forests. This seems to be a step towards developing the timber wealth of the north of the island, which has long lagged behind the older timber industry of the south established by the Japanese. In the Primorskiy kray, construction started on another major new timber and wood-working factory at Novomikhaylovka, in 1971, to be completed during the current ninth plan. As it is planned to contain a colophony and timber sawing works as well as plywood, fibre-board and chipboard plant, to process more than 1 million cu.m. of timber daily, it should be a most important addition, eventually, to the Far Eastern timber processing industry. A motor road is to be built to link this works with the Varfolomeyevka station on a branch line of the Ussuri railway, so as to provide an outlet for its products. There are many small timber centres in the well-wooded parts of the Khabarovsk kray, some of the most important of which are in Komsomol'sk and its new town Amursk. Amursk has saw-milling and wood-working factories as well as the large new cellulose-cardboard combine forming a landmark in the development of the Far Eastern wood-chemical industry. It started to work in 1968 and makes viscose, fodder yeast, ethylene spirit and fibre-board.

Apart from the need to develop the Far Eastern timber industry for domestic requirements, the Soviet government has the long-term aim of exporting this timber to the timber-deficient countries of south-east Asia, the Indian sub-continent and Australia (the 'Pacific Rim'). The Soviet Far Eastern timber export ports of Nakhodka and Vanino are being enlarged and equipped with the latest type of loading machinery, supplied by Japan, and the timber-carrying fleet is also being expanded, according to Soviet reports, to promote this trade. However, much remains to be done in regard to the organisation of Soviet exports before Far Eastern timber can compete satisfactorily with the well-organised exports of high quality Canadian and American timber, in Pacific markets, such as Australia.

Soviet interest in the forest wealth of the Far East is reflected in the recent establishment of some local scientific institutions, devoted to research on forestry problems. Thus, a Laboratory of the Economy and Biology of Timber is now functioning, as part of the new Far Eastern Scientific Centre (Vladivostok), in the Suputinka reservation, south-east of Ussuriysk. Its special field of research is investigation into methods of testing the viability of trees and it has been credited with discovering the causes of the desiccation of the famous Ayan fir, one of the chief commercial species of timber in the Far East. The Suputinka reservation is a pre-revolutionary foundation and, being situated in a heavily forested area, should be a good site for this laboratory. Its own work is connected with the preservation and study of typical Ussuri semi-tropical flora and fauna.

The development of the timber industry in the three eastern regions of the R.S.F.S.R. (west Siberia, east Siberia and the Far East), between 1940–71, is summarised in the following table. It shows the production of timber and timber products in the eastern regions between 1940 and 1971 and also their share of the total R.S.F.S.R. production of the different branches of the industry, during this period:

Timber Production of the Eastern Regions and % of Total RSFSR Production[6]

	1940	1971
Removal of commercial timber (million cu. metres)	27	99
% of total RSFSR	26	36
Production of sawn wood (million cu. metres)	8.1	31
% of total RSFSR	28.2	33
Production of cellulose (th. tons)	—	1,143
% of total RSFSR	—	23
Production of paper (th. tons)	0.9	319
% of total RSFSR	0.1	8.7
Production of cardboard (th. tons)	0.7	443
% of total RSFSR	0.6	21

Source: Nar. Khoz. RSFSR v 1971g. Moscow 1972

Between 1940 and 1971, production of the lumber and processing sections of this Siberian industry increased considerably and both now make respectable contributions to the R.S.F.S.R. industry (the main all-Union supplier) though the new Siberian paper industry has still a long way to go to catch up on European Russian production. In recent years, nevertheless, there has been a steady shift to the timber stands of the eastern regions as those of European Russia declined through over-felling. There is an almost limitless prospect of expansion of the timber industry in the east, where it was roughly estimated, in 1967, that less than 50% of the forests had yet been opened up for commercial purposes.

Fur Farming. The whole forested area of the Soviet Union from the Urals to the Soviet Pacific coasts and Sakhalin is the natural habitat of different species of valuable fur-bearing animals. Among the most important of these animals are the sable, the ermine, the mink and squirrel and there are a large number of less valuable but useful species. The status and organisation of the Siberian fur industry (once a dominant factor in the Russian economy) have basically changed in the last fifty years since the Soviet Revolution. Though fur and fur materials (originating for the most part in Siberia) still have a high prestige value in Soviet foreign trade and earned 44.7 million roubles in 1970, this only represented some 0·4% of the total value of Soviet foreign trade, corresponding to the same percentage (in Tsarist roubles) in 1913.

Soviet Exports of Furs and Fur Materials (in roubles)

	roubles	% of total Soviet exports
1913	5,100,000	0.4
1938	21,600,000	9.4
1950	37,400,000	2.3
1960	41,600,000	0.8
1965	52,100,000	0.7
1969	47,500,000	0.5
1970	44,700,000	0.4

Source: Nar. Khoz. SSSR v 1970g.

[6] West Siberia east Siberia and the Far Eastern region.

The Russian fur industry had been drastically declining in the century before 1917 and in the words of a Soviet report 'the Soviet government received the miserable remains of the (Siberian) fur riches from the Tsarist Government and an unorganised hunting industry.' Reputable Tsarist writers confirmed the disastrous effects of rapacious over-hunting and the corrupt practices used to extract pelts from the native trappers, especially in Yakutiya and Transbaykaliya, the sources of the valuable sable, ermine and silver fox pelts. In particular, the precious Vitim or Barguzin black sable, 'which only lives in Russia', was again almost exterminated when hunting this animal was prohibited for three years, in an attempt to preserve it, in 1912. But overhunting of the sable remained a constant threat to the survival of the Siberian sable in the Soviet, as in the Tsarist, period.

The fur industry was placed on a new basis in the late twenties, when the Soviet government established the first fur-farms, thus reducing the traditional dominance of individual trappers and hunters in this industry. It is now estimated that at least three-quarters of Siberian fur comes from caged animals bred in these farms, which are organised on a collective basis into state, collective and cooperative farms, while a diminishing number of licensed hunters operate outside the collectivised system. These fur farms are situated mainly in regions where they can rely on a food supply based on the waste products of the local agricultural, fish, whale or silk-winding industries. If care is not taken to keep the animals free from disease and to handle them properly, the farms can run into trouble and incur financial losses. Thus, it was reported that a high percentage of Yakut farm pelts were defective in 1967 and that many fur farms were working at a loss, owing to poor organisation and careless handling of the animals.

The Soviet fur farms expanded in the sixties, to the extent that their production formed about 83.7% of Union procurements. As far as Siberia is concerned, Soviet reports say that 70% of the northern output is from fur farms. Failing exact statistics, it may therefore be assumed that the proportion of Siberian fur as a whole procured from these farms is somewhat higher than this. As a result of the development of fur-farming in Siberia, the U.S.S.R. now occupies second place, after the U.S.A., for the production of caged animal mink pelts and first place for caged blue fox and silver and black fox pelts. In line with international fashion trends, a wide range of mutation shades of mink, sapphire, pearl, dark brown are being produced.

As collective-state fur farming has expanded, the numbers of individual trappers and hunters has fallen. They now only contribute about 10% of Soviet procurements of Siberian pelts. It is, however, claimed that their furs from the wild are superior to those from the farms, a claim which, in turn, is challenged from the fur-farm interests. In fact, the extent to which individual hunters are still active probably varies from area to area. One press report notice stated that during the 1972 winter season '8,000 hunters were engaged in producing pelts in Yakutiya and were transported to the inaccessible places by helicopter or to tundra and taiga by reindeer sledges.'

Soviet fur production is heavily concentrated in eastern Siberia and Yakutiya which between them produce about one-third of all Soviet procurement of furs including two-thirds of the sable, almost two-thirds of the squirrel and ermine pelts.

The area round Lake Baykal is the habitat of the most valuable fur-bearing animals, the sable, mink and squirrel. The Barguzin sable, 'the king of fur animals', is specially prized but has had a precarious history for many years. Following a disastrous period of over-hunting, sable hunting was totally forbidden in the U.S.S.R. in 1935–41, so as to reinforce or re-establish sable stocks. By 1961, according to Soviet sources, the sable had been fully re-established within the limits of its distribution at the beginning of the seventeenth century and the government was receiving almost the same quantity of pelts as 300 years ago. But this again proved to be only a temporary reprieve. 'Alarm' about the position of the sable was expressed in a detailed statement by a Soviet east Siberian biologist in 1972 (*Pravda* 30.9.1972). Pelt procurements had fallen in the Irkutsk and Sverlovsk oblasts, the Altay kray and the Buryat A.S.S.R. (the main sources of supply) and in some areas the number of sable (according to this report) was reduced to the critical level of the thirties. Experiments had proved the impossibility of breeding the sable satisfactorily in captivity and that the characteristic rich black pelts could only be obtained from wild animals. Nevertheless, the hunter's payments had been cut so that he was no longer interested in financial aspects of his job. As a result, the existence of a sort of black market in sable was openly admitted in this *Pravda* report. 'Private sales, especially in areas of new constructions and places where large numbers of expeditions are working have assumed considerable dimensions', it was stated. If the present trend continues, it is estimated, that the sable 'catches' may be reduced ten-fold within 30–50 years and the animal even again threatened with extermination by the contemporary transport situation and the growing population. Whereas Irkutsk hunters formerly penetrated the taiga with some 16,000 horses, there are now no horses and no satisfactory alternate transport has been provided.

During an investigation of the Sayan area in 1972, more details came to light about the new situation in the taiga which was detrimental to both the fur-bearing animals and the government procurement of pelts (*Pravda* 14.11.1972). 'A number of industrial fur enterprises were examined and infringements of the traditional system of work were constantly found. The professional hunter as such had ceased to exist. He has been replaced by the "casual type". He gets as much as he can, selling as much as he can. If it is estimated that the government official pays 30–50 roubles for a sable pelt and "the black market" 100–150 roubles, it is obvious to which purchaser the "casual type" [synonymous in Russian with poacher] turns for business.'

It is not only the sable that is affected by poaching. It had reached such a level in east Siberia in 1973 that the popular musquash fur cap, for example, was no longer to be found in the shops. The former flourishing State procurements of this pelt had fallen heavily or by one quarter, by 1971. *Pravda*'s sensible conclusion from this state of affairs was, that the procurement prices for musquash should be raised, so that the hunter would think it worth his while to bring his pelts to the government.

But there are more attractive interesting aspects of the Siberian fur situation than poaching. In the first place, the large sable Nature Reserve on the Barguzin

Hills running down to Lake Baykal deserves mention. It was created in 1916 to restore the depleted sable stocks, and was taken over in 1923–26 by the Soviet government, which has subsequently shown special interest in it. One of the main activities of the Sable Reserve has been the introduction of sables into new areas with very encouraging results, especially in the Urals.[7] It is a curious feature of Soviet statistics that unlike other Siberian fur-bearing animals for which more specific data is available, no annual statistics of the sable catches are published. Statistics of the percentage of various species in the total state purchases of pelts in 1956–59 showed sable pelts at 11%, squirrel at 15.8%, muskrat at 13.7% and fox at 11.1%, but this was not apparently followed up by later information.

It is difficult to arrive at any firm conclusion about the present position of the valuable Siberian sable. While *Pravda*'s scientific correspondent was expressing serious concern about the threat to its survival, in the same year (1972) *Izvestiya* reported that there were between 600,000 and 800,000 sable in Siberia and the Soviet Far East. The best squirrel pelts also come from the Barguzin area where local pride in the animal is shown by the heraldic device of a squirrel sitting on a silver ground. The adjacent Yakut A.S.S.R. is also very rich in valuable fur-bearing animals. More than half of the all-Union supply of white fox and ermine and a third of the mink come from Yakutiya. Many fur farms in the Khabarovsk and Primorskiy krays also produce mink and black and white foxes in considerable quantities.

Licensed hunters for fur-bearing animals in remote areas of the taiga should, in principle, be supplied with various aids for more comfortable, successful hunting, such as improvements in hunting equipment, mobile trailers and shelters, radio communication between bases and production sectors and sometimes even helicopters for transport. But in fact, the supply system is often far from satisfactory. Some local Siberian reports, for example, complain of the lack of special clothing for fur trappers and of the poor quality of the traps 'which do not withstand Siberian frosts in the fur-rich Sayan taiga and are too heavy' and of difficulties in obtaining light automobiles or motor cycles, 'out of turn', for the hunters.

All the native peoples of Siberia are highly skilled in the traditional crafts of trapping and hunting wild animals and in some areas they provide their main means of livelihood (apart from the reindeer-herding). It is an open question whether they really want modern means of communication, such as radios or helicopters, or whether these hunting aids are not rather devised to accommodate non-native elements engaged in fur-farming and hunting. Moreover, it is difficult to ascertain how far the native peoples now participate in the new fur-farming system or have been affected by it.

Some native trappers are apparently dissatisfied with the rates they receive for their pelts which are certainly much lower than market rates. This emerged clearly in a speech by the Evenk delegate to the Supreme Soviet in 1965. Referring to the efforts to introduce modern economic and technical methods of fur-trapping into

A full account of Soviet conservation of natural resources will be found in Philip R. Pryde's *Conservation in the Soviet Union*, Cambridge University Press, 1972, to which I am indebted or these details.

his Evenkiysky National Okrug, long known as 'Sable Land' and containing traditionally famous sable, ermine and squirrel-hunting grounds, he complained of the 'irrational system of wages' and the high turnover of workers owing to the lowering of 'material stimuli'. He stressed that prices fixed for furs should be based on the real cost of production in difficult natural conditions. The general tone of his speech suggested that the fur trappers, long exploited by the Tsarist government, were not even now under the Soviet government getting a fair deal.

A decree of the all-Union Council of Ministers, introduced in 1968, which required the respective authorities to devote more attention to hunting and the breeding of fur-bearing animals and ordered a 50% rise in the procurement price of pelts from the far north, might be regarded as an official reaction to these trapper grievances.

In the Tyumen' oblast of west Siberia where there are 'dozens of wild animal breeding farms', lack of qualified staff including hunters and animal breeders, was reported to be an acute problem in 1972, in spite of the technical institutes set up expressly to train this type of expert. It would appear that the native trappers in the far north of Siberia prefer to continue with their traditional hunting methods and have apparently shown little enthusiasm for this kind of professional training. The result is that the fur farms according to *Ekon. Gazeta* (27.7.1972) are obliged to take on 'people who are ignorant of the special technology of the maintenance and breeding of fur-bearing animals in captivity'.

The fur farms in the far north of Siberia are relatively few and confined to areas where fishing is regularly possible and not only seasonal, because of the freeze-up of the coastal waters, or where fish and/or meat offal is available to feed the animals. This for the most part means the Magadan and Avachinsk (Kamchatka) regions where farms are situated near fishing bases of the trawler fleet which can supply the necessary fish. 'They provide the government annually with thousands of pelts'.

In Siberia, as elsewhere in the developing world, industrialisation and far-flung mining enterprises have encroached on the age-long habitats of the fur-bearing animals and driven them further and further into the taiga and away from the new human settlements. The threat to their natural habitats from deforestation has thus been further increased. Soviet conservationists are keenly aware of these dangers and anxious to avert them, but when they come up against a strongly-entrenched, industrial ministry, indifferent to wildlife, it is no easier in the Soviet Union than in the west to obtain their goodwill.

Fisheries. Siberia and the Soviet Far East contain very rich sea and river fisheries. The Far Eastern fishing industry (*Dal'ryba*) is of all-Union importance owing to the volume and variety of catch and the value of its exports of fresh and canned fish as earners of foreign currency. It has gained enormously in strength and status since 1913, when it was of relatively minor significance, with little more than one-tenth of the Russian catch compared to the Caspian Sea industry, producing over three-quarters of the national catch. Now, about one-third of the total Soviet fish catch comes from the Far Eastern industry and some 40% of

Soviet canned fish products is also of Far Eastern origin.[8] This is a major industry in the Soviet Far East, employing some 160,000 fishermen; about 20% of all Far Eastern workers are engaged in one job or another connected with the fisheries. But because of its proximity to markets in European Russia, eastern and western Europe and probably its greater efficiency, *Zapryba* (the Atlantic based Soviet fishing administration) still has the edge over *Dal'ryba*.

The northern Pacific fishing grounds of the Soviet Far East contain the world's largest stocks of salmon and crab, as well as a great variety of other fish, especially herring. The crab beds are located in the Okhotsk and Bering seas, while the west coast of Kamchatka is the main crab fishing ground. Kamchatka is not only the centre of the Soviet crab industry, but also of the world crab industry, more than 80% of the world's canned crab being processed from Kamchatkan crab. Intensive fishing of crab by the Japanese since they were allowed back into these fishing grounds after World War II, in 1956, is believed to have lowered the crab catch and the processing of crab in recent years, according to Soviet sources.

There are four main fishing bases where fish is handled and processed: the Primor'ye, Kamchatka, the Amur river and Sakhalin. *Dal'ryba* is the chief government organ in overall charge of this industry. The home fishing grounds of the north-east and north-west Pacific include the Japan Sea, the Sea of Okhotsk and the Bering Sea and extend from Peter the Great Bay, to Sakhalin and Kamchatka, along the Aleutian islands to Bristol Bay in Alaska.

The Soviet Far Eastern fishing fleets do not confine their operations to the home coastal waters of the Far East.[9] There is increasing official interest in extending *Dal'ryba's* fishing activities southwards to the Indian, south Pacific and Antarctic waters. However, in spite of considerable modifications in the design of ships originally intended for coastal fishing, this fleet is not yet sufficiently well equipped for profitable fishing in tropical waters, or equipped for deep sea and pelagic fishing.

Throughout the 1960s, the Far Eastern fishing fleet was reorganised on a more efficient basis. New types of vessels, including large refrigerated ships and floating factory ships were added and considerable modernisation and expansion took place. The floating canneries produce a major share of the Soviet Far Eastern canned fish especially salmon and crab. This fleet also includes the important whaling fleets which operate out of Far Eastern ports, two in the vicinity of the Kuril, Commander and Aleutian islands and two mainly in the Antarctic waters. Overfishing of certain species of whales has led to various international agreements on the regulation of this industry in which the Soviet Union has to a certain extent participated as well as in international whale research. In 1972, it agreed to cooperate in the Inter-

[8] I am greatly indebted to Mr. P. Dibb's excellent essay: The Soviet Far Eastern Fishing Industry: A Geographical Assessment (Dept. of Geography, Nottingham, 1970) for details reproduced in this section, with his permission.
[9] According to a survey published in 1969 by the Fisheries Dept. of the U.N. Food and Agricultural Organisation (FAO) on the extent of the territorial sea limits claimed by the countries of the world, the Soviet Union's claim of territorial sea limit was 12 miles but did not define its exclusive fishing zone.

national Observer Scheme and accordingly the Soviet Union, Japan and Norway signed an agreement for an exchange of observers between factory ships operating in the Antarctic region and for fixed quotas of whale catches.

There has been a huge increase in the Far Eastern catch in the last forty years. It rose from less than 162,000 tons in 1928, to 2,056,000 tons in 1966. But, as Mr. Dibb points out, a large percentage of this catch was inedible fish and only some 711,400 tons were used for food, 'as a result of fishermen's attempts to fulfil planned quotas which were set too high and without any regard to quality differentials'. Most of the inedible fish is made into fertiliser, but as agriculture is poorly developed in the Soviet Far East, the surplus had to be hauled long distances throughout Siberia at great expense. To stop this wasteful trend, a new form of incentive payment was introduced in 1968, by which fishermen's wages are geared to the catch of edible fish.

In the sixties there was a sharp drop in the salmon and crab catches. This occurred in the first place as a result of over-fishing and, subsequently, because of restrictions introduced to prevent overfishing. Kamchatka, the centre of this crab and salmon fishing, has lost much of its former importance to Vladivostok and even Nakhodka, where the ocean-going fleet is concentrated and the fish can be sent by rail to markets in the west of the country (though the organisation of this transport leaves much to be desired). Flotillas of two large administrations: *Dal'morprodukt* (Far Eastern Maritime product) and *Vostokrybkholodflot* (Eastern fish refrigeration fleet) are based in Vladivostok. Their floating factories, large refrigerators and whale bases, operate from the Northern latitudes to Antarctic waters. Long-range prospecting is also carried out in the Pacific and Indian oceans by scientific research ships. Moscow reported in 1971 that, by 1975, Vladivostok's fishing harbour would be able to receive vessels of any displacement and its handling capacity would be increased by nearly 50%.

The lack of rail communications, adequate port and repair facilities and labour problems, have adversely affected the position of the Kamchatkan fishing industry in recent years. Soviet sources reported a high absentee rate in the industry in the latter half of the sixties. As a result of these difficulties and 'idleness', planned production fell short to the tune of several million roubles. The 'flight of labour' was also high among migrant Kamchatkan fishery workers, until the new regional wage incentives were also made applicable to them. Thousands of seasonal workers are annually assigned to the Far Eastern fisheries, including students, at great expense to the State, resulting from the high cost of transporting them from European Russia and the financial loss to the factories from which many are temporarily removed.

The Far Eastern fishing industry is now reported to be operating at a profit (though long operated at a loss). In his careful analysis, Mr. Dibb attributes this change to the introduction of a more realistic pricing policy under the new economic reforms. He quotes the case of frozen cod, in which the production cost per ton, pre-1968, was 390 roubles and the selling price only 270 roubles, and frozen Pacific herring for which demand is falling, but which was selling for 580 roubles per ton, though it cost only 180 roubles per ton to produce. 'Anomalies still exist'.

he concludes 'and complaints are voiced about inflexible prices in relation to changing market positions.'

Over 50 per cent of the edible fish landed in the Far East in 1965 was frozen and this proportion is probably much the same today. Production of salted herrings, always so popular with the Russian people, has declined, however, owing to the difficulty and expense of procuring salt for the necessary processing. Fresh or chilled fish do not play a significant role in the Far Eastern fishing industry because of the long distances involved in transport to the main market in European Russia.[10]

The most important market opportunities are now for canned fish, headed by the big export sales of Far Eastern crab and salmon. After a reorganisation of the Far Eastern canning industry into a smaller number of more efficient and larger centres, nearly 2½ million cans were produced in 1965, half of which came from floating canneries. And this output has continued to increase. Nevertheless, the Atlantic-based canneries are still the largest producers of Soviet canned fish.

With a view, it would seem, to catching up with the more sophisticated international packing of some fish products and the preparation of others, an exhibition and tasting of imported, foreign canned fish and preserved fish products was held in Vladivostok in 1966. Nine countries exhibited their products: Denmark, Spain, Italy, Sweden, Norway, Iceland, West Germany, France and the Netherlands. As a result of this experience, it was announced that the Maritime kray would begin to manufacture fish pastes in tubes according to the Swedish method and to pack Far Eastern fish products 'in glass jars with screw tops'. The outcome of these modest initiatives is not known. A straw in the wind, perhaps, is that most of the fish sold to Japan is reported to be unprocessed and includes even the fish heads. 'It is not enough to get the fish out of the sea . . . it is more important to prepare it in better shape for the national table', announced N. Nosov, the Head of the Chief Fishing Dept. of the Far Eastern Basin in 1971. He recognised the big demand for such fish products as balyk (smoked sturgeon), fish sausages, pel'meny and all smoked fish, but admitted that the necessary canning equipment and workers were lacking to produce them. As far as the labour problem is concerned, the causes are the same as throughout Siberian industry. To quote Nosov again: In order 'to fix' the workers, it is necessary to speed up the rate of living accommodation construction and the provision of cultural-domestic requirements for fishermen and workers at the fishing ports and ship repair works.

The lack of coordination between trawler capacity, freezers and refrigeration transport is another cause of much fish wastage and financial loss, which is increased by excessive delays in ship repairs in the coastal docks. Paul Dibb has summarised the situation in the Far Eastern fishing industry in 1970 and its future as follows: The prospect is for the Far Eastern fishing industry to continue its role as an important supplier of fish to an estimated 55–60 million Soviet citizens and as the source for at least one-third of Soviet fish and fish products exports. The disadvantage of distance from the main consuming centres in the U.S.S.R. will be offset increasingly by sales of fish to nearby Japan. But *Dal'ryba* will have to pay closer attention to quality controls for edible fish and also to the need for supplying

[10] cf. P. Dibb, op. cit. p. 157.

an improved variety of fish currently in demand, both within the Soviet Union and overseas. Moreover, in the next Five Year Plan (1971-75) more capital investment will have to be earmarked for the Far Eastern fisheries if the acute shortages of port facilities and labour are to be overcome.' And in fact, the ninth five-year plan does specially mention the need to develop the ship repair capacity and fishing ports of the Far Eastern basin and to introduce new progressive methods of prospecting and catching fish. All these planned tasks have been actively followed up subsequently.

Internationally, the Soviet and Japanese fishing industries are closely connected and highly competitive in Far Eastern waters and primarily in the north Pacific.[11] To a much lesser extent and up to the present mainly on a scientific basis, contacts have been established between the U.S.A. and the Soviet Union in regard to their common oceanographical and fishing interests in the north-western Atlantic and north-eastern sector of the Pacific Ocean. Further cooperation in regard to 'common and complicated problems' in these fields is now urged by the Soviet side. A high Soviet scientific official has expressed the hope that following the Brezhnev visit to the U.S.A. in 1973 'Soviet and American scientists, including oceanographers, will receive still greater possibilities for joint researches'.

It may not be inappropriate to mention here that the Chinese have joined in the widely expressed suspicion of espionage regarding Soviet Far Eastern and other fishing vessels. These Chinese allegations were, as might have been expected, indignantly denied by Tass (3.8.1973). 'The Chinese N.C.N.A. has come out with another falsehood' it declared. 'This time it has announced that Soviet fishing vessels sailing in the world's oceans are engaged in nothing more nor less than piratical and spying activities. As to facts – the N.C.N.A. has none, and cannot possibly have any.' Whatever the 'facts' in this matter, these Chinese suspicions have received wide publicity and support in the foreign press.

The Far Eastern maritime fisheries are strongly reinforced by the great inland fisheries of Siberia. The large rivers and lakes of the country are an important source of freshwater fish, which provide food for thousands of local inhabitants and also employment in many places lacking other industries. The great Yenisey and Lena rivers, though producing a considerable volume of fish, are not as rich in organic matter and, therefore, in fish as might be supposed from their length and volume of water. The Amur, however, has a very important freshwater fish industry, based on the large quantities of valuable types of fish such as salmon and kaluga (a sturgeon found in eastern waters) found in the river. West Siberia has a major fishing industry which produces about a fourth of all the freshwater fish of the Soviet Union. Almost half of Soviet sturgeon and other valuable fish is caught in west Siberia. The chief fishing centres are the Ob' and the Irtysh rivers and the estuaries of the Ob' and Taz. The annual catch amounts to some 60,000 tons. Apart from the fish consumed fresh locally, most of this west Siberian fish is sent to the fish factories in the Irtysh and Taz estuaries and in the middle and lower Ob' districts for processing and export.

[11] This subject is more fully discussed in Chapter 12 below.

chapter nine

Transport

Rail. The economic development of Siberia has long been retarded by the lack of good rail and road communications and, in the Far East, maritime transport. The first step taken to rectify this situation, and ease the long arduous trek through Siberia for travellers and goods, was the construction of the Trans-Siberian railway at the end of the nineteenth century. This great feat of railway engineering still overshadows any subsequent railway development in this region: 6,000 miles long, and presenting the builders of the track with the greatest hazards from the climate and the terrain, the completion of the Trans-Siberian may be said to have changed the economic face of Siberia. It had linked Chelyabinsk in the Urals with Vladivostok on the Pacific by 1904, *via* the Chinese Eastern railway and Harbin. Owing to careless planning, the railway finally cost over £150 million, much more than the original estimates, while the failure to foresee difficulties of supply and terrain and unpredictable natural disasters, took a heavy toll of the workers' lives. A northern spur of the Trans-Siberian, the Amur railway linking Kuenga to Khabarovsk was only finished in 1916. A great bridge, one and a half miles long, carried the railway over the Amur at Khabarovsk, whence the line was later continued south through the Ussuri railway, to Vladivostok. It is now completely double tracked and electrification has reached the Baykal area and is continuing beyond.

Stalin's pre-war industrialisation plans, and the new Soviet interest in developing Siberian raw materials, in turn necessitated the construction of a number of new railways to make these materials more accessible to plants and factories. The *Turk-Sib* railway linking the Trans-Siberian railways with the Central Asian network was a bold project and the most important railway construction of the first three five-year plans. It ran between Lugavoy in southern Kazakhstan and Novosibirsk (1,442 km.) and was intended to carry Siberian grain and timber to areas of Central Asia lacking both and bring Central Asian cotton to Siberia.

It was not the success expected, partly because of constructional difficulties and largely because the projected Siberian timber and grain supplies were not regularly forthcoming for Central Asia.

Mining and metallurgical developments in the Kuzbas and the Altay during the thirties produced another spurt of railway construction in Siberia, mainly inter-connecting these mines and plants. The shuttling of coal, coke and ore between the Urals and the Kuzbas to supply the great new Second Metallurgical Base at Stalinsk (Novokuznetsk), put the main Trans-Siberian line under a very heavy additional strain, which was further increased by economic developments in East Siberia and the Far East. A spur of the Turk-Sib, the Rubtsovsk–Ridder (Leninogorsk) railway, facilitated the working of the non-ferrous resources of the Altay. Lines were also built to link the large new Karaganda coal fields with the Trans-Siberian and with the Balkhash copper smelter, some 504 km. further south in Kazakhstan.

In the Far North, a narrow-gauge railway (70 miles long) was built in 1937 to link the new mining-metallurgical combine at Noril'sk with Dudinka on the Yenisey. After the war, this line was converted to broad gauge and another narrow gauge line was built between Noril'sk and the associated Talnakh mines, in 1965.

During this period a few other new railway lines were constructed in east Siberia and the Far Eastern Region, but less was done in the field of communications in either region than might have been anticipated in view of the state of tension between Japanese-occupied Manchuria and the Soviet Union's Far Eastern border areas.

On the eve of World War II and subsequently, the Soviet rail links with Outer Mongolia and China were greatly strengthened by extensions of the Trans-Siberian railway over the Soviet-Mongolian frontier. Outer Mongolia was connected by rail for the first time in 1939, with the Soviet Union, through the construction of a five-foot gauge line between Borzya (a station in east Siberia on a spur of the Trans-Siberia starting at Chita) and Choybalsan, the chief town in eastern Mongolia. Borzya is also the junction, *via* the Manchurian frontier station of Zabaykal'sk, for the Chinese Eastern Railway line, through Harbin to Vladivostok (since the Sino-Soviet conflict, it is no longer possible to travel from Siberia to Vladivostok by this trans-Manchurian route, which is considerably shorter than by the Amur railway). The Buryat-Mongolian capital of Ulan-Ude was connected by a new 213 miles long railway with the frontier town of Naushki. These lines were of major strategic significance for the Soviet Union, when the crunch came with the Japanese in Manchuria in 1938–39 and in 1944–45. They were also economically important in getting Mongol supplies of meat and cattle to the Soviet Union during the war and later, while Soviet equipment for the post-war industrialisation of Outer Mongolia largely depended on these railways. The Naushki line was later extended to Ulan Bator and was fully operational by 1950. The much publicised 1,115 km. long Trans-Mongolian railway (five-foot gauge and single track) connecting Ulan-Bator with the Chinese frontier and rail system was a tri-partite Russian-Chinese-Mongolian construction and was opened to traffic in 1956. It was estimated to shorten the distance between the Soviet and Chinese capitals by 700 miles.

Between 1933–36, the 1,687 miles long stretch of the Trans-Siberian further east, between Ulan-Ude and Khabarovsk, was double-tracked. This measure provided badly needed reinforcement for a sector of the Trans-Siberian then greatly over-strained with an increasing load of heavy freight, for the defence build-up of the Far Eastern Region. Moreover, in 1940 Khabarovsk was linked by rail with the new town of Komsomol'sk-na-Amure, 213 miles to the north. As a result Komsomol'sk gained access through Khabarovsk to the Siberian rail network which was most important for its growing industrial development.

Considerable interest was aroused, in the pre-war years, by the announcement of a plan to build a trunk line (known as the B.A.M.) from Tayshet, on the Trans-Siberian railway, to an undesignated terminal on the Pacific coast. This line was to run through mostly wild and unexplored territory and when completed would be about 1,200 miles long. Forced labour was used on this difficult job and construction was started on both ends of the line. Then, with the outbreak of the war, a mysterious silence blanketed all further news of its progress until, in 1972, this B.A.M. project was resurrected. All that is known with any certainty of its earlier progress is that the Lena sector from Tayshet to Ust'-Kut was started in 1938.

In July 1945, an important extension of the Amur railway linked Komsomol'sk-na-Amure (the rail terminal) with the Pacific port of Sovetskaya Gavan', the best natural harbour on the Gulf of Tartary. This Pivan'–Sovetskaya Gavan', line was finished just in time to be extremely useful for the transport of Soviet troops for the seizure of Sakhalin and the Kuril islands from Japan, in 1945.[1] In fact, this 277 mile long railway started from Pivan', on the other side of the river from Komsomol'sk. Trains have, therefore, to be transported from one shore to the other by special ferries, or along tracks stretched across the ice in winter. Thus, this railway, which seems on the map to run non-stop to Sovetskaya Gavan', actually runs into the river barrier at Komsomol'sk. In order to eliminate this time-wasting inconvenience, it was decided in 1965 to build a bridge across the Amur, to be completed in 1970. This Amur bridge proved a most difficult construction owing to the great depth of the river at this point, the sharp fluctuations in the water level, the fierce frosts and winds and the icy winter conditions, which create very complex constructional problems. Moreover, the labour force was largely inexperienced in this kind of work. The result of all these difficulties is that the construction period has now been protracted to the ninth five-year plan period (1971–75).

After World War II, intensified Soviet interest in the development of Siberian economic resources, initiated a new period in railroad construction in Siberia. Apart from many smaller branch-lines of mainly local significance, the most important new lines were the Central and Southern Siberian lines, the Abakan–Tayshet railway, and the completion of the Tayshet Ust'-Kut Trans-Siberian spur to the Lena river port of Usetrovo.

The South Siberian line (in spite of its Siberian designation), traverses a long stretch of Kazakhstan before reaching its Siberian terminal in the Kuzbas. It was completed in 1953 by forced labour. Starting from Tselinograd in the heart of the Virgin Lands, it is a 700-mile extension of the Magnitogorsk–Karaganda line, now double-tracked and electrified. It provides an essential link through the Barnaul junction for Virgin Lands grain, moving west or eastwards to east Siberia and the Far East, *via* the Trans-Siberian railway. Many other products of industrialised north Kazakhstan are also given an outlet by this railway.

In the same category of importance is the Middle or Central Siberian line (745

[1] cf. H. Tupper, *To The Great Ocean*, p. 422.

miles), partly completed in 1966, though under belated construction since 1950, but only finished in 1972. Its starting point is Kustanay, whence the line runs through Kochetav-Irtyshskoye (with a branch line to Omsk on the Trans-Siberian railway) Kamen'-na-Obi to the *Srednesibirskaya* (Middle Siberian) station of Barnaul, where it joins up with the South Siberian railway. Work is nearly completed on the change-over from single track to double on this line. Some other branch lines of the Trans-Siberian railway going south should be mentioned: Tatarsk–Karasuk–Kalunda, which intersects both the Central and South Siberian railways; the line to Biysk leading into the wooded steppes of the Altay and, most important, the large rail network connecting the Kuzbas and the Trans-Siberian and the many industries of the Kemerovo oblast. Asino, with its extention northwards to Belyy Yar and south to the Trans-Siberian by a branch line from Tomsk, has become an important all-Union timber-processing centre, based on its large and rich timber resources. Like the well-forested areas of western Siberia, now traversed by the Ivdel–Ob' and the Tavda–Sotnik lines, the establishment of a modern timber industry only became economically possible with the arrival of the railways.

A number of railways essential for the various big economic development schemes which have taken place in eastern Siberia, since the war, radiate from Tayshet and Abakan. Work on the Tayshet railway (discontinued during the war) was resumed in 1945. The important stretch running to Ust'-Kut *via* Bratsk was completed in 1954. It was essential as a supply line for the new Bratsk hydroelectric power station and all the industries subsequently based on it. Ust'-Kut connects with the Lena river port of Osetrovo, from which there are regular river services into the heart of Yakutiya. Thus, Yakutiya gained a new link with European Russia, through the Trans-Siberian network at Tayshet. This Tayshet–Ust'-Kut railway has also played a vital role in the development of the valuable natural resources of the area. This applies in particular to the Korshunovo iron ore deposits and the forestry industry of the middle Angara Valley, neither of which could have been developed without the aid of this railway.

Double-tracking started in 1972. From Khrebtovaya, a station between Bratsk and Ust'-Kut, a new line was opened in 1973 to the site of the big Ust'-Ilimsk hydropower station now under construction, thus enormously facilitating transport for men and materials formerly entirely dependent on very indifferent roads. The Mama mica deposits and Bodaybo gold-fields to the east of Ust'-Kut are also linked with this Lena railway through the Vitim–Lena waterway.

It seems to be definite Soviet policy, at the time of writing (1973) to continue construction of the discontinued B.A.M. railway, starting from Ust'-Kut. This line, it is assumed, will in turn become the eastern sector of the *Sevsib* (northern Siberian railway), a 5,000 mile long railway project announced by Soviet sources in 1966. Work from the western sector railhead of Tyumen' started in 1965. There have been very unsatisfactory reports of its progress towards Surgut, the middle Ob' oil centre, where rail transport is urgently needed by the rapidly expanding oil-gas industry. Having reached Tobol'sk, this line was still ploughing its difficult course through bogs and marshes to Surgut in 1974. The track will then run eastwards, *via* the confluence of the Angara-Yenisey rivers, and link up with the eastern sector of the railway at Ust'-Kut. From the meagre detail so far released by the Soviet authorities about this railway, it is believed that beyond Lake Baykal, on the way to Komsomol'sk, the track will be laid from 240 to 435 miles north of the Trans-Siberian and the Chinese Amur frontier – a great strategic advantage over the older railway course. In the magnitude of the enterprise, the area to be covered and the difficulties of construction, this north Siberian line stands comparison with its predecessor, the Trans-Siberian railway, and again bears witness to the great tradition of the Russians as railway builders since the last century. It was originally estimated that this huge engineering project might take 15–16 years to complete, but the valuable economic resources, still largely under-developed in the regions traversed for lack of transport, and the strategic interest of the Far Eastern sector, may well be factors inducing a shorter timetable, in spite of the heavy capital costs involved in its construction (see Postscript).

Abakan, the capital of Khakassiya, has in recent years become an important railway and industrial centre, though for so long only known for the primitive iron mines in its vicinity (now organised on modern lines). Situated in the Minusinsk Plain renowned for its mild climate and fertility (as well as for an ancient civilisation), railway building here is not subject to the usual Siberian hazards of climate and terrain. To the north, a line from Abakan crosses the Trans-Siberian railway at Achinsk and extends to the big Maklakovo-Abalakovo timber centre on the Yenisey. To the west, Abakan is connected with the Kuzbas rail network, through Novokuznetsk, and can thus ship its iron ore direct to the Kuzbas metallurgical plants. In the north-east, it has a second connection with the Trans-Siberian through the Abakan–Tayshet railway, completed after many delays in 1965. This line traverses some of the most difficult, inaccessible terrain in Siberia, with many rivers and high mountains to cross and little or no development to make the line pay, for the present. Both the Abakan–Tayshet and the Achinsk–Abalakovo railways were criticised by the Krasnoyarsk kray Party secretary in 1966, because of the large capital investment tied up in their construction, before the two regions had been subject to proper economic planning. The Abakan railways will doubtless assume a new importance with the development of the many-sided Sayan hydroelectric project. This network is the only one in the vicinity of Sayan while a good motor road (80 km. long) connects Abakan with Shushenskoye close to Mayna, the actual site of the Sayan H.E.S. Thus, the Abakan links with the Trans-Siberian railway should initially provide an essential means of transport for construction and other supplies for the Sayan H.E.S., and later for the varied industries planned in connection with the H.E.S.

Apart from these established railways, many Siberian railway projects float in and out of the Soviet news media, but are, apparently, not yet seriously considered by the planning authorities. There are, however, a few lines for which exceptionally strong economic claims have been made by interested local parties and expert supporters and which might be expected to materialise in the not too distant future. In the first place, these are the Salekhard railway, the Trans-Siberian line to the copper mines of Udokan and the Bam-Chul'man extension of the Amur trunk line.

top: Removal of logs from an
Irkutsk forest
bottom: Rafting logs on the river
Angara, Krasnoyarsk kray

The Salekhard railway was a Stalinist project and planned to run some 700 miles through Arctic Siberia to Igarka, on the Yenisey. It was abandoned after his death in 1953. Owing to the atrocious conditions in which it was built, by concentration camp labour in the freezing Siberian wilds, it was known as 'Mertvaya Doroga' (The Road of Death)[2]. At the time of construction there seemed little or no point in building a railway through a very sparsely inhabited wilderness, with no known economic prospects. The situation has now been entirely changed by the discovery of enormous gas fields in the area of the partly dismantled and deserted railway track. The west Siberian petroleum enterprises are now keen on the reconstruction of at least the Salekhard–Nadym sector of this railway, so as to facilitate the movement of supplies to the great gas fields in the neighbourhood of Nadym (at Medvezh'ye). But for the moment the problem remains undecided, owing to the opposition of the railway authorities on the score of costs.

There is general agreement among the foreign and Soviet experts concerned with the development of the huge copper reserves at Udokan, situated some 300-odd miles north of the Trans-Siberian railway in a primitive permafrost area of the Chita oblast', that mining operations cannot start before a railway, however costly, is built from some point on the Trans-Siberian railway, probably Mogocha to Udokan. Though it had been decided in principle to develop these mines, nothing had been decided about the railway or other aspects of this important development until 1974. The area will now be crossed by the Baykal-Amur railway (see Postscript).

The intermittent discussions about the need to build a metallurgical base in the Far Eastern region, invariably raise the question of linking the large coking coal deposits it Chul'man, in southern Yakutiya, by a new line to the Amur railway. The need for this line has strong local support while establishment of the Far Eastern metallurgical base was decided in principle some years ago. The Japanese interest in Chul'man coking coals has frequently been made clear, but apparently Japanese participation in development was dependent on agreement about the necessary infrastructure and, primarily, a railway. The Soviets have now started to build with promised Japanese cooperation and the 110-mile spur from Bam station on the Trans-Siberian railway to Tyndinskiy, half-way to Chul'man, has been constructed (1972) while work proceeds on the track to Chul'man.

Further east, the island of Sakhalin is traversed from east to west by a new line crossing the narrowest part of the island from Arsent'yevka to Il'insk (26 km.). It is now possible to transport goods to the east coast (from the west coast opposite the mainland) without going through the oblast centre far south of the Isthmus. This is of considerable economic importance to the island, already traversed by the North-South railway. It was also reported from Sakhalin, in 1970, that the last steam locomotive was taken out of service and replaced by diesels.

A Soviet sea and rail container service known as the 'Siberian Land Bridge' is

[2] The conditions under which this line was being built before it was abandoned were described in detail in an article in *Novy Mir* (no. 8. 1964).
[3] For further discussion of Udokan copper see relevant section 'Non-ferrous metallurgy', p. 101.

Sorting furs in Yakutiya

now operating between the Soviet Far Eastern ports of Nakhodka-Vladivostok and Japan. The scheme was originally proposed by the Swiss container-operating organisation, Transcontainer. Japan is expected to be the main user of this service; a special container complex is being built at Nakhodka, the chief container port, supplied with special Japanese equipment, including an automatic crane, capable of off-loading containers of up to 40 tons from flat wagons, straight into ships' holds. Japanese trucks for handling containers will also be used at the terminal, and all this equipment was planned to be installed and put into service by the end of 1973. It was reported in 1971 that the Soviet Far Eastern line had assigned three cargo vessels, each of which would carry 45–50 containers, to the Nakhodka–Japan route in connection with the container traffic between Europe and Japan, through the U.S.S.R. The first batch of containers consigned to Europe *via* the U.S.S.R. arrived from Japan in 1971. By 1973, 1,500 containers from Japan were carried monthly on the Trans-Siberian railway to customers in Europe. Uniorient, a mixed Soviet-Japanese company, organises this trade.

This new Soviet venture has apparently gained much from British experience in the container-ship service, between Hull and London-Tilbury. The Chief of the Commercial Traffic Section of the Soviet Railway Research Institute[4] originally stated that Soviet containerisation would be largely based on British Rail's experience. Complex discussions took place in 1972 in order to link this Trans-Siberian container service with the East European rail-network and thus enable west European containers to be shipped to Nakhodka overland. Meanwhile, the U.S.S.R., Czechoslovakia and Hungary have agreed to unite in building a freight station near their common borders so as to enable 20-ft. transcontainers to be trans-shipped between the wide-gauge Russian railway wagons and the European standard gauge. The aim of these plans would be to eliminate the present bottle-necks arising from the trans-shipment of containers at the Soviet Baltic ports. At the Pacific end of the traffic, transport was at first hampered by poor stevedoring facilities at Nakhodka, and Soviet failure to provide scheduled special freight trains to accommodate the containers from Japan. This service seems now to have overcome its various teething troubles, and it is expected that there will be savings both of costs, up to 30% and of time, reduced to 20–23 days, compared to the shipping routes to Europe. For example, an experimental container train from Finland bound for Japan *via* the Soviet Union in 1972 took three weeks, or half the time of sea transport.

Two measures were taken in 1971 to facilitate Soviet trade by rail with North Korea. Work on the reconstruction of the Soviet rail terminal at the Soviet-Korean border Station of Khasan began in 1971. New tracks of different gauge have been laid and freight platforms are being built. A Soviet-Korean railway freight agreement was signed in Khabarovsk for 1972, to accelerate handling of trains and increase the flow of goods traffic between the two countries. From the Soviet side, oil products, coal, timber and machines are exchanged for Korean rice, cement and fertilisers, Khasan is planned to become one of the major transfer and marshalling

4 According to a report in *The Financial Times*, 25.1.72.

points in the Soviet Far East. It is situated at a politically crucial juncture of the Soviet, Korean and Chinese frontiers, across the Tuinangan river bridge.

From this survey of the development of railway transport in Siberia in the Soviet period, some general trends and facts emerge. The Trans-Siberian railway remains the chief carrier throughout the entire area, with 90% of the traffic in west Siberia, the most highly industrialised sector. In spite of the many new feeder lines and to a certain extent on account of the accruing freight, it is still heavily overloaded. This situation is now being to some extent eased by the new pipelines eastwards and westwards from the Tyumen' oil deposits[5] which when completed will take much of this heavy freight from the Trans-Siberian railway.

There are constant complaints in Soviet sources of the gratuitous and uneconomic crosshauls, especially of sawn and round wood, between east Siberia, west Siberia and the Far East, which also greatly increases the strain on the railways.

The density of railway per kilometre of the Siberian territory remains extremely low and also varies considerably from west to east. It is most highly concentrated in the Kusbas with 13.7 km. per 1,000 sq. km. falling to 1.2 km. per 1,000 sq. km. in the enormous Tyumen' oblast, containing great stretches of tundra-permafrost, only recently acquiring some economic significance with the discovery of the large local oil-gas fields.

Since the outbreak of the Sino-Soviet conflict, the sparsity of lines in the eastern areas of Siberia and especially the vulnerability of the Trans-Siberian line are apparently matters of some concern to the Soviet military authorities. In the 1,481 miles between Mogocha and Vladivostok the railway is seldom more than 50 miles from this frontier. This situation may well explain the final decision to build the *Sevsib* railway some 240–435 miles north of the Trans-Siberian railway and the adjacent Sino-Soviet frontier along the Amur in the Far Eastern sector. Otherwise, most railway construction has taken place, since the war, in central and eastern Siberia, in response to the many transport demands from industrialisation schemes. On the other hand, the lack of transport facilities is holding up development of other resources known to exist in presently inaccessible areas. To quote a recent Soviet report: 'In order to expedite the development of the productive forces of the Eastern regions a large-scale transport construction [scheme] is necessary. The lack of reserves of traffic capacity on a number of existing railway lines connecting the eastern regions with the Urals and the European parts of the U.S.S.R. to a certain extent complicate the development of industrial and capital construction in the East; the poor development of a network of rail and automobile roads in regions of new exploitation (of resources) is a brake on the rate of opening up new natural resources in this zone.'

This state of affairs could be illustrated from many parts of Siberia. But the blockage of mining development in the north-west Buryatiya for lack of transport is as good an example as any other. Here in the Sayan-Tunkinskiy area there are allegedly reserves of high-quality asbestos, bauxite, graphite, nephrite and many rare and non-ferrous metals. The rich Bokson bauxite alone might be useful raw material for the east Siberian aluminium industry (now dependent on remote

[5] For details of Siberian oil and pipelines, cf. Chapter 5: Energy.

nepheline raw material). The extremely high quality graphite was once used by the famous Faber pencil company, but the mine was abandoned after the Revolution owing to transport difficulties. Admittedly the terrain is extremely difficult for road or rail construction, 'it looks like primeval mountain chaos', but if Faber could get the graphite out a century ago to make the internationally known pencils, the time seems ripe in the late twentieth century for more vigorous efforts to work these valuable mines.

With the advance of industrialisation and the opening up of many formerly uninhabited areas, Siberia's need for an expansion of the present railway system is obvious. But there are many factors severely limiting, or at least delaying, rail construction and indeed all transport in Siberia and the Far East. In the first place, the formidable costs, especially in the large areas of permafrost, where both construction and maintenance of railways is extremely expensive and much the highest in the Soviet Union. The great distances between centres of industry and population also increase construction costs, as well as the costs of moving freight between these widely separated places.[6] Apart from costs, railway construction in most of Siberia is hampered by peculiar difficulties, arising from the harsh climate and other natural conditions.

Roads. The urgent need for a big Siberian road building programme is even more strongly stressed in Soviet sources than the emphasis on railway requirements and 'roadlessness' is frequently deplored in many areas. This is especially true of the east Siberian and Far Eastern regions, where hard surface roads are few and far between and very expensive to build. Even dirt tracks are often lacking in potentially rich timber districts, though this situation is now improving with the progress made with narrow gauge railways and more passable forest tracks.

The chief trunk motor roads in these two areas are between Never-Yakutsk and through to Magadan; Irkutsk–Kachug; Minusinsk–Kyzyl (the capital of the Tuva A.S.S.R.); Ak-Dovurak(Tuva's asbestos centre)–Abaza; Lensk–Mirnyy and the Tunkinskiy *trakt* highway, traversing the Irkutsk valley to the border of Outer Mongolia at Mondy and beyond. Mondy is the site of the famous Sayanskaya Observatory, where valuable scientific observations of the magnetic field of the sun were made for the Year of the Quiet Sun (1964–66). Along this *trakt*, large herds of Mongol cattle pass annually into the Soviet Union, to increase its meat stocks. In the huge 'roadlessness' of Siberia, these few arterial roads are of the greatest importance. This is particularly true of the great Magadan–Never trunk road traversing both the Kolyma and the Aldan gold-fields. It was built simultaneously with many minor roads in this area, under conditions of dreadful hardship, by concentration camp labour during the last war. It now provides a reliable and relatively short means of transport between east Yakutiya and the Trans-Siberian railway. Another important highway in the Primor'ye starts from Sokol'chi and follows the railway to Nakhodka, Vladivostok and Khabarovsk and thence along the Amur

---

[6] A detailed analysis of Siberian transport costs and other difficulties is given in *Siberia and the Pacific* by Paul Dibb.

into east Siberia. About a third of all freight transport is by road in the Far East. The Chuyskiy *trakt*, a 617 km. long motor road, connects Biysk with Outer Mongolia having traversed the mountains, rivers and many other obstacles in the Gorno-Altayskaya autonomous oblast.

Road building in Siberia, owing to the nature of the terrain, and the generally harsh environment, is often most difficult where it is most acutely needed. In the Tyumen'-middle Ob' oil fields, for example, road construction is complicated by the marshy-forested terrain and the floods, while in the gas-fields further north, permafrost and boggy tundra are very intractable obstacles. Similar difficulties are encountered in all the northern areas of Siberia. Apart from these physical obstacles, the extremely high cost of road building throughout Siberia must be taken into account. In the non-marshy forested areas of east Siberia, the cost of building 1 km. of first class road has been officially estimated to be half a million roubles (much higher than construction of 1 km. of railway). It must therefore be astronomical in the Tyumen' region of bog and permafrost.

Throughout Siberia the motor road network is developing relatively slowly in relation to the growing numbers of motor vehicles and need for hard surface roads, which are very unequally distributed throughout the region. According to *Sovetskaya Rossiya* (25.2.1971), this situation is causing the State large annual financial losses. For many years, Soviet policy has favoured rail and air transport over roads (especially highways), probably on account of the great distances between many towns and urban settlements and the high and often unremunerative cost of road building. It has hitherto been virtually impossible to cross Siberia by car, owing to the lack of a practicable motor road. But this impasse is to be rectified by the decision to build a 7 m. wide motor road, from Moscow to Chita, construction being scheduled to start in 1973. This projected Trans-Siberian highway will run through Ufa, Chelyabinsk, Omsk, Novosibirsk, Krasnoyarsk, Irkutsk and Ulan-Ude on its way to the present projected terminal at Chita, but no doubt will eventually be extended further east to some point on the Pacific, possibly Nakhodka.

Far Eastern transport, especially inland transport, has advanced more slowly than most other branches of the economy and is still inadequate for the region's requirements, particularly in the remote regions of the north. While, according to official sources, industrial production has risen six times in the Soviet Far East since pre-war, hard-surface motor roads have increased less than three times and the railways still carry more than half of all freight in this region.

Rivers. The Siberian river system most usefully complements both the rail and road network, and in many regions of the north where neither roads nor railways exist, is often essential. The usefulness of these rivers varies greatly from region to region. With the exception of the Yenisey, none of the great rivers like the Amur, the Lena or the Kolyma are navigable up-stream from their estuaries for ocean-going ships. The great Lena estuary is entirely unnavigable, blocked by islands and numerous tributaries. Its port is actually to the east of the estuary, at Tiksi, where much of the freight from and for the Lena is unloaded. This navigation impasse at the mouths of many Siberian rivers discharging their waters into the Arctic, is solved by the use of fleets of barges which are used to trans-ship freight from the ocean-going ships for distribution up-stream. Siberian river navigation is, of course, seasonal and only lasts during the summer months, while the rivers are free of ice. When frozen hard, the rivers also provide indispensable winter roads.

According to the ninth five-year plan, Soviet river transport is to increase 24% by 1975, and in Siberian northern conditions the percentage will probably be higher. The importance attached to river transport is reflected in many steps now in train to improve it. Throughout Siberia, old river ports, like Novosibirsk, are being modernised with the installation of electric gantry-cranes and other heavy equipment, while many new ports are being established to serve the oil-gas industry of western Siberia, the developing timber and other industries. Thus, new river depots are being constructed at Surgut, Tobol'sk and Nizhnevartovsk to handle oil freight and supplies for the petroleum industry and Novosibirsk is to have a second river port, to deal with the increasing volume of freight passing through.

The transport situation continues to be acute in the lower Ob' basin where the ground is frozen for most of the year, and becomes impassable bog and marsh during the short summer. In this area, hydrofoils have been introduced to improve the movement of supplies for the gas industry. Efforts are also being made to deepen the Nadym river and build a river port at Nadym, now confronted with the very difficult problem of collecting gas from the Medvezh'ye fields some 50 km. north of Nadym.

Owing to the very poor development of either rail or road transport, the rivers have an important role to play in both east Siberia and the Far Eastern region. The more powerful rivers, with the exception of the Amur, run northwards from the inhabited centres, so supplies for many districts in the taiga-tundra zone are largely provided by the rivers during the short navigable season. Thus, the Yenisey and the Lena with its chief tributary the Aldan connect the towns of Noril'sk, Igarka and Yakutsk with the railways. But other rivers like the Nizhnyaya Tunguska and the Angara are less useful for navigation owing to the numerous rapids along their courses, but do supply some stretches of lateral transport to the Yenisey. The nature of the terrain in the north and north-east of the Far Eastern region, where there are many valuable mines, makes transport development extremely difficult. The expensive round journey involved in sending supplies from Yakutsk to the tin-mining region of Ese-Khaya, on the Yana river, is a good example of the problem. As direct communication is barred by the great Verkhoyansk mountains, supplies have to travel down the Lena to the Arctic, then across the Laptev sea and then up to Yana river, a journey of over 1,260 miles, before reaching their destination (though Yakutsk and Ese-Khaya are only 240 miles apart as the crow flies). Moreover, tin concentrates from the Ese-Khaya plants may take up to a year to reach the Novosibirsk smelter, owing to transport complications.

Osetrovo, the busy Lena port at the Ust'-Kut rail terminal in east Siberia, has been built up in recent years, to serve as the trans-shipment point for supplies passing some seven hundred miles down stream to the new Lena port of Lensk (formerly the small Mukhtuya river settlement), whence they are transported by road to the Yakutsk diamond centres, the Vilyuy H.E.S. and further east to the heart of central Yakutiya. A ship-building industry to cope with this river transport has also been established at Osetrovo and a number of supporting winter roads built from Lensk into Yakutiya.

River traffic on the Lena has been increasing in recent years and equipment installed at Osetrovo and Yakutsk to improve loading and unloading. This is not so at the smaller intervening ports according to V. Dubrovsky, the head of the Lena steamship administration. He complained in 1973 of the lack of 'coastal bases' along the banks of the Lena, which then carried 80% of supplies for Yakutiya including machinery, clothing, oil, construction materials and vegetables. Lack of river craft for this traffic was no longer a problem, but there were problems connected with unloading and storage for the unloaded goods. Owing to the lack of storage facilities, loaded goods often lie in 'the open air' along the banks of the Lena, the Aldan, the Indigirka and the Vilyuy, he stated. Unlike Yakutsk and Osetrovo, these ports are departmental, but the departments concerned seem little concerned about conditions on the landing stages and as a result of a shortage of refrigerators and storage depots, there were great losses of perishable foods. The situation on the Yana, which traverses a major mining area, seemed particularly neglected for import-export operations as there were not even the most simple docking facilities at Ust'-Yana, Kazach'e or Verkhoyansk. Dubrovsky also criticised the Chief Administration for Oil Supply for inefficiency in moving oil to Yakutiya from Osetrovo. New docks and powerful pumps, he said, had been installed at Osetrovo and the tanker fleet organised, but nothing had been done to adjust low-powered pumps and pipelines along the Lena, with the result that ships were held up and tankers could only discharge their oil with great delays.

In the southern zone of the Far Eastern Region, the Amur, in spite of its length and volume of water, is not the major transport artery which it was before the Amur railway track was laid, roughly parallel to the course of the river. In fact, goods, especially heavy freight, are preferably shipped by rail (which is cheaper and more efficient) rather than by river. As the lower reaches of the Amur and its wide and complicated estuary are not navigable to ocean-going ships, the value of the river as an outlet to the Pacific is also greatly reduced. Now, a 14 km. long canal is being built between Ozero Kizi and Bukhta Tabo on the Tatar Strait, by which it is hoped to increase the navigability of the Amur through this second outlet to the sea.

Sea. Many measures have been taken to improve and expand maritime transport in the Far Eastern and Arctic waters of Siberia since the last war. Formerly, the only port of any international or coastal significance was Vladivostok. It still retains its dominant position as the Far Eastern Naval base, but its commercial importance, though still considerable, is diminished by being closed to foreign shipping (and foreigners), for reasons of security. On the other hand, a number of small ports, with only the most primitive equipment, have recently been expanded and modernised. The aims behind these measures are varied. There is the need for better port facilities for the increasing coastal trade especially with Japan.

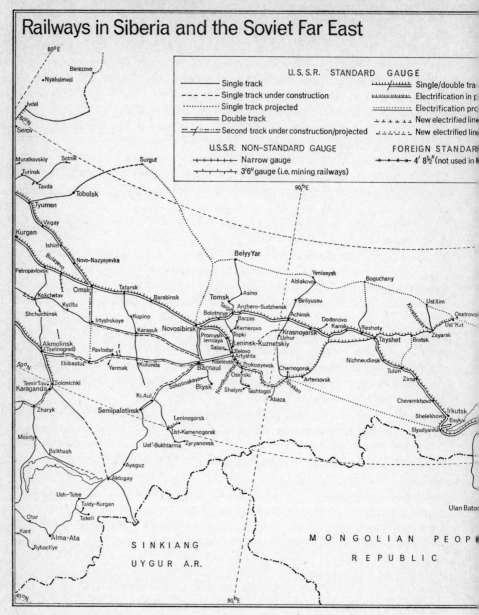

Railways in Siberia and the Soviet Far East

The post-war attempt to develop trade with the countries of the 'Pacific Rim', including south-east Asia, India and Australia also requires better organisation of the Far Eastern mainland ports. And then there are the pressing demands of the important Far Eastern fishing and commercial fleets, for much improved shore installations as these fleets expand.

The new Soviet-American relationship will also have an impact on the Soviet Far Eastern ports. It seems that the former contacts between the Russian Far

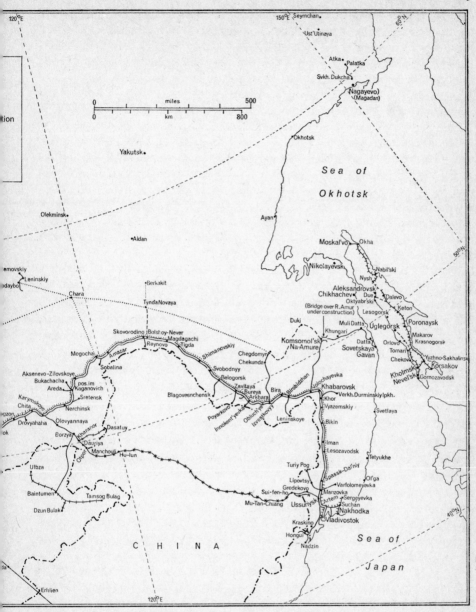

Eastern mainland and the West Coast of the United States which were discontinued after the 1917 Revolution are now to be revived. Two delegations of American officials from Seattle and Long Beach (California) visited Nakhodka in 1973, to examine its docking facilities and discuss the handling of Soviet vessels at Seattle with the Far Eastern Shipping Line. Later, the Sunkist company of California delived a consignment of lemons to Nakhodka and 'expressed a desire to become a permanent supplier of citrus fruits to the Soviet Far East'. There would certainly be a big market for this citrus fruit throughout Siberia, should the Soviet trade organisation decide to import it. The development of Yakutsk natural gas should eventually make considerable demands on the Far Eastern ports, as large shipments of equipment arrive from Japan and the United States for this project, and in time the liquefied natural gas is shipped by tanker to Japan and the West Coast of America. It is difficult to anticipate how far these contacts will go or whether the atmosphere of cordiality across the Pacific could blossom into two-way Soviet-American tourism, apart from purely commercial contacts.

The Soviets are undoubtedly interested in extending their Far Eastern shipping operations. A clear indication of this aim was the establishment of the Singapore-Soviet Shipping Agency, a branch of the Far Eastern Steamship Company, organised early in 1968 for trade with south-east Asia and India. Later came press reports that the Russians were attempting to compete with British and European shipping lines, with 36 cut-price sailings a year, in the Australian trade. The matter was eventually settled by agreement with the Russians to cut their sailings to 12 a year north bound and rather fewer south bound.

The chief ports participating in the present forward-looking Far Eastern maritime transport programme are Nakhodka-Vrangel, Sovetskaya Gavan'-Vanino and the relatively less important Slavyanka, Pos'yev and Nagayevo (the port for Magadan). Undoubtedly, improvements have also been made in the naval base of Vladivostok, but these operations are shrouded in secrecy. Japan is playing a leading role in implementing this port-modernisation programme, in the commercial port of Vladivostok as in the other Far Eastern ports, especially with equipment.

Nakhodka, about 120 km. north of Vladivostok, and situated on a semi-circular harbour, is rapidly becoming one of the largest and best equipped waterfronts in the U.S.S.R. In 1971, it was reported to have an annual turnover of 8,000,000 tons. For some years now, it is being built up to replace Vladivostok as the main commercial-container port in the Soviet Far East and to accommodate vessels up to 120,000 t. capacity. Its great advantage over other Soviet Pacific ports is that, like Vladivostok, it can be kept open (with the aid of ice-breakers) throughout the year. The modern equipment (mostly made in Japan) installed in the last twenty years includes floating docks and a 100-ton floating crane. Three deep-water quays are under construction (1972), with berths for large vessels. Nakhodka acquired a new floating dock, in 1972, which was manufactured in Klaipedia and towed 15,000 miles across 'three oceans' from the Baltic to the Far East. It is to be used in the ship repair works of the maritime fishery enterprise. When construction is complete, Nakhodka will also be the largest oil trans-shipment base in the Soviet Far East, with accommodation for tankers of over 40,000 tons displacement; the tanker fleet should ultimately consist of 15 tankers. By 1971, it had almost doubled its capacity to 4 million tons and the oil storage had also greatly increased since the base opened in 1968. Japan, East Germany, Bulgaria and Poland are all building ships and tankers for this Far Eastern fleet.

Nakhodka is the centre of Soviet Far Eastern international trade. No exact statistics of this trade are published in the Soviet Union. But Japan, Vietnam, the east European countries and occasionally Australia, are among the countries with which the port has trading or other connections. Supplies for Vietnam are shipped from Vladivostok and Nakhodka to Hayphong as well as along the Chinese railways to the Vietnam land frontier. Nakhodka also serves many north Pacific Soviet coastal ports, in the first place Nagayevo, and reinforced hulls have been installed on ships plying along this route.

Vrangel, on the opposite side of the Bay of Nakhodka (with which it is to be connected by road), is being constructed as a large deep-water port with equipment supplied by the Japanese, at an estimated cost of $45 million. Eventually its primary aim is to relieve congestion at Nakhodka; control of all cargo operations is to be automatic, and it will have the first specialised complex for the trans-shipment of coal in the Far East. Vrangel port is to be connected with the Suchan mines (now renamed Vostochnyy) by the first road and rail bridge in the Far East, now being constructed over the lower reacher of the Suchan river. Eight quays are to be built and much modern port machinery is to be installed. It is estimated that when this work is finished, Vrangel's handling capacity will be about half that of Nakhodka.

The third major port development scheme in the Soviet Far East is now in train in the big Sovetskaya Gavan' harbour, where the twin ports of Sovetskaya Gavan' and the new port of Vanino are situated. The Severnyy ship repair yard at Sovetskaya Gavan' is being expanded and modernised and two new floating docks added to its facilities, one of them built in Sweden. Vanino was selected as the terminal of the new ferry boat service between Kholmsk in Sakhalin and the mainland, across the Tatar Strait. After various constructional hitches, mainly at Vanino, the service was commissioned in June 1973. *Sakhalin I*, the first ferry boat to be operated on this line, was built in Leningrad and has a top speed of 18 knots. She is one of a new *Sakhalin* series of four ferries and is designed like an ice-breaker 'to withstand the heaviest ice conditions in the Tatar Strait'. *Sakhalin I* has a special, four-track railway deck and the passage of trains from land to ferry in this way is planned to eliminate the former laborious loading and unloading operation in Vanino. It can carry tractors and motor vehicles as well as passengers and other freight, and can make the 144 km. crossing in nine hours according to Soviet reports. Soviet sources estimate that economies in operating the ferry will amount to two million roubles annually and that the initial costs of construction will be recouped in about three years. It is too early to judge whether these optimistic prognostications will be justified. But the inauguration of this ferry service is another reflection of Moscow's interest in reinforcing the mainland links with Sakhalin and developing the island's economic resources. At the present time, however, it would not appear that the volume of traffic between Sakhalin and the mainland was such as to require this ferry boat service though, weather permitting, it should be a convenience for any train traffic from the mainland to Sakhalin.

The Sakhalin Shipping line is mainly concerned with coastal shipping but also conducts some foreign cargo business. The Ministry of the Merchant Marine plans to allocate 33 modern vessels to the line, including the four ferries which will operate on the Vanino–Kholmsk route. Other measures are aimed at bringing this remote island out of its former isolation, by establishing overseas trading links with foreign countries. There has been mention, for example, in Soviet sources of a Sakhalin-Australian shipping service.

Apart from being the mainland terminal of the Sakhalin train ferry, Vanino specialises in processed timber freight and has been equipped with an overhead timber handling installation. Vanino timber exports are expected to reach 2,500,000 cu.m. when all the new quays come into service. The port is also linked overland with the Amur railway through the branch line from Volochayevka (Khabarovsk) to Sovetskaya Gavan', and thus has an outlet to the wide ramifications westwards of the Trans-Siberian railway.

Smaller Far Eastern ports like Pos'yet, Slavyanka or Nagayevo have relatively poor facilities for handling passengers or cargo, though there are development plans for all of them in the offing or in train. Pos'yet, for example, is being equipped as a commercial port with new docks specialising in the handling of timber, oil and coke freight and Slavyanka, 10 km. from Pos'yet, is being organised to become the biggest ship repair base in the Soviet Far East, while Nagayevo, increasingly important as the port for Magadan city, now has a fourth berth commissioned in 1971 and is equipped with gantry cranes and automatic loaders and some other modern machinery.

Other ports or portlets along the Primor'ye and north Pacific coasts, are mostly engaged in the fishing industry. Soviet sources contain many complaints of inefficiency and delays in the Soviet Far Eastern ship-repair bases, as a result of which progress in the local fishing industry is often retarded. These difficulties are to a large extent caused by poor repair facilities, while big labour shortages arising from workers' dissatisfaction with living conditions and the high labour turn-over in the ship repair yards constantly disrupts their work.

Coastal shipping fulfils many functions in the areas of the Soviet Far East north of the operating radius of the Trans-Siberian railway and which are extremely important in view of the lack of adequate alternative communications between the north and the south of this huge area. Ice-breakers headed by the atomic ice-breaker, *Lenin* (out of service for some years, but reported to be operating again in 1972) are an essential seasonal adjunct of coastal shipping in these northern Pacific waters.

Coastal sea trips are a recent new attraction for Soviet Far Eastern citizens and are used to bring them into closer contact with the adjacent islands and their peoples. An annual cruise is organised from Vladivostok (but not available to non-Soviet citizens), in which high-lights are visits to Sakhalin, the hot springs and volcanic lands of Kamchatka and some of the major Kuril islands, including Shikotan, in dispute with Japan since it was seized by the Soviets after the last war. This cruise visits mink farms and archaeological remains in the Kurils and the little known Sedim Bay on the Amur delta, where Soviet guides recall that the Russians established a whale fishery in 1871.

All shipping along the Soviet Pacific coast and around the islands is controlled by the amalgamated Far Eastern Shipping Corporation. It was formed in 1964 from the Sakhalin, Far Eastern and Kamchatkan directorates, and has been very active subsequently in modernising its fleet, buying new ships and increasing the volume and range of its operations.

Air. Throughout Siberia and the Far Eastern region, the lack of rail and road communication is partly made good by the intensive penetration of even the most remote areas by aviation. Fares are relatively cheap and practically every inhabited hamlet has its airstrip and is linked with the main airlines radiating from local cities like Khabarovsk or Krasnoyarsk, and thus eventually connected with Moscow. As new industrial centres develop, there is a continuous expansion of airlines to serve them. Thus, Bratsk, for example, which had no air (or other means of transport) twenty years ago, is now linked by air with Moscow and Irkutsk as well as Ulan-Ude, Krasnoyarsk, Yakutsk, Mirnyy, Tomsk, Simferopol and other Russian towns. Regular passenger and mail services function normally in winter on the Moscow–Arctic routes, and throughout Northern Siberia and the Far East passenger transport is mostly by air. Seaplanes for geologists, fishermen and hunters were being introduced in 1970 in the north of the Krasnoyarsk kray, where lakes and rivers provide good landing facilities. There are also winter services operating from Khabarovsk to the Tatar Straits and the coasts of the Sea of Okhotsk, while direct flights between Vladivostok and Magadan were being planned in 1972. And it is reported that aircraft, Il-62s, carry nine times as many passengers on the Khabarovsk–Moscow route as the railways. Further north, in Chukotka, helicopters are extensively used where the terrain does not provide safe or suitable landing grounds for planes. The first MI-6 helicopter 'the biggest in service anywhere',[7] and used mainly for large items of freight, flew over the Pevek–Bilibino route in 1970 and should be most useful to this remote mining area. Other helicopters are also in use in the north, notably the MI-8 and the smaller MI-4.

Apart from its network of domestic airlines, Siberia is now of international air significance through the so-called 'Siberian Air Corridor'. This has come about as a result of international agreements between Aero-flot, Air-France, Japan, U.K. and Scandinavian Air Lines, signed in 1970, on the joint operation of the new Paris–Moscow–Yokyo service. This route across Siberia is operated by these companies, each of them making two flights a week (in 1972). The new service saves four hours, compared with the route over the North Pole, and takes about $10\frac{1}{4}$ hours. The Russian equipment used is the TU-114 128 passenger turbo-prop plane. Moscow would certainly also be interested in flying Moscow–Tokyo and beyond, while tapping the west-European market for its Siberian corridor and entering the Trans-Pacific route to the U.S. west coast from Tokyo.

Among other aviation developments in the Far East, the construction of a new air terminal at Komsomol'sk, with 'all passenger amenities', to take some of the air cargo pressure off Khabarovsk may be noted. The airport aimed to be operational according to plan in 1973 and Il-18, TV-114 are among the aircraft which can land there.

The Northern Sea Route.[8] Though it plays a relatively small part today in the Siberian transport system, mention must finally be made of

[7] cf. T. Armstrong. ISEGR Occasional Papers, no. 2. October 1970, University of Alaska, p. 15.
[8] This section is substantially based on two authoritative works by Dr. T. Armstrong: *The*

the Northern Sea Route in view of its unique position in the Arctic, its romantic origins and the great efforts of heroic sea captains who contributed to its achievement over the centuries. This is the route that connects Vladivostok with Murmansk through the perilous waters of the Arctic.

The Northern Sea Route (as it is known today) originated in the sixteenth-century attempts of British mariners to find a north-east passage to Cathay and did not then get beyond the Kara Sea. They were followed by other sea captains of many nations, apart from the Russians, who edged their way to the estuaries of the Ob' and the Yenisey and eventually, towards the end of the nineteenth century, the northern passage was covered to its eastern extremity at the Bering strait by A. E. Nordenskiöld in the *Vega*.

A considerable trade in Siberian exports of timber, bristles, butter and other local produce and in imports of foreign goods for inhabitants of the lower reaches of these Siberian rivers, the Ob', the Yenisey, the Lena and the Kolyma, was built up before the 1917 revolution. Progress was also made under the Tsarist government on navigational aids and the study of ice conditions, in the Arctic.

Subsequently, the Soviet government showed great interest in developing the route as 'a usable waterway'. Money was generously expended on Arctic scientific research, floating ice-stations, improving charts and providing ice-breakers to escort ships using the route. As a result of all this work, it has been proved possible to make the through passage from either end in one short summer season. But it is officially regarded as still more practicable at present to divide the passage into two sections. Thus, ships are sent eastwards from Murmansk to the Yenisey estuary, where metallurgical products from Noril'sk and timber from Igarka can be collected, and westwards from Vladivostok to the mouth of the Kolyma river and Pevek and further West, where isolated communities have to be supplied with necessary goods and mining products despatched.

A large flotilla of ice-breakers (of which the flagship is the atomic ice-breaker *Lenin* (with 44,000 h.p., the second largest in the world) regularly escorts these vessels to their respective destinations. As a result of continuous research into the behaviour of the sea-ice in the Arctic and the reinforcement of the Soviet ice-breaker fleet, the Arctic 'season' has been lengthened to four months and sometimes even more, according to weather conditions.

In spite of the navigation skills and aids developed by Soviet scientists, 'the service area of the Northern Sea Route has tended steadily to diminish' in Dr. Armstrong's opinion. It has been eroded, as he notes, by the enormous growth of air transport and by the extension of the rail link to the Lena river (at Ust'-Kut). It is mostly used to serve isolated settlements remote from the rivers Ob', Yenisey and Lena, all of which are now intersected by the railroad.

This situation might have been dramatically changed if the Soviet proposals, put forward in 1967, to introduce an international service between European ports and Japan *via* the Northern Sea Route had been adopted. In fact, they met with no

Northern Sea Route. Soviet Exploration of the North East Passage. Cambridge University Press. 1952. *Soviet Northern Development, With Some Alaskan Parallels and Contrasts.* ISEGR Papers No. 2. October 1970. University of Alaska.

response from foreign firms in either Japan or Europe, who were obviously reluctant to enter this hazardous unknown seaway without cargo ships specially strengthened to cope with Arctic conditions, in spite of the Soviet assurance of navigation aids and the shortened time and reduced costs of using the Route. There is a considerable difference among experts as to whether economic or strategic aims predominate in determining the large Soviet expenditure which has gone into improving the Route. Both have, undoubtedly, largely influenced Noscom's decisions on this matter over the years.

chapter ten

Population and Labour Problems

The most striking feature of the population situation in Siberia and the Far Eastern Region is the disparity between the enormous land-mass of this territory (12,766,000 sq. km.) and its relatively insignificant population of 25,354,000. Thus, east Siberia and the Soviet Far East alone, which form more than half the entire territory of the Soviet Union, contain little more than 10% of its population. Some idea of its size may be gauged from the fact that Yakutiya alone is larger than India (pop. 500 million) but has a population of only 664,000.

The Population of Siberia and the Soviet Far Eastern Region
(According to the Soviet censuses of 1959 and 1970)

	1959	1970	Increase 1959/1970 in %
West Siberia	11,252,000	12,110,000	8
East Siberia	6,473,000	7,464,000	15
Soviet Far East	4,834,000	5,780,000	19.6
USSR	208,827,000	241,748,000	15.8

Between the 1959 and 1970 censuses, the share of both east and west Siberia and the Soviet Far East in the total Soviet population declined as a result of the continuing heavy exodus of workers to other parts of the Soviet Union. In these three regions, both the natural increase and the birth rate, which had been far higher than the respective Soviet averages pre-1959, fell heavily between 1960–70. In west Siberia, the natural increase declined from 20.9 per thousand in 1950, to 7.6 per thousand in 1967, and was below the respective Soviet average natural increase of 9.8 per thousand. In the same period, the west Siberian birth rate fell from 32 per thousand, to 14.8 per thousand, also below the Soviet average rate of 17.4 per thousand. The fall in the birth rate in the Soviet Far Eastern region was even more dramatic, from 42.5 per thousand in 1950 (by far the highest in the Soviet Union), to 16.7 per thousand in 1967. Nevertheless, the population growth in the Soviet Far East while still below the numbers required to work the region's farms and industries, increased above the Soviet average (15.8%) between 1959–70, by 19.6%.

These trends run contrary to Moscow's demographic aims for Siberia, which were reflected in the exuberant prognostications of Soviet demographic experts in the fifties and early sixties that Siberia would need, and reach, a population of some

A Nganasan reindeer breeder
(Taymyr National Okrug)

80,000,000 by 1980 or 1990, to provide the labour necessary to execute the major economic plans. Little is now heard of these optimistic population estimates. The huge Far Eastern region, for example, almost as big as Australia, had a population of only 5,780,000 in 1970, while the adjacent island of Sakhalin lost over 30,000 of its people in the inter-census period, in spite of the efforts to attract migrants, by playing down its atrocious climate, and the rapid rise in population after its annexation by the Soviet Union in 1945.

The Siberian population is very unevenly distributed. The southern areas are most thickly populated and the average density varies greatly even between north and south of the same region. This is notably so in the case of the Tyumen' and Irkutsk oblast and the Krasnoyarsk kray. In fact, the inflow of millions of settlers to the land and towns of Siberia, resulting from the impulse given to the opening up of the country by the completion of the Trans-Siberian railway at the beginning of the twentieth century and which continued to the outbreak of World War I, now shows a steady reverse trend, with Siberian migration deficits in recent years. This has happened in a period when settlers were urgently needed to operate the new enterprises of the expanding Siberian economy.

A constant feature of both Tsarist and Soviet Siberian colonisation policies has been the restriction of recruitment of migrants to their own peoples, mostly from European Russia, and peasants. In this, Russia's policies sharply differ from the American multiracial 'open door' policies, as a result of which millions of skilled and unskilled agricultural and industrial workers from Russia, Poland, Italy, Germany, Britain, Ireland, Scandinavia, etc., settled in America in the nineteenth–twentieth century, thereby enriching its thrusting young economy with their manifold skills.

Not surprisingly, the harsh climate of the Far North for long confined the population to the small numbers of the native peoples. But with the development of mining in such Far Northern areas as Noril'sk, the Kolyma gold fields and Chukotka for example, the population, largely consisting now of Russian and other non-native workers, has increased round these industrial enterprises. The same thing has happened in the former wilderness of north Tyumen' with the discovery there of its important oil and gas reserves.

Urbanisation and the rapid growth of certain big cities, old and new, is a characteristic of Siberia's population (as indeed of the Soviet Union as a whole).

Population of Some Siberian Towns

	1939	1970
Angarsk	—	204,000
Bratsk	—	155,000
Irkutsk	250.000	451,000
Krasnoyarsk	190,000	648,000
Magadan	27,000	92,000
Noril'sk	14,000	136,000
Novosibirsk	404,000	1,161,000
Omsk	289,000	821,000
Tyumen'	79,000	269,000
Yakutsk	53.000	108,000

A Frontier Guard looking
eastward towards Alaska from
Chukotka on the Bering Strait

There are many other places like Bratsk which in 1939, before the hydroelectric station and its associated industries were built, were only tiny hamlets and are now becoming fair-sized cities. The adverse aspect of this increasing urbanisation is the sharply diminishing rural population, which has poured into many of the towns in search of better living conditions and wages. The labour for the new oil and gas industries of north Tyumen', for example, has to a large extent been recruited from the south Tyumen' agricultural areas which are now themselves suffering from a severe lack of workers. In some years the net outflow of the rural population in west Siberia has been as great as 50%, exceeding the total natural increase, and these migrants were mostly young people from age groups best suited to agricultural work.

Since the annexation of Siberia by Russia in the seventeenth century, the Russian population has increased to such an extent that it has long outnumbered the various small pockets of native peoples scattered throughout the territory from the Urals to the Pacific.[1] Thus racially, as well as politically and culturally, Siberia today is essentially a Russian land.

The crucial population problem in Siberia and the Soviet Far East is the 'flight of labour', a Soviet phrase denoting mobility of workers anywhere in the Soviet Union but of particular relevance to the position throughout Siberia and the Soviet Far East. Since the closure of the big concentration camps which ran the main construction-mining sites in the harsh northern areas of this territory in the fifties, and the abolition of the drastic laws prohibiting workers from leaving their jobs voluntarily under pain of the severest penalties, this exodus from east to west has become the 'scourge' of Siberia's economic development.

While official pronouncements regularly stress the need for immigrants, the exodus of Siberian workers to the more attractive southern areas of the Soviet Union continued throughout the sixties. An investigation by the Siberian Department of the all-Union Academy of Sciences, revealed a very high percentage of departures from the north Tyumen' oil fields, 56% from the Surgut oil industry and 87% from that of Nefteurgansk, while west Siberia as a whole was estimated to have lost 350,000 workers between 1959 and 1967. This 'flight of labour' causes considerable disruption of work plans and is very costly to the State amounting to 75–80 millions of roubles annually according to one Soviet source and much more according to others, owing to the high costs of moving and settling migrants. Some Soviet experts believe this money would be better spent on improving housing and amenities. Against this background, the prospects of getting the millions of migrants required to operate the big development schemes in Siberia and the Far East to the end of the century are not promising.

Labour for Siberia and the Soviet Far East is recruited and directed to specific agricultural and industrial enterprises by *Ognabor*, the R.S.F.S.R. Central Directorate for Resettlement and the Organised Recruitment of Workers and its branches at local levels. Workers who want to participate in this 'voluntary' organised

[1] For details of the population of the native areas and peoples cf. following section of this chapter.

migration conclude working contracts at their places of domicile and registration and receive free passages to their new place of work and the promise of 'accommodation in hostels on arrival' among other concessions. Labour contracts concluded by men and women from 18 years of age, are for one to five years, according to the location of the enterprise and its needs of production. On completion of the contract, these workers receive a return passage home for themselves and their families. Notices are frequently broadcast regarding the recruitment of labour for settlement in the Far East and the advantages offered to intending migrants. One such notice was broadcast at the end of 1972 to attract settlers for the Maritime kray. It stated that migrants would be granted subsidies and provided with 'well-appointed housing' and household plots at the place of settlement. It was later reported that these settlers would be coming from the Krasnodar kray and Yaroslavl, Penza and Ryazan' oblasts. The sequel to these often unrealistic advertisements, especially in regard to the promised housing, must be regarded as disappointing, as long as the flight of labour continues in the Far East.

Apart from largely ineffective verbal exhortations, the responsible ministries and other state agencies involved must devote closer, more practical, attention to this problem if it is to be solved and must give heed to the mass of expert and well informed local opinion on the subject, which up to date has been largely ignored. The Twenty-fourth Party Congress once more voiced the Government's long-term aim of settling stable cadres of workers, especially skilled workers, in Siberia and the Far East. But so far this policy has been to a large extent foiled by the continuing exodus of both skilled and unskilled workers.

The unanimous verdict of Soviet experts is that the high level of the 'flight of labour' from Siberia and the Far Eastern region is caused by the low living standards, especially in housing, the irregularity of food and other necessary supplies, and their high cost, and the inadequate provision of cultural-service requirements, e.g. schools, hospitals, shops, in many of the newer towns and industrial settlements. The food situation was graphically illustrated in a report by *The Times* correspondent who visited four towns, in eastern Siberia and the Soviet Far East in 1970. 'I saw no meat in any official shops', he reported, 'except for frozen (animal) heads and lungs and sometimes sausage for which there were long queues. There was proper meat in the markets but it was very expensive and there, too, there were queues.' (*The Times* 18.12.1970)

In order to attract workers of all categories to the construction sites and other jobs in Siberia, the Government has passed a number of measures providing for wage increments, extra leave and other privileges, for workers in the Far North and other places in Siberia and the Soviet Far East, where conditions were much more rigorous and food and other necessities more expensive than in European Russia. A stupid mistake was made in 1960 when the previous coefficients of wages in the northern areas were abolished. Soviet experts calculated that the abolition of the northern allowance in 1960 diminished real wages to about the same level as those in the Central European area of the Soviet Union. The result was an increased exodus of workers, which reached 30–35% annually in some regions, such as Magadan oblast. It was particularly high in the construction and timber industries.

The majority of those departing were young people and workers who had spent up to a year in the North and included mainly qualified specialists.

Dr. Terence Armstrong gave a first-hand description of the problems created by these cuts when he visited Yakutsk in 1967 (on the eve of their abolition). 'Evidence was not lacking that these increases were urgently required. One resident in Yakutsk told me that the extra pay he received was virtually all spent on the higher cost of living. By this he meant not only more fuel, heavier clothes and higher prices on the kolkhoz market but also the increased price of "brand" items in the shops. I had thought that these items were sold at the same prices throughout the country, but he told me that there was about a 10% increase in Yakutsk. As a result, many would-be immigrants had either left or never come. This was especially true of skilled people. Clearly no major progress has been made in improving amenities for northern workers (this was to have been the compensation for the 1960 cut in extra pay).' (*Polar Record*, No. 89. 1968)

This unsatisfactory situation was partly retrieved by the decree of 1967. It restored the privileges abolished for the northern territories in 1960 and extended them to various categories of workers formerly excluded and also to southern areas of Siberia and the Far East equated to the north, but not previously eligible for these benefits. Further allowances followed in 1969 to improve conditions for migrants. The latest measure dealing with wages in Siberia was passed by the Supreme Soviet in 1972; it established a minimum wage of R.70 a month, with a simultaneous increase in the wages and salaries of medium-paid workers in the production branches, and these scales were to be introduced first of all in the Far North. In 1973, the new wage conditions are to be introduced for blue and white collar workers in industry and other production branches in all the areas of the Far North, Siberia and Urals. At the time of writing, the information available about these new wage conditions is too vague to warrant any assessment of how far they provide a solution to the regional labour problem. The discrepancies between industrial production and workers' amenities still requiring reform were squarely stated by a Yakut deputy to the Supreme Soviet in December 1972. Having recalled that in recent years Yakutiya had considerably strengthened its construction base and completed various productive enterprises, he continued: 'The rate of construction of dwellings lags behind the rapid rate of development of the productive forces of the Republic. The lack of accommodation and cultural service amenities leads to the flight of labour.'

A basic defect of all the Siberian incentives to date, in terms of wage increments and regional coefficients, is the lack of correspondence between them and the actual cost of living in different places. In fact, Soviet agencies responsible for fixing wages and coefficients are, in the view of a leading Soviet specialist, 'badly acquainted with comparative standards of living and even real wages in various places ... The Siberian exodus is due to the region's backwardness in living standards, compared with other areas of the country. To establish a basic level of real wages in the eastern regions, it is necessary to estimate the additional expenses of the population connected with the natural conditions, relatively weak transport system, enormous distances, miserable conditions for holidays at times of regular leave, and the necessity in many cases of journeys for rest and cures to remote western regions'.

A mass of material in the Soviet press and other sources reflects local dissatis-faction with living standards, the discrepancies between real and nominal wages, and the total inadequacy of even the increased differentials of 1967–68 to meet local costs of food, clothing, heating and other necessities.[2] The root of this trouble was revealed some years ago, in the calculations made by N. P. Kalinovskiy regarding real and nominal wages in Siberia and the Far East. His conclusions were that 'a person would have to spend 41 per cent more on food, 47 per cent more on clothing, 16 times as much on heating outlays, and more than twice as much on transportation (including holiday trips to European resorts) to attain the same level of material comfort as in the Centre.'

This statement is limited to personal expenditure. Siberian citizens in many of the new towns which have arisen around major construction sites in Angarsk, Bratsk and such like places, also suffer great hardship from the lack of adequate public services: schools, hospitals and other necessary social amenities, for which no level of wages can compensate. This situation was analysed in detail in a revealing study by the Chairman of the Irkutsk *obkom* Planning Commission, P. P. Silinskiy, who laid the blame for it on the cuts imposed mainly by *Gosplan* R.S.F.S.R., and by other Central State agencies in the budgetary estimates submitted for these purposes, especially in the new towns, by the local planning authorities. The result was that it was financially impossible to proceed with the necessary construction programme to provide housing and other amenities for the workers. It seems per-missible to conclude that similar cuts by the Central agencies such as *Gosplan* may be responsible elsewhere in Siberia for the inadequacy of housing and other amenities.

A few concrete examples, of how workers in different parts of Siberia are affected by these failures to live up to official promises of social services, may better illustrate the present situation as seen by those directly concerned. 'There is a decree but there is no living accommodation' heads a signed letter from a group concerned with conditions in the town of Yeniseysk (*Pravda* 29.7.1971). Recalling the instruc-tions of the Twenty-fourth Congress of the C.P.S.U. to develop housing and improve social-cultural conditions at accelerated rates, so as to encourage a further flow of immigrants to the Far East and eastern Siberia, they complained that the construction of housing at the Maklakovo-Yenisey timber industrial complex re-mained and remains behind industrial construction: 'The colophony-resin factory should begin production next year and will then require 400 workers. But where are they to live? Miserable sums for housing have been allotted by the Ministry of the Cellulose-Paper Industry of the U.S.S.R.'. It was also stated in this letter that in another local plant some hundreds of additional qualified workers were needed. 'But there is no housing for them.' The ineffectiveness of central orders was clearly reflected in this situation, which remained unchanged in spite of a special Ministerial order, specifically aimed at improving living conditions in this Yeniseysk industrial complex.

[2] Readers interested in a fuller analysis of these regional differentials are referred to Paul Dibb's work:*Siberia and the Pacific* Praeger, London. 1972, to which I am also indebted.

Another letter in *Pravda* (16.11.68) voiced the grievances of the citizens 'wearing out the doorsteps' of the repair shops in their fruitless efforts to get their various domestic appliances repaired, and the bureaucratic attitude of some Soviet officials to their complaints.

In yet another case quoted by *Pravda*, a badly needed poultry factory near Tomsk could not be operated because no steps were taken to provide a workers' settlement although it was intended to employ 400 workers there. The reason was not uncommon: 'The Ministry of Agriculture is doing nothing about financing the housing'. In fact, workers' housing more often than not still has a low priority in the official budgetary allocations to construction sites throughout Siberia

To quote Silinskiy again: 'People who construct new industrial complexes, new towns and workers' settlements, build roads, clear the taiga, require well-built houses, schools and children's institutions, shops, cultural-domestic and medical institutions. . . . But this is seriously obstructed by the erroneous method of planning productive, housing and cultural-domestic construction in areas of new development. All of this must be created in a coordinated scheme (a complex) with productive construction'. But what actually happens, to the great detriment of non-productive construction (as housing etc., is termed), is that productive and non-productive construction are planned by separate bodies with no coordination, while inadequate capacity in the construction organisation often means that housing and social requirements have a low priority. As a result of this 'irrational' system, the construction of factories and plants gets started before there is proper provision for workers' housing or other amenities.

The emphasis in this survey on the population-labour problems of Siberia and the causes of the costly flight of labour throughout the territory must not be interpreted as meaning that no decent housing exists in this region, but rather as showing the inadequacies of Soviet policy on this crucial problem. The larger Siberian cities certainly contain big blocks of the usual type of housing, adequate if unattractive and familiar to all acquainted with the drab urban buildings of Moscow or Leningrad. But the economic future of Siberia lies increasingly in the new industrial sites being carved out of formerly uninhabited places in the taiga and even the tundra of the Far North. The need to retain a stable labour force to develop these new resources of energy and minerals by suitable housing and other public amenities is, therefore, obviously of exceptional importance.

It is encouraging to note that a few of the latest Soviet Siberian industrial projects have mentioned in their publicity that a workers' settlement would be built in advance of the actual production plant. If this becomes general practice, it would mean a basic change in the old government priorities and inevitably go far to solve the present labour problem, in Siberia.

chapter eleven

Relations with the Native Peoples of Siberia

Groups of native peoples are to be found widely dispersed throughout Siberia and the Soviet Far East. They differ greatly in numbers and linguistic-cultural traditions, the strongest numerically and culturally being the Yakuts and the Buryats, the Altaytsy and the Khakasy. Together they form one of the most varied and fascinating ethnic mosaics in the world.

Soviet policies towards these peoples, since 1917, aimed at completely supplanting the régime prevailing under Tsardom, which was indiscriminately condemned for its 'greed and corruption'. Lenin's words regarding the 'patriarchal, semi-wild and even actual wildness' of the non-Russian population of Siberia provided guidelines for shaping the Soviet attitude to their traditional social organisation and customs.

While there was a good deal of truth in the Soviet charges of rapacious exploitation of the Siberian natives by Tsarist officials, in the collection of the *yasak* or fur tribute, and the predatory practices of the Russian traders in the Siberian fur business and their responsibility for introducing drunkenness and disease among these peoples, certain more positive aspects of the Tsarist administration need mention to complete the pre-Soviet picture. In the first place, there was no attempt to destroy the 'internal autonomy' of the natives and they thus enjoyed a large measure of self-rule through their tribal organisation of justice and other matters in their usually small social units. The Speranskiy 'Statute for the administration of natives' (1822)[1] which remained in force until the Soviet revolution, aimed specifically at protecting the natives from official or other Russian exploitation. Unfortunately, owing to the corruption of Tsarist officialdom, it was virtually a dead letter from its inception. Unlike other colonial masters, the Russians were entirely lacking in racial prejudice towards the Siberian natives and marriage between the races was frequent. But very little was done for native education or medical care under the Tsarist régime (which in fact did little better for millions of its own Russian peasants). Still, it is to its credit that it did not interfere with the traditional native pattern of life and left the social organisation based on the clan intact, coexisting in a type of

---

[1] For a fuller treatment of this subject cf. Dr. T. Armstrong's *Russian Settlement in the North*: Parts I and II. Cambridge 1965. It is impossible to deal adequately with this complex subject here.

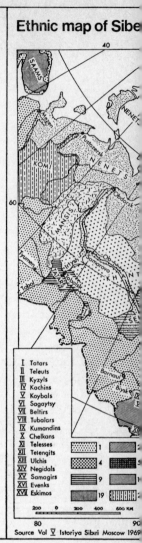

Ethnic map of Sibe

Peoples of the Slavonic language group: 1 Russians (and Kamchadaly). *Peoples of the Turcic language group:* 2 Altaytsy (Altay kizhi, Teleutiy, Tubalary, Kumandintsy, Chelkantsy, Teleky, Telengity); 3 Shortsy; 4 Khakasy (Kyzyl'tsy, Kachintsy, Koybaly, Sagaytsy, Bel'tiry) and Chulymtsy; 5 Tuvintsy; 6 Tofalary; 7 Yakuty; 8 Dolgany; 9 Siberian Tatary. *Peoples of the Mongolian language group:* 10 Buryats. *Peoples of the Tungus-Manchu language group:* 11 Evenki; 12 Negidaltsy; 13 Eveny; 14 Nanaytsy (and Samagiry); 15 Ul'chi, 16 Oroki; 17 Udegeytsy; 18 Orochi. *Peoples of Finnish language group:* 19 Saamy; 20 Komi. *Peoples of the Ugorskiy language group:* 21 Mansi; 22 Khanty. *Peoples of the Samoyed language group:* Nentsy; 24 Entsy; 25 Nganasany; 26 Sel'kupy. *Peoples of the Eskimo-Aleut language group:* 27 Eskimos; 28 Aleuts. *Peoples of other language groups:* 29 Chukchi; 30 Koryaki; 31 Itel'meny (North-east Paleo-Asiatics); 32 Yukagiry; 33 Nivkhi; 34 Kety; 35 Ainu; 36 Uninhabited places.

Source Vol V Istoriya Sibiri Moscow 1969

indirect rule, for administrative purposes with the Imperial Russian administration. In some cases, this native organisation had reached a high social level for regulating problems within the clan and in relations with other clans. It certainly did not merit, in the case of the Tungus (Evenk), for example, the derogatory epithets of 'primitive' and 'dark' applied to it by Soviet ethnographers, largely, it would seem, to justify its destruction by the Soviet régime.

The 'Declaration of Rights of the Peoples of Russia' issued soon after the 1917 Revolution, including the right to 'free development of national minorities and national groups' also applied in theory to the native peoples of Siberia, who knew nothing of 'the power of the landlords' or the 'power of the autocratic generals',

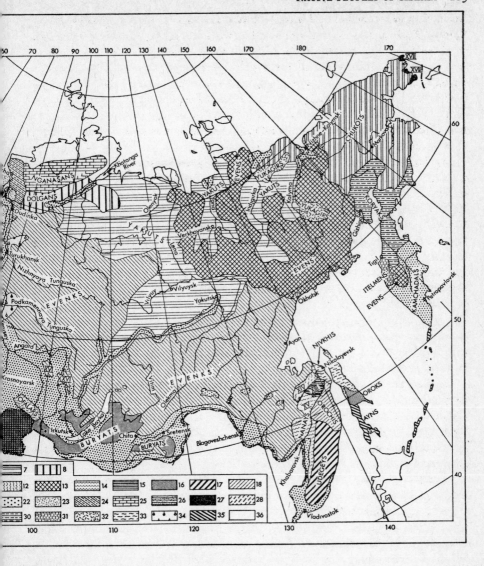

from which the workers and peasants in other parts of the country, were 'freeing themselves'. From the time of the establishment of Soviet power, the Bolsheviks were, however, busy with many measures to overcome the cultural-economic backwardness of the Siberian native peoples and the elimination of much in their traditional way of life, which differed from European Russian and especially Soviet-socialist standards. There was never any question of them developing 'freely' according to their own lights and traditions.

In the first place, an intensive campaign was waged against the general illiteracy of these peoples and their ignorance of modern medicine. Only the Yakuts and the Buryats were to some extent literate and had a certain sense of national identity.

But new alphabets had to be devised by Soviet linguists for the scriptless peoples of Siberia. These alphabets were first based on the Latin script, but this was changed to Cyrillic in 1937. School books had then to be provided and schools built to educate native children. As so many of these peoples were still nomadic, the *internat,* or boarding school, was the type of school favoured by the Soviet authorities, though it was not at all popular with the native parents, who were suspicious of the long and unusual separation from their children that it involved. There were also some nomadic schools which taught illiterate parents as well as their children, and also gave simple instruction in personal hygiene.

The formulation of these new Soviet cultural-educational policies was complicated by the extremely intricate, ethnic-linguistic basis of the many small groups of Siberian peoples and their different levels of advancement. The methods adopted for the more primitive peoples may be exemplified from the experience of the Chukchi, one of the smaller and originally most illiterate of the group. It is obviously impossible here to deal separately with the various individual peoples. Before the Revolution, the Chukchi were entirely illiterate with the exception of the few who had attended the one Chukchi school at Uelen. These would have been taught in Russian, as there was no written Chukchi until after the Revolution, when Soviet scholars created a Chukchi script. From the formation of the Chukchi National Okrug (District) in 1930, schools began to spread, apart from the cultural bases which were mainly intended for adults. By 1951, there were 84 middle, seven-year and primary schools in the Okrug, teaching about a thousand children as well as *internats* for more than 1,200 pupils.

Teachers for the increasing numbers of schools in Chukotka have been trained for years now at the Anadyr Pedagogical Institute, where many of the students are Chukchi boys and girls. The Khabarovsk Pedagogical Institute and the Herzen Pedagogical Institute also train teachers for Chukotka. Since the middle fifties, individual Chukchis have made the grade to be admitted to a Soviet university and some have studied in Leningrad University, or other universities nearer home.

Yakutsk University, founded in 1956, as a training college in the heart of this native territory, is now a recognised university, with some 4,000 students and an enlarged curriculum offering courses in medicine, agriculture, geology, civil engineering, etc. It attracts many native Siberian as well as Russian students. More than 60% of the specialists trained at Yakutsk University in the sixties belonged to the native peoples of the Yakut A.S.S.R. Further east, at Ola on the bleak shores of the Sea of Okhotsk, in Magadan oblast, there is a school specialising in various branches of animal husbandry peculiar to the region, such as reindeer herding, and mainly intended for native breeders such as the Koryaki and the Chukchis.

Special facilities exist to encourage children of Northern ethnic groups like the Chukchis or the Yakuts to continue their education after school. Thus, native students who get a passing out 'C' grade at school may be accepted at a university, without entering the usual competition compulsory for all other students. Russian is the language of instruction at Siberian universities and often causes difficulties for native students, educated up to university level in their native tongue. In order to overcome this problem, they are given special training in the Russian language on entering the university. These students also receive a northern bonus in addition to free board, housing and medical care, like workers in the North.

Tribute is frequently paid by the Soviet press to notable instances of cultural achievements by individual Siberian natives. Thus, when a Chukchi or other member of this group makes the grade as a pilot, an engineer, or in some other profession, a photograph of the successful character accompanied by a laudatory caption will appear in one or other of the metropolitan newspapers, to encourage others to do likewise.

In line with the advance in literacy, many Russian books and translations have been published in Chukchi (and of course also in the other Siberian languages). According to Soviet sources more than 4,000,000 copies of books were published in the last 30 years, for example, in the Chukchi language, though how much this grand total consisted of original works, how much of the usual preponderance of Marx-Leninist texts, in translations, was not stated. A local newspaper *Soviet Chukotka* is published in Chukchi and Russian (no copies of which are available in the west, because of the general Soviet ban on subscriptions to any daily papers issued in Siberia). The Soviet communist propaganda organ *Blotnot Agitatora* (Notebook of the Agitator) is also published in both languages. One Chukchi writer, Yuri Rytkheu, has achieved all-Union recognition from his articles and stories published in Russian in the top level literary journals *Novyy Mir*, *Ogonëk* and the Moscow daily press. He accompanied the Canadian author Farley Mowat on his Far Eastern trip as guide and interpreter and later visited Canada, where the impression given was of a Chukchi with a veneer of western sophistication and a hard drinker. Only one generation literate, Rytkheu likes to expound the blessings brought by Soviet civilisation to his people and also to recall the simple illiterate existence of his parents and his childhood near Uelen, in Chukotka.

The Soviet policies for the promotion of literacy and education in the native areas of Siberia had their counterpart in the field of public health. During the Tsarist period, the Siberian native peoples for the most part relied on the exotic ministrations of the Shamans (a sort of witch-doctor, or sorcerer, often with hypnotic powers) in case of illness and epidemics, e.g. smallpox, or influenza, which took such a heavy toll of lives when they struck a district. This situation soon engaged the attention of the Bolsheviks. Even in such remote areas as Yakutiya and Chukotka, feldshers, or partly trained medical assistants, were sent out to teach simple practices of hygiene and first aid, while hospitals were little by little set up throughout the native areas. Having been so long accustomed to the Shamanistic magical rites, the Siberian peoples at first shunned western medicine through ignorance and fear. But when the Shamans were at last publicly driven out of business by Soviet officialdom (they long survived the official ban clandestinely and may even now continue to exist to a relatively small extent), the new medicine was gradually accepted and its efficacy in wiping out the former dreaded epidemics was recognised.

Education and public health were thus among the most positive aspects of the new Soviet policies in the native areas of Siberia. The other policies, aimed at a drastic 'reform' of the traditional native economy, were much more controversial and from the beginning ran into stiff opposition from all the Siberian native peoples. This was particularly the case among the northern peoples whose economy was based solely on reindeer herding, trapping and hunting. The Soviet decision to collectivise the reindeer herds and settle their nomadic owners in villages (for abstract ideological reasons) ran directly contrary to the proper conduct of reindeer herding, which requires pasturing over vast areas of tundra. Owing to widespread uprisings and disturbances among the peoples concerned, this 'reform' was not completed until the early fifties. These irrational collectivisation policies were often enforced by incompetent and brutal non-native officials, sent into the native areas to enforce the law: to a large extent their conduct intensified the bitter native resentment against this economic 'reform'. Collectivisation brought immense hardship to the reindeer peoples who, in many cases, preferred to slaughter their animals rather than have them collectivised and be themselves denomadised. Denomadisation involved settlement in Russian-type villages where they could no longer live in their mobile huts, such as the *yarangi* of the Chukchi and the Eskimo (possibly unhygienic but in many ways preferred by them as nomadic herders) and which they had used for centuries.

It took more than a decade for Moscow to recognise the folly of enforcing its collectivisation policy in northern Siberia, against the general local opposition and the injury done to the peoples concerned. Eventually a more rational approach was adopted and a modified system of collectivisation, better adjusted to partial nomadic pasturing of the herds in the tundra, was introduced.

From the late fifties, reindeer herding has become a new source of income for the native breeders, in areas where mining is being developed. The influx of miners to the Far North from European Russia and other parts of Siberia, needing a western diet, popularised reindeer meat as the only source of protein available and good prices are paid for it. Reindeer are also hired as pack animals, both by miners and geological expeditions, where other transport is scarce. As a result of these improved conditions, the herds have been increasing. In the Far Eastern region alone, the home of such big breeders as the Chukchi, the Koryaki and the Yakuts, there were 1,345,300 reindeer in 1970 compared to 1,147,600 in 1961. But this increase has not yet reached the 2 million of 1929, before the disastrous impact of forced collectivisation.

Apart from the traditional occupations of reindeer herding and trapping wild animals, it is difficult to ascertain to what extent the Siberian native peoples work in mining, or the other new industries now being developed in their homelands. The published information is both unsatisfactory and extremely meagre and is mostly confined to general trends. Though mining dominates the industrial production of Yakutiya, it appears that the Yakuts only form a small percentage of the mining workers though, exceptionally, they form a high percentage of the diamond mining workers.

One Soviet explanation of this situation is that the gold, tin, mercury mines and the diamond industry have arisen far from the main areas inhabited by the native populations, while the collective and state farms of these areas themselves experience an acute lack of workers. This explanation is not entirely convincing. It could be that the reason why some of the native peoples apparently do not engage to any extent in mining or other industrial enterprises is simply that they prefer their traditional occupations, or that, on the other hand, they do not easily master the use of complicated mining and other industrial equipment. The fact that the native peoples were not eligible for the special rates of pay in northern industry until 1960 (the situation subsequently is not quite clear) may also have been a deterrent to their participation in mining, not at best an attractive occupation.

The First Secretary of the Yakut *obkom* referred to this question at the Twenty-fourth Party Congress in 1971 in typically vague terms which nevertheless should be quoted: 'The Far North is also inhabited by many native peoples. Together with those engaged in traditional branches of the economy, they actively participate in industrial production, industrial labour. Now Yakuts, Evenki, Eveni, Chukchi, Yukagiry and others with all the Soviet peoples are moving in one system to the heights of communism.' This statement does not contribute much to a precise analysis of the situation, nor does a study by the Siberian Department of the Academy published in 1970. The information concerned the percentage of national cadres engaged in the various branches of industry in Yakutiya in 1963. Accordingly, 10% were engaged in industry and 76% in agriculture, the latter a rise from 43% in 1950. No indication was given of the nature of this industry, or whether it was mining or not, nor of the position after 1963. Since the opening up of the west Siberian oil-gas industry, references occasionally appear in Soviet sources to the participation of the Khanty-Mansi and other local native people. But the information given is also very vague and no statistics of numbers have been noticed. References to them are sometimes found in *Neftyanik* (the official journal of the oil-gas ministry). Thus: 'The multi-national working force in west Siberia also includes the native peoples. A Khanty-Mansi [of whom an illustration was published] who came from a fishing village of the Far North, mastered the complex equipment of the oil industry, with the aid of experienced workers ... Sons and grandsons of hunters, sleigh-drivers not even able to sign their names, now drive through the taiga not harnessed reindeer but powerful bulldozers and work in exploration parties, on oil pipeline routes, on derricks, equally with all who participate in developing the reserves of this very rich area and its "pearl" Samotlor.' (No. 11,1972) While it is impossible without much precise information to decide how far this native participation in industry goes, in either west Siberia or the Far East, there is clearly some participation.

All the major industrial enterprises throughout the native areas of Siberia, such as the Kolyma goldfields or the Chukotsk tin and gold mines, are administered by remote control by the relevant all-Union ministries and agencies, like *Gosplan* and *Gosstroy* in Moscow, and policy regarding these enterprises is decided by them. It is not within the competence of the local bodies on which the native peoples concerned are represented. The reactions of these peoples to the development of the mines and other natural resources in their midst is a delicate question, almost impossible to investigate satisfactorily under Soviet conditions. But rumbles of discontent do occasionally come to the surface, both about the effect of mining, for example, on native habitats, or the extent to which the peoples of the mining areas benefit from the removal of their gold and other valuable raw materials.

A complex framework of new political institutions was devised for the native areas of Siberia after the Revolution, to accompany the planned economic re-organisation of native life. This consisted of a hierarchy of administrative units which mostly took shape, after various experiments, in the 1930s. The impressive terminology applied to these units suggested a much greater degree of autonomy than any of them actually possessed.[2] Thus, the more compact and advanced native groups, the Yakuts, the Buryats and the Tuvintsy (since 1961), were given the status of autonomous republics (A.S.S.R.); and at a lower level of this administrative hierarchy, national okrugs and national oblasts were established; for the smaller groups there were national okrugs; the Khanty-Mansiyskiy, the Yamalo-Nenetskiy, the Taymyrskiy (Dolgano–Nenetskiy), the Ust-Ordinskiy and Aginsky Buryatskiy, the Evenkiyskiy, Koryakskiy and the Chukotskiy national okrugs, and three autonomous oblasts: the Gorno–Altayskaya, the Khakasskaya, the Yevreyskaya (Jewish). The autonomy of these various national units is severely limited by the overriding authority of the central Soviet and Party organs and, closer to hand, by the subjection of the decisions of each national unit to the approval of the immediately superior organ in the Soviet system. Thus, decisions of the Supreme Soviet of an autonomous republic must be approved by the Supreme Soviet of the R.S.F.S.R., though this would not be immediately apparent from the ambiguous clause in the U.S.S.R. Constitution to the effect that 'The Supreme Soviet of an autonomous Republic is the sole legislative organ of the Autonomous Republic'.

Within this framework, the native peoples do have a considerable say in matters of local concern, through participation in their regional Soviets and always so long as their *desiderati* do not conflict with the policies of the Central government. They have a right to representation, according to fixed quotas, in the Council of Nationalities of the Supreme Soviet, but with the exception of the Buryat A.S.S.R. and the Yakut A.S.S.R., none of the Siberian native peoples are sufficiently numerous (statutory minimum number 300,000) to participate in the Council of the Union.

Unlike the areas inhabited by other Siberian native peoples who have been subject to Russian rule since the annexation of Siberia by Tsarist Russia in the seventeenth century, Tuva (or Uriankhai as it was then known) was never conquered by the Russians, but formed part of the Chinese Empire until the Chinese Revolution of 1911. In the ensuing troubled years of civil war and strife, Tuva was claimed by Outer Mongolia before it passed into the Soviet orbit. Under increasing Soviet influence, a Tuva People's Republic was set up in 1921, but at this stage Tuva did not constitutionally belong to the Soviet Union. This situation changed in 1944, when the Tuva People's Republic was incorporated in the Soviet Union, in circumstances obscured by the war and the remoteness of the country, as an autonomous oblast of the R.S.F.S.R., thus losing even its former theoretical independence. In 1961, its status was once more changed, and the Tuva autonomous oblast was elevated to the rank of an autonomous republic.

Between the 1926 and 1959 censuses, a great change took place in the character

[2] For an analysis of the constitutional position of the Siberian native peoples cf. Chapter 3.

of the national composition of the populations of the native areas of Siberia and the Soviet Far East, in most of which the natives formerly predominated. The development of natural resources, and particularly of mining, in the native areas of the north and south of Siberia resulted in a large influx of migrant Russian and other non-native workers. This trend was intensified in the next inter-census period between 1959 and 1970, when many additional resources in such remote areas as the Chukotskiy Okrug and north and west Yakutiya were opened up. According to Dr. Armstrong's calculations,[3] there were probably between 40,000 and 50,000 Russians living in the north (including the European north of Russia, with which I am not here concerned), at the end of the last century, rising to 100,000 in 1926.

By 1959, there were 1,600,000 Russians, according to the census, in the same area of the Soviet North. These statistics admittedly cover the European Russian North as well as the northern areas of Siberia. But, in default of more exact figures, they nevertheless clearly enough reflect the rapid expansion of the Russian element in the Siberian North since 1926.

In the three autonomous republics of Yakutiya, Buryatiya and Tuva, where there are the largest compact native populations in Siberia, the Russian population is also increasing, exceeding the native element in the three republics according to the 1970 census. These larger native units are distinguished in Soviet statistics from the smaller so-called 'little peoples', most of whom live in the northern areas.

Autonomous Republics of RSFSR. (in thousands)

Name of ASSR	Total Population 1959	1970	Change from 1959 to 1970 %	Russians 1959	%	1970	%	Change from 1959 to 1970 %	1959	Titular nation (nations) % pop. 1970	% pop.	Change from 1950 to 1970 %
Buryat	673	812	20.065	503	74.6	597	73.5	18.688	136	20.2	179	22.0	31.618
Yakut	487	664	36.345	215	44.2	314	47.1	36.047	226	46.4	286	44.0	26.549
Tuvinian	173	231	34.302	69	40.1	88	38.3	27.536	98	50.7	135	58.6	37.755

Source: Sovetskaya Rossiya, 20 May, 1971. Percentages of population growth estimated by Roman Szporluk 'n "The Nations of the U.S.S.R. in 1970", Survey, Autumn 1971.

Though the Russians are numerically superior to the titular population in these three areas, both the Buryats and the Tuvintsy nevertheless in the inter-census period (1959–70), showed higher rate of increase than the Russians, who therefore suffered a slight if only relative decline. In Yakutiya, the Russian increase, relatively and absolutely, at the expense of the Yakuts, was maintained. In spite of such a large influx of migrants, the total population of Yakutiya (664,000) is still extremely small both in relation to the size of the territory and to the labour problem which is often acute in the major mining industries.

In all the national *okrugs*, the homelands of the smaller native Siberian groups, the titular native peoples are now a minority encompassed by a Russian majority.

The measures taken to improve health and education have not resulted in any significant overall increase in the numbers of the native peoples of Siberia and the Soviet Far East, and where there were increases between 1959–70, they were tiny. A comparison of the following statistics with earlier census results, suggests that some of these peoples have either been assimilated to larger groups like the Russians,

[3] cf. T. Armstrong, op. cit. pp. 58, 188.

or the Yakuts, and so are not mentioned in the census list or are on the verge of extinction.

Native Peoples of Siberia

	Number of People of given nationality (in thousands)		Percentage who consider the language of the group to be their native lanbuage		Percentage of those in 1970 who command the Russian language as well as their own or as a 2nd language
	1959	1970	1959	1970	
Buryaty	252	313	75.9	67.6	73.9
Tuvintsy	100	139	95.1	92.8	40
Yakuty	233	295	89.3	82.7	45.2
Khakasy	56	65	86.4	84.2	81.6
Altaytsy	45	55	89.2	88.1	67.0
Little Peoples of the North, Siberia and Far East of which:					
Nentsy (Samoyeds, Yuraks)	23	28	84.7	83.4	64.0
Evenki (Tungus)	25	25	55.9	51.3	71.4
Khanty (Ostyaks)	19	21	77	68.9	78.5
Chukchi	12	14	93.9	82.6	75.7
Eveny (Lamuts)	9.1	12	81.4	56	60.5
Nanaytsy (Golds)	8	10	86.3	69.1	88.7
Mansi (Voguls)	6.45	7.7	59.2	52.4	86.3
Koryaki	6.3	7.5	90.5	81.1	82.7
Dolgany	3.9	4.9	93.9	89.8	72.2
Nivkhi (Gilyaks)	3.7	4.4	76.3	49.5	94.9
Sel'kupy (Ostyak Samoyeds)	3.8	4.3	50.6	51.1	88.9
Ul'chi (Ol'chi)	2.1	2.4	84.9	60.8	95.7
Yaami (Laps)					
Udegeytsy	1.4	1.5	73.7	54.4	90.8
Itel'meny (Kamchadals)	1.1	1.3	36	35.7	97.3
Kety (Yenisey Ostyaks)	1	1.2	77.1	74.9	80.5
Orochi	.8	1.1	68.4	48.6	95.7
Nganasany (Tavgi Samoyeds)	.75	1	93.4	75.4	66.6
Yukagiry	.4	.6	52.5	46.8	
Eskimosy (Asiatic Eskimos)	1.1	1.3	84	not listed	not listed
Aleuty (Aleuts)	.4	.4	22.3	not listed	not listed

Source: Soviet census 1970

The 1,300 Soviet Eskimos and the 400 Soviet Aleuts were apparently regarded as too small to have a regular place in the Soviet census return, so they were relegated to a footnote and no information was listed for their language position in 1970 (in 1959 the Aleuts were well on the way to losing their native language as only 22.3% considered it to be their native language). But insignificant numerically though both groups are, they live in areas of considerable ethnological and strategic significance. The Eskimos inhabit the extreme north-eastern tip of Chukotka facing Alaska across the narrow Bering Strait and the Aleuts the Komandorskiye Islands, 500 miles east of Kamchatka in the North Pacific. The Siberian Eskimos are blood brothers to the Eskimos of Alaska and Canada, while the majority of the Aleuts live in the United States. The social-economic progress of the Eskimos under Soviet rule, as contrasted with their 'neglect' by the American and Canadian governments is a favourite topic of the Soviet press (which overlooks the awkward fact that, whereas the North American Eskimos are increasing, the Soviet Eskimos are not increasing and even declining since 1917). Soviet ethnographers also show considerable interest in Eskimo culture 'the sphere of expansion of which extends from Chukotka to Greenland' and stress that the solution of many questions of the ethnogenesis of the peoples of north Asia and north America is linked with the 'Eskimo problem'.

The information given in the above census table about linguistic trends among the Siberian native peoples, and especially the numerically smaller groups, shows a steep decline in the numbers who regard the language of their group to be their native language and the strong linguistic influence of Russian. Even in the case of the Yakuts, the strongest of these northern natives and who seem to have held relatively tenaciously to their language, the percentage who regard Yakut as their native language fell from 97.6% to 93.6% between 1959 and 1970. Less than half of the Yukagiry (46.8%) or the Orochi (4.88%) were reported to regard their native language as their own. While the census does not actually state what language these peoples had adopted in preference to their native tongue, the high percentages listed of those who command Russian as well as their own, shows that as might be expected Russian is the major linguistic influence. The Orochi are among the 14 native peoples who are still scriptless and are only taught Russian in the primary school.

In Siberia, Russian cultural assimilation has been an inevitable concomitant of Russian rule since the annexation of Siberia in the sixteenth century and this has continued during the Soviet Russian period. In Tsarist days the process was known as Russification and was comparable in its way to the British cultural influence in Ireland or to that of the French in their colonies. Nationally and internationally, this was acceptable according to the conventions of the day.

Marxist-Leninist ideology, however, totally rejects the old idea of Russification with its strong political overtones and the notion therefore that there is any similarity between Tsarist Russification and Soviet linguistic-cultural policies, promoting cultural assimilation, is repudiated out of hand in the Soviet Union. But, in fact, there is not such a great difference between Tsarist and Soviet policies in this matter. Thus, according to Soviet ideology, the Russian language has an important role to play in the 'progressive process . . . of the convergence and fusion of peoples' and 'fusion of peoples' into a Great Russian mould is a long-term aim of all Soviet nationality policies. Given the predominant Russian demographic-political position in Siberia, and the weakness of all the Siberian native groups, it would seem only a matter of time before they and their respective cultures are assimilated by Russian influences and virtually disappear. 'Millions of peoples of different nationalities consider Russian culture to be their own culture and the Russian language their own language,' commented *Pravda* on the 1970 census results. When national convergence leading to fusion with Russian culture, i.e. assimilation, is official policy in the Soviet Union, concern about the languishing or disappearance of any native languages or cultures would be out of place in the Party's main organ.

The attitude of many Soviet ethnographers and other scholars who have devoted their lives to the study of Siberian native peoples and cultures is very different.

Their research and first-hand investigations are recorded in a large volume of distinguished work on Siberian ethnography, languages, history, anthropology, archaeology and archaeological sites of very great value to all seriously interested in Siberia and its peoples. In Chukotka, for example, archaeologists have made some remarkable finds such as, in the first place, the contents of the now famous Uelen grave which established the existence of an ancient Eskimo culture. Soviet ethnographers have produced excellent monographs on the different native peoples, their folklore has been studied and taken down 'live' while there are still people to record it. Side by side with this work of scholarship, a number of learned bodies, museums and libraries have been founded in places like Chukotka, where nothing of the sort formerly existed. Thus, there is now a Chukotsk Regional Museum in Anadyr, the capital of Chukotka, which has assembled a special collection of Chukchi and Eskimo bone carving and other handwork, and publishes periodical *Zapiski* (Transactions), dealing with local cultural matters. Magadan has its own publishing house as an adjunct (perhaps) to the very active North-Eastern Complex Research Institute in Magadan. This work has been largely accomplished in the harshest physical conditions and, until the most recent times, in places devoid of elementary western living facilities. Since the outbreak of Sino-Soviet hostilities in the Far East in 1968, there has been a noticeable tendency on the Soviet side to attempt to buttress the official line about this frontier with somewhat dubious and loaded arguments borrowed from this scholarship, with some curious results. Thus some of the smaller native peoples living in the frontier areas have acquired a new image in Soviet publicity, while the cultural-political influence of the Chinese before the Russian conquest has been played down. One of Academician A. P. Okladnikov's learned papers on the historical development of the peoples of Asia, for example, was quoted to the effect that 'research had proved that a highly developed culture, more ancient than any in China or Japan, had been established on the banks of the Amur by the ancestors of the Nanaytsy and other peoples of the Soviet Far East.' This is an intriguing idea, but would probably get short shrift from Chinese cultural historians.

In general, however, it is not 'the highly developed culture' of these native peoples that dominates Soviet publicity about them, but rather their great social-cultural advancement under Soviet guidance. A typical article recently described the visit of a group of Soviet journalists and 'foreign television correspondents' to the Nanaytsy village of Naykhin on the lower Amur, 'in search of the exotic old way of life', as it had been described by V. K. Arsen'yev in 1908. Then, 136 people lived in 18 *fanz* with earthen floors and smoking stoves covering everything with a thick layer of soot. The Nanaytsy were 'threatened with extinction'. But instead of the anticipated 'exotic scene', this group found a thriving fishing industry with modern boats and equipment, modern houses and an *internat* for the children of the hunters and fishermen. Cattle breeding and vegetable growing had been introduced, both hitherto unknown. These formerly illiterate Nanaytsy now had 60 teachers and 20 doctors replaced the old Shamans. 'During 50 years of Soviet power', concluded this *Pravda* story, 'the Nanaytsy had given the country writers, scholars, an artist, a composer and other promising intellectuals.'

It is noticeable that whether by accident or design, the 'little peoples of the

Soviet Far East' are invariably presented in a favourable light in Soviet sources. They are always good, generous, kind . . . and 'baddies' apparently never crop up among them. Moreover, in Soviet publicity about native areas, there always seem to be the necessary schools, houses and other amenities (the lack of which is so often complained of by industrial workers). All this would be more credible if the picture of native existence did not so uniformly redound to the credit of the Soviet system.

Official satisfaction with the impact of Soviet power on the 'little peoples of Siberia' is dominated by the undoubted success of the literacy and public health campaigns and the more controversial social-economic reorganisation imposed on them. In this euphoria, the peculiar character of the 'old order' evolved over centuries by the Siberian peoples themselves is not given its due, except by anthropologists and other scholars. It was a remarkable achievement to have mastered their extremely harsh environment so well, while their intelligence and ingenuity was shown in the intricate hunting and fishing gear they produced from the few materials at hand and in fashioning their attractive clothes from fur and skins. Their knowledge of wild life was exceptional and the admiration of all who came in touch with them.

The only overall picture we have of how these peoples have adjusted to the new socialist order derives from Soviet sources. But to what extent it is true to fact, gilds the lily, conceals dissatisfaction with the impact of mining and the bulldozer on the reindeer's tundra, or mute criticism of the revolutionary changes in native life in the last half-century, is not known and cannot be known with any assurance until it is possible to investigate these matters at first hand. Meanwhile, facile conclusions about the present situation had best be avoided.

chapter twelve

Scientific Research in Siberia

Scientific research in Siberia is not a mushroom growth forced into existence by the October revolution, though the Soviets can justly claim to have greatly expanded its scope after the revolution. Since the eighteenth century, state-financed and private expeditions explored the geography and geology, the flora and fauna of Siberia, while many intrepid and highly intelligent private scientist-explorers ventured into the wilds to add their contributions to the growing store of knowledge of this new Russian land mass, its natural resources and native peoples. Moreover, there were many men of a scientific bent of mind among the Russian and Polish exiles, who applied themselves, with great assiduity and success to a study of their surroundings in the remoter parts of Siberia and the Far East. An outstanding example of this dedication is the geographical work of Prince Peter Kropotkin, during his years of exile in East Siberia.

From the time of Peter the Great, Russian sovereigns and the many new learned bodies of later years like the Imperial Russian Geographical Society, the University of Moscow and the St. Petersburg Botanic Garden, promoted scientific research in Siberia. The life, customs and languages of the Siberian native peoples were also studied by pioneer Tsarist ethnologists and archaeologists, many of whose learned works are still essential reading in their respective fields.

In Siberia itself, a wide range of scientific investigations was conducted under the auspices of the first Siberian University, opened at Tomsk in 1880. Nor must the keen interest shown by Gennadius V. Yudin, a wealthy Krasnoyarsk distiller, in collecting materials dealing with Russian and Siberian ethnology, archaeology and bibliography be overlooked, and the fact that his collection, shipped to Washington in 1907, formed the nucleus of the now famous Slavic Division of the Library of Congress.

Clearly Siberia was no scientific wilderness in pre-revolutionary days (in spite of its many rapacious officials and traders). There were still many gaps to be filled, notably in a much more exact identification of the rich natural resources of the territory and the utilisation of science to promote economic development. But a fine tradition had been established before 1917 on which Soviet scientists and scholars could, and did, later build.

Undoubtedly, the most important step taken by the Soviet government to promote scientific research in Siberia, was the establishment in 1957 (following a decision of the Party Congress), of the Siberian Department of the U.S.S.R. Academy of Sciences. It was built on the outskirts of the west Siberian city of Novosibirsk, among the conifers and birches of the virgin Siberian taiga. Known as the *Akadem-gorodok*, this new academic township was extremely fortunate in its first Director, Academician M. A. Lavrent'yev, a man of independent mind, and a distinguished specialist in the field of hydro-dynamics, winner of both a Stalin prize for research and the Order of Lenin. He was able to attract a brilliant group of scientists in many fields to Novosibirsk to take charge of the various scientific institutes being established there and to avail themselves of its excellent laboratory and other research facilities. The staff is some 25,000 strong and the cost of establishing this remarkable institution is believed to have been about 200 million roubles.

The Siberian Department eventually brought under its direction the affiliates of the all-Union Academy of Sciences already existing in Novosibirsk, Ulan-Ude, Irkutsk, Yakutsk, and the Far East (Vladivostok and Petropavlovsk-Kamchatka), and to this extent represented a decentralisation of the all-Union Academy's former centralised administration. The Moscow Academy, of course, still retains final authority over all these bodies, including the Siberian Department, but much less directly than formerly.

While recognising the importance of pure scientific research, the primary objective of the Siberian Department was officially stated to be the application of science to the problems of the economic development of Siberia and the Far East. This orientation of the Siberian Department's work gave it exceptional authority in investigating and advising on Siberian economic problems. Academician Lavrent'yev is personally much concerned about the need for close cooperation between science and industry. But after some years of experience of life in Siberia, he has had to admit that 'a direct leap from science to industry has unfortunately not always been successful. Great efforts by both sides have frequently failed to produce the desired results, each side blaming the other'. At his suggestion, the Government therefore decided to set up a number of design bureaux and experimental enterprises at Akademgorodok, to act as intermediary stages between a scientific discovery and its application in the national economy. According to Lavrent'yev, 'these must become places where young people can learn to use new techniques in an industrial and yet scientific environment, so that we can hand over to industry not just blueprints, but also young people who have played a creative part in developing new techniques.'

A new University was opened in Novosibirsk in 1959 to train young specialists for advanced research work in the various institutes of the Academy. These bodies fluctuate in number according to scientific need and possibilities, but there were recently 15 institutes, employing 13 regular members and 43 corresponding members of the all-Union Academy of Sciences, as well as 2,000 to 3,000 young scientists. The practical orientation of research at the Institute of Economics may be regarded as typical of other specialist institutes in their respective fields. Among these economic research problems are investigation of the distribution of industry and the complex development prospects of different areas in conjunction with labour productivity problems.

In spite of the disappointments referred to by Academician Lavrent'yev, there have been many scientific investigations in the Siberian Department which have directly benefited agriculture and industry. In addressing the Annual General Meeting of the all-Union Academy of Sciences in March 1973, the President, M. V. Keldysh, mentioned the work of the Institute of Cytology and Genetics of the Siberian Department, in collaboration with the Siberian filial of the all-Union Institute of Plant Growing, in creating a type of spring wheat 'Novosibirsk-67' now successfully used in many parts of Siberia. Among achievements in the field of earth sciences, he stressed the research done in the Geology and Geophysics Institute of the Siberian Department in demonstrating how promising in terms of oil and gas are the rock masses of the intermediate, tectonic complex of the west Siberian shield.

Under the impetus largely of the Siberian Department many new scientific institutes have been established in Siberia and the Soviet Far East. Some of these bodies are subordinate (Filialy) to the Siberian Department and some come directly under the all-Union Academy in Moscow. Irkutsk contains a cluster of high-ranking scientific institutes and is a worthy site, with its old intellectual traditions, for a branch of the Siberian Department of the Academy. The Institute of Geography of Siberia and the Far East is probably the best known internationally of these bodies. It has several research out-stations in various parts of Siberia and is responsible for the publication of a number of widely respected journals, e.g. the *Doklady* (Reports), 2–4 issues annually, and the *Sibirskiy Geograficheskiy Sbornik* (annual) (Siberian Geographical Collection). It has produced a fine atlas of Irkutsk oblast, and its Atlas of Zabaykaliya should soon appear (if it has not already appeared). The largest of the many Irkutsk institutes is the Institute of Terrestrial Magnetism, the Ionosphere, and Radio Waves. A new scientific centre is now being built in Irkutsk to coordinate these various institutes.

Further east, Yakutsk has developed a number of scientific bodies of exceptional interest. One of the most expert and interesting is the Permafrost Institute, containing eight laboratories entirely devoted to permafrost problems, such as subsoil water and cryology, in the best natural conditions for this research, as Yakutsk itself is built on permafrost extending for hundreds of miles on all sides of the town. These studies are also of great practical interest to other countries like Canada and Alaska, which have permafrost problems. The second International Permafrost Conference was held in Yakutsk in 1973 and gave foreign experts from 14 countries an opportunity of learning at first hand of Soviet success in building towns, gas pipelines and dams in the permafrost. There are several other scientific institutes in Yakutsk, notably of biology and economics.

The Far Eastern Scientific Centre, established in Vladivostok in 1970, already bids fair to become one of the most important scientific bodies in the country. Its director is Dr. A. Kapitsa, the brilliant and very active son of the famous Academician P. Kapitsa. It is regarded as a feather in his cap that his new Centre is directly subordinated to the all-Union Academy in Moscow and not to the Siberian Department of the Academy in Novosibirsk. The range of its scientific work is very wide. Moreover, scientific institutes in Magadan, Kamchatka, Khabarovsk, Sakhalin and Blagoveshchensk, with a total staff of 4,000, come under its aegis. A large academic 'townlet' on the lines of the Novosibirsk *Akademgorodok* is being built during the current plan period for this Centre, in a suburb of Vladivostok. One of the main functions of this Centre and its affiliated institutes will be to work out solutions to economic and production problems in the Soviet Far East and to investigate latent raw material resources. Thus, the Geological Institute is investigating deposits of tin, gold and polymetallic ores both on land and on the continental shelf, and it has a station in the Tetyukhe-Kavalerovo region to study problems of the industrial-chemical pollution of the sea. Both the new Pacific Institute of Oceanology (set up in 1973), and the Institute of Marine Biology, are concerned with reproduction problems of the biological resources of the oceans. This Institute of Marine Biology was also engaged in 1972 in hydro-biological research on the Komandorskiye islands, which included studies of the tidal and upper sub-littoral areas at a depth of 30 metres.

A very comprehensive programme has been prepared for the new Economic Research Institute of the Far Eastern Scientific Centre and if effectively implemented, the impact on the region's economy should eventually be considerable. The Institute, for example, is instructed to provide forecasts of the development of the Far Eastern region's productive forces up to the year 2000; to study the application of the economic reforms to the region's enterprises and to make recommendations for improvements. It will also have to study the export-import policies of countries in the Pacific area, including Japan, Canada, Australia and Latin America. The wide range of scientific research to be conducted by 19 scientific establishments, under the auspices of the Far Eastern Scientific Centre on the shores of Amur Bay, is thus remarkable, even in outline, and the result will be awaited with considerable interest by foreign scientists in their respective fields.

The more limited scientific work now being done at Khabarovsk has a good deal of local value. In 1972, the Far Eastern branch of the all-Union Institute of Mineral Raw Materials in Khabarovsk was elevated to the status of a Far Eastern Institute in its own right, owing to its importance in investigating more thoroughly the resource base of this large and only partly surveyed territory. The task of studying the economic background to trade between the Soviet Far East and Japan, S.E. Asia and Oceania was hitherto concentrated in the Khabarovsk Laboratory of Export-Import Specialisation (subordinate to the Siberian Department of the all-Union Academy) and it is not yet clear how this work will now be coordinated with the rather similar assignment of the new Vladivostok Economic Research Institute.

The North-Eastern Complex Research Institute at Magadan, as its name suggests, is closely concerned with economic-production problems of the great mining industries of the Kolyma and Chukotsk regions. Its energetic director, Academician N. Shilo, is a gold expert and gets a good deal of publicity in the metropolitan press with his frank criticisms of the bureaucratic procrastination which, in his view, is holding up the economic development of the north-eastern areas of the Far East in which he is especially interested. Costs do not apparently enter into his appraisals of official policies, but otherwise he often scores good points without risk of official rebukes. In order to facilitate its research on geological and mathematical problems, a third Minsk 32 computer was installed at this Institute in 1971.

The proliferation of Siberian scientific research also extends out to Sakhalin and the Kuril islands. A Maritime Geology Laboratory was established as part of the Sakhalin research institute, in 1971, with the object of investigating the in-shore waters of Sakhalin and the Kurils, and estimating the distribution of deposits of oil and gas, metals and other minerals.

Based on Vladivostok, a number of Soviet maritime expeditions have been engaged in research in the home waters of the Soviet Far East and remoter oceans. In 1971, for example, the veteran of Soviet science ships, the *Vitaz*, with 65 scientists aboard did extensive research into the biological resources of the world's oceans and the behaviour of fish and mammals, during a four-months' voyage. The *Vitaz* sailed as far south as Australia, Tasmania and New Zealand and touched at various Pacific island ports. As a result, interesting short reports on these islands and their peoples, their way of life and costume, as observed by the scientists, were published in the Soviet press, but attracted little attention in the west.

In the same year, the *Dmitriy Mendeleyev*, a vessel belonging to the Oceanological Research Institute of the all-Union Academy of Sciences, sailed to New Guinea, the New Hebrides, Samoa and Fiji, and the islands and atolls of Oceania, to carry out a number of investigations into problems of marine geophysics, hydro-biology and other scientific fields. Soviet scientific vessels from Vladivostok also participated in various international research programmes. Among these was the 'Tropical Experiment' in 1971–72, in the east Atlantic, part of the comprehensive Global Atmospheric Research Programme. The main objective of this 'Tropical Experiment' expedition, according to Soviet scientists, is to obtain quantitative data about the heat and moisture transfers from the ocean to the atmosphere in tropical regions. These problems are also being investigated from the Atlantic to the Arctic oceans. According to western scientists participating in the Experiment, Soviet scientists are cooperating harmoniously in this international work.

Early in 1973, there was an intriguing and unexpected development of Soviet-U.S. scientific cooperation in the strategically delicate area of the Bering Sea. Here a joint series of experiments was organised to study the natural environment from outer space. From the Soviet side, the weather ship *Priboy*, the special Il-18 aircraft equipped as a flying laboratory, and representatives of a number of scientific institutions in Moscow and Leningrad participated. On the American side, there was the N.A.S.A. plane 'Convair-999' containing probably the latest, most sophisticated U.S. scientific devices, and the ice-breaker *Staten Island*. The American delegation was led by Leonard Jaffe of N.A.S.A. and the Soviet delegation by Aleksandr Vinogradov, Vice-President of the U.S.S.R. Academy of Sciences. The two delegations met in advance to discuss their respective research results in geology, geomorphology, land utilisation, glaciology and oceanology, but it is not clear whether they visited their respective planes and their equipment, or indeed met at all in the Bering Sea. The Soviet base for the Bering expedition was Mys Shmidta, on the north-east coast of Chukotka. *Pravda* reported very favourably on the 'good spirit of cooperation and mutual understanding' prevailing throughout the expedition. Whether the Soviet objectives in authorising these investigations in a usually very strict security area were purely scientific, or whether they also wished to have a close look at the latest N.A.S.A. plane, must remain an open question.

The Soviet expeditionary fleet has been basically reorganised in recent years to enable it to participate more adequately in international research work. Formerly it consisted mainly of re-equipped transport steamers, fishing trawlers and similar craft. But now special vessels of the *Academician Kurchatok* class have been built and furnished with modern scientific equipment and a computer centre. Apart from its purely scientific interest, the information collected by these Soviet expeditions must also be of strategic value to the Soviet government.

There are a few scientific stations of unique interest in Siberia which should be mentioned in this brief survey. Among these stations is the Sayan cosmo-physical observatory of the Institute of World Magnetism and Ionosphere, situated on the highest peak of the Chasovaya mountain in east Siberia. It is equipped with a large coronograph, a horizon mount telescope and other sophisticated instruments. Some interesting discoveries may also be anticipated from the south-Siberian geographical observatory now under construction near Shushenskoye, with the task of studying the Minusinsk plain 'a place possessing unique climatic properties' (as a result of which the famous Pazyryk grave treasures were preserved intact after hundreds of years).

The wide range of scientific institutions now established in Siberia and the Far East in turn prompts the question as to the extent to which relations have been built up with industry and agriculture, resulting as originally intended in specific advantages for the Siberian economy. It is impossible for a scientific tyro like myself to answer this very complex question here with any assurance but some straws in the wind may be worth mentioning in this connection. The critical attitude of various experts of the Siberian Department of the Academy, both to the conduct of the Siberian economy and of various policies of the central industrial ministries and agencies in Moscow, seems to suggest that the influence of the scientists is far from being as effective as it was originally intended to become. The Siberian geologists would appear to be in a special category among scientists, proving their worth to the economy by their frequent valuable mineral discoveries and often winning their tussles with Moscow about the necessity of prolonging difficult, but ultimately successful, prospecting (as happened prior to the discovery of west Siberian oil).

In default of more definite information on this important question, it is tempting to recall the criticism of the work of the Academy of Sciences of the Kazakh S.S.R. by Rashidov, First Secretary of the Uzbek S.S.R. (in 1966), though admittedly it may not be relevant to Siberian conditions. While acknowledging the Academy's achievements in medicine, nuclear and radiation physics, and other theoretical fields, the Uzbek party chief stated that 'scientific successes carried out so far have found only limited application in the republic's industry. During the last five years only 14% of the work done by the Kazakh Academy's institutes and other higher scientific establishments has actually been used in production.' 'This state of affairs', continued Rashidov, 'has been brought about by the considerable amount of research work which is of little theoretical or practical value, and by the rather inflexible attitude of the industrial workers themselves, who are reluctant to use the latest achievements of science.'

Perhaps in the case of Siberia, it might be nearer the mark to place much of the blame for the often disappointing impact of scientific research on Siberian industry and agriculture, on the rigidity of senior officials in Siberia and the ineffective instructions of the ministries who direct them. The low percentage of scientific inventions and proposals actually applied in Siberian industrial enterprises must also to a large degree be attributed to the wholly inadequate numbers of trained technological cadres in these enterprises, capable of testing and applying these scientific inventions and other recommendations. But Mikhail Lavrent'yev, the director of the Siberian Department of the Academy, still believes in the importance of the development of science in Siberia. In an interview some years ago, he is on record as saying: 'I think Siberian science has a great future. There are many highly important scientific problems which will require for their solution vast amounts of electricity, large areas of land and extra-strong materials. These are precisely what Siberia has in abundance. The establishment of scientific centres and the construction and utilisation of huge research installations such as will be required, for example, to solve the problem of controlling thermonuclear reaction, will be cheaper there than in the European part of the country.'

chapter thirteen

Economic Relations with Japan

copartnership projects and trade in Siberia and the Soviet Far East

Soviet economic relations with Japan in the Far East are both complex and potentially very extensive. They include the issues raised by their conflicting interests in the north Pacific fisheries, barter trade, and the proposed Soviet-Japanese economic cooperation in the development of various Siberian natural resources.

The North Pacific Fisheries. Soviet-Japanese fishing interests have been competing for supremacy in the rich fishing grounds of the north Pacific, to go no further back than the first World War. The Japanese at first gained the upper hand after the 1917 Revolution, when they were able to extend their fisheries and canneries most profitably on to the Soviet Far Eastern mainland. This situation rapidly changed with the Japanese evacuation of Sakhalin in 1925 and the subsequent vigorous development of Soviet fisheries and canneries along the Far Eastern coast to Kamchatka and in floating canneries on the high seas. The Soviet victory over the Japanese in the second World War destroyed the former prosperity of Japanese fishing enterprises in these north Pacific waters. In particular, the rich fishing grounds off the Kurils and south Sakhalin, annexed by the Soviet Union after the war, were barred to the Japanese by the twelve-mile limit imposed by Moscow and they lost their former very valuable concessions in the Kamchatkan salmon rivers. Since the Soviets had command both of the sea of Japan and the vast Sea of Okhotsk, the Japanese, to whom these fisheries are of the greatest national importance, both as a source of food and of canned fish export products, were in a poor bargaining position in their negotiations with the Soviets to improve matters.

Following the announcement of the termination of the state of war between the Soviet Union and the Japanese in 1956, a ten-year Soviet-Japanese Fishing Agreement was signed in 1957, which regulated their respective fishing operations in the north Pacific. It was agreed that a Soviet-Japanese Conference on fisheries problems would be held annually, alternately in Moscow and Tokyo, to fix quotas for the salmon and crab catches. The Japanese were disgruntled at the reduced quotas assigned them by the Soviets, but the latter alleged overfishing by Japanese fishermen and concern about the dwindling stocks of north Pacific salmon and herring.

Since then, the Japanese have also been constantly annoyed about the arrests of their fishermen and the confiscation of their boats and gear by Soviet patrols, when caught fishing in traditional Japanese fishing grounds, from which they are now banned by the post-war Soviet regulations. Latterly, the Soviets have sometimes released 'on humanitarian grounds' Japanese fishermen caught fishing in the waters round the south Kuril islands. Concessions have been made to 'small fishermen' regarding crab and tangle fishing in the restricted Habomai and Shikotan waters (but not off the larger Etorofu or Kunashir, Kuril islands). The Japanese are also interested in obtaining 'safe fishing' rights in the rich Hokkaido fishing grounds, surrounding their homeland island, where they fished for years before the second World War.

At the last meeting of the Soviet-Japanese Fisheries Commission in 1972, out of a total salmon catch of 90,000 tons in north-western Pacific waters, over 80,000 tons were allocated to Japan. It was furthermore agreed that as the Sakhalin and Hokkaido herring stocks had been exhausted, decisive measures were required to rebuild stocks. At the same time, a joint control system for whaler mother-ships in the northern Pacific was agreed in Moscow. Observers from one country will travel in mother ships of the other, to ensure that whaling is carried out under the rules of the international convention. It is hoped in this way to preserve and restore whale stocks in the Pacific, which have been seriously depleted in recent years. Japan's quotas of king, snow, and blue king crabs were all reduced at this 1972 meeting of the Commission. As a result of a special agreement for one year, a total of 330 Japanese boats will be allowed to gather sea-tangle (a type of seaweed highly prized in Japan) off Kaigara Island (east of Hokkaido) and Japan will pay the U.S.S.R. 12,000 yen for each boat engaged for a year in this fishing, which is the main livelihood of the small fishermen in the area.

The Japanese crab fishing industry would suffer great losses if the Soviet claim to the whole of the continental shelf off Sakhalin and Kamchatka were fully implemented. Mainly for this reason, it is assumed, Japan is still not willing to sign the U.N. Continental Shelf Convention (of 1958). On the basis of the Continental Shelf Treaty, the Soviets put forward proposals for very severe restrictions on Japanese crab fishing in the Primor'ye, west Kamchatka, east Sakhalin and the Amur Delta areas in 1969. After 50 days hard-fought negotiations, on the eve of the opening of the fishing season, the Japanese agreed to restrictions in these areas (less than originally demanded by the Soviets) and the complete banning of tanner crab fishing in Primor'ye and other crab fishing in Olyutorskiy Bay area (north-east Kamchatka). The squeeze had begun.

The Treaty under which the United States returned Okinawa to Japan in 1971 brought the ever simmering issue of the southern Kuril islands, annexed by the Soviet Union in 1945, to the boil again in Japan. Both sides indulged in a good deal of verbal sabre rattling on this score without significantly damaging their mutual relations. The Soviet Minister of Fisheries, Ishkov, accused the Japanese of linking the fisheries question with their 'Northern Territories claim' (as they are known in Japan). This would be quite a natural association, in view of the valuable fisheries lost to Japan round the south Kuril islands as a result of the Soviet 12 mile limit.

For their part, the Soviets were using their superior power in the north Pacific to bring pressure to bear on the Japanese, through the threat of further restrictions on their vital fishery interests, to weaken the Japanese-American alliance and force Japan to sign a Peace Treaty on Moscow's terms.

While still maintaining a rigid policy on the territorial issue, a noticeably more friendly note pervaded Soviet statements about Far Eastern relations with the Japanese, following the Soviet Foreign Minister Gromyko's visit to Tokyo and President Nixon's visit to Peking in 1972. Emphasis was laid on Moscow's willingness to discuss outstanding fisheries problems and interest in increasing trade and economic cooperation with Japan. The culmination of this easing of tension was the announcement some months later that preliminary negotiations, prior to formal talks on the conclusion of a peace treaty, would be held in September 1972. The talks were duly held, with no positive result up to the end of 1973.

Soviet-Japanese economic cooperation in Siberia and the Far East. The idea of Soviet-Japanese copartnership in a number of development projects in Siberia first emerged, literally out of the blue (for Japan had long been regarded as the Soviet Union's Enemy No. 1 in the Far East), during a visit to the Soviet Union of a large Japanese delegation in 1962. These proposals have now been under contentious discussion for a decade, but to date the only projects to be implemented are the joint development of the Amur basin timber reserves and the construction of a new port at Vrangel Bay, the twin port of Nakhodka. The Japanese are also supplying special equipment for the container terminal now being built at Nakhodka itself. Progress on other copartnership proposals has long been held up, not by any conflict of views on the substance of the projects, but by disagreements on financial or political issues. The line taken by Soviet spokesmen is that while Japanese technical assistance would be welcomed in the development of Siberia, the Soviets are perfectly capable of tackling these development schemes single-handed. To quote one of these statements: 'The Soviet Union is opening up the natural wealth of Siberia and the Far East by its own efforts, but it certainly does not decline the additional advantages offered in this task by mutually advantageous cooperation with Japan.' The truth behind this complacent pronouncement is that the Soviets now realise that with Japanese, American, or other foreign technical assistance and capital investment the development of Siberian economic resources can be given a great spurt forward, compared to the more uncertain, slower progress achievable under Soviet socialism without the technological aid and cooperation of advanced industrial countries such as Japan.

The details of the first Amur timber deal were fixed in an Agreement signed in 1968 which provided that, during a three-year period starting in 1969, Japan was to supply technical assistance and machinery as well as specific quantities of footwear and clothing for the timber workers, in return for Soviet shipments of some 7.2 million cu.m. of lumber and 20,000 cu.m. of sawn timber. Although some 70% of Japanese housing is made of wood, there have been difficulties in absorbing these large quantities of timber by the Japanese construction industries. The financial accounting for this complicated business agreement was the subject of protracted discussion before the two sides made concessions to achieve agreement, in 1968, at meetings attended by the Soviet Foreign Trade Minister N. Patolichev. Thus, the Japanese Export-Import Bank reduced its usual interest rate on machinery and equipment from 6.5% to 6%, while the Russians agreed to pay 20% rather than 10% down and 5.8% rather than 5.5% on the remaining account. This agreement was renewed and expanded in 1971. Complaints have also been made by some Japanese timber firms about the quality of Siberian timber compared to American, and the somewhat arbitrary attitude of the Soviet Far Eastern export agencies towards the seasonal-specification requirements of the Japanese timber market (due, it would appear, to their ignorance of, or indifference to, the way the market functions in a capitalist country like Japan).

Probably more important is Japan's part in the technical re-equipment and enlargement of the important Far Eastern port of Nakhodka and in the construction of its new twin deep-water port on the other side of Vrangel Bay. Since the closure of Vladivostok to commercial shipping, the expansion of these and other Far Eastern ports was necessary to deal with the increasing coastal trade, in the first place with Japan, and eventually with countries of the 'Pacific Rim'. The new ambitious $50 million dock project at Vrangel Bay, some 30 km. north of Nakhodka, as embodied in the Soviet-Japanese Agreement of 1970, should relieve both the congestion at Nakhodka and the shortage of manpower at the docks. The Japanese will supply equipment and machinery for the Soviet construction of the planned coal and woodchip handling facilities on the docks. As a result of this Japanese assistance, Wrangel port operations will be largely automated, so as to make it independent of the inadequate supply of local labour.

Apart from the above agreements already concluded with Japan, the extent of Soviet interest in obtaining foreign technical assistance for the development of Siberian-Far Eastern economic resources may be seen in the variety of projects for this purpose still in the pipeline and under intermittent discussion with Japan since 1962, and the more recent Soviet proposals for economic cooperation with the United States.

One of the most important of these projects was for Soviet-Japanese cooperation in the extension of the Tyumen'–Irkutsk pipeline (completed in 1964) some 4,000 km. further east to Nakhodka. But as west Siberian oil began to flow, Moscow decided to build a much longer pipeline to Nakhodka starting from Tyumen' oblast and covering some 7,800 km. When completed, this pipeline would be the longest in the world and would seem to be a necessity for the success of the Soviet plans for an eastward outlet for Tyumen' oil and exports in tle first place to Japan. It should also relieve the already overloaded Amur railway of oil tanker traffic between Irkutsk and the Soviet Far East.

According to the original Soviet-Japanese project, Japan would supply the technical know-how and equipment, such as the 48 in. diameter pipe with capacity up to 70 million tons per annum, to transport oil over this great distance, pumping stations, etc., and be repaid in crude oil. In the protracted discussions subsequently, over the financial terms involved in this proposed deal, the Japanese found the

Soviet capital-investment demands exorbitant and financial circles in Japan were not earlier prepared to underwrite the unusually long credit terms demanded by Moscow. Agreement was finally reached in principle on Japanese participation in the construction of this pipeline in mid-1973, in view of the threatening energy crisis and the importance of this pipe to both sides. Accordingly, when completed, Japan will receive 25,000,000 tons (not the originally mentioned 40m. tons) of Soviet oil annually, which in the words of a Soviet statement 'will contribute greatly to the stabilisation of Japan's oil supplies'. In fact, however, the stipulated quantity would only represent a tiny fraction of Japan's enormous oil requirements and imports of some 200 million tons annually. Still, it would be a useful additional source to offset against the more remote and uncertain Near Eastern supplies and, incidentally, dwarfs China's contract for one million tons a year. Before concluding this agreement with Japan, the Soviets had started on their own to construct the Anzhero–Sudzhensk–Irkutsk section of this 48 in. pipe. By 1973, it was reported to be proceeding and likely to reach Irkutsk by the end of the year. This was not achieved.

Apart from the Tyumen' oil pipeline, Japan has also been involved in discussions with the Soviet government about participation in the development of the west Siberian oil industry. After protracted discussions, the Soviet government extended a definite invitation to the Japanese, in 1972, to participate in this copartnership project, on the familiar Soviet barter basis, by which the Japanese would be paid for their financial and technological cooperation in Tyumen' oil. A large Japanese delegation was then permitted for the first time to make a preliminary survey of these oil-fields. Technical circles in the west expected at this time that the Japanese would draw on the advanced oil technology of Gulf Oil, one of their affiliated companies, if they finally became copartners in this development project. Many contentious issues of finance, credits and prices had to be ironed out to the Japanese satisfaction before agreement could be reached. A Soviet commentary announced in mid-1973 that 'full-dress negotiations are under way on the Tyumen' oil project and problems such as the Japanese Government's extension of bank credits are to be studied soon'. There the matter rests at the time of writing.

Japanese participation in the development of Siberian copper, iron ore, coal and the respective infrastructures, has also been sought by Moscow, and qualified interest expressed in such cooperation by the Japanese. One of the most difficult and expensive of these proposals concerns the exploitation of the Udokan copper mines.[1] Soviet estimates of the volume of capital investment required for the Udokan project, about $700 milliard, far exceeded the limits of Japanese calculations. These remote Udokan mines would undoubtedly require large capital investment to create a workers' settlement with housing and other amenities, roads and a railway to connect with the nearest station on the Trans-Siberian, some 500 km. to the south. It is now generally thought that the Soviet financial demands are too high, for these purposes, to be carried by one country. Having inconclusively discussed Udokan with the Germans, the French and the Rio Tinto Zinc Corporation, as well as the Japanese, the idea of an international consortium to handle the

[1] Fuller details of these mines are given in the respective section of Chapter 6.

complicated finance of this huge undertaking was being canvassed by the Soviet government in 1970–71. Nothing yet seems to have come of the idea that the Rio Tinto Zinc Corporation might form part of such a group, to handle Udokan finance in cooperation with Japan for metallurgical-technical assistance and probably with a third country as well. Subsequently, Udokan vanished from Soviet news reports, at least for the time being (1973).

Japanese collaboration in the exploitation of the Chul'man coal mines and the iron of the Khabarovsk and Amur krays would seem to have a more immediate chance of materialising than some of the other copartnership projects. These mines (which contain good coking coal) are more accessible and lie in a more tolerable climate than either Udokan copper, Yakut or Tyumen' oil and natural gas. Once the relatively easy communications problem was solved, and energy possibly supplied by the Yakutsk natural gas development scheme (now apparently under active consideration), the capital investment required would be much lower than in the other projects under consideration. The fact that the Soviets have already started to build the railway, which will link the Chul'man coal mines with the Amur trunk line, suggests either that they are planning to go ahead alone in opening up these reserves, or that they may be hoping to accelerate cooperation with the Japanese, by improving the local communications (see Postscript).

Before agreement can be reached even on this relatively simple deal, the Japanese would presumably have to be satisfied, not only that the financial terms were acceptable, but that regular coking coal and iron supplies would be forthcoming from these Soviet mines. This would be an important consideration if they were to switch from their previous supply sources in the U.S.A., and more recently in Australia, where the iron mines are richer and well developed. These sources, being more remote from Japan than the Soviet Far Eastern mines, involve higher transport costs but can be relied on for regular deliveries while the record of the Soviet State Export organisations in the Far East in this respect is not encouraging.

In the Far East, Soviet-Japanese discussions about the joint development of natural gas have also been proceeding since 1966 without agreement being reached on terms. The original proposal was that Sakhalin natural gas should be exported through a 1,480 km. long pipeline to Hokkaido, to feed the Japanese petro-chemical industries in Muroran. The Japanese would be paid for their technical assistance in constructing this pipeline with Sakhalin natural gas. The two parties found it difficult to agree on prices and credit terms, but the negotiations broke down altogether when the Russians abruptly switched the proposals from supplies of Sakhalin gas (the reserves of which they now declared to be much smaller than originally estimated) to natural gas from the remoter Yakutsk fields. This would be a much more difficult and expensive operation and involve the Japanese in the construction of a pipeline through rugged and largely uninhabited country to the port of Magadan (as it was then proposed), liquefaction of the gas, and its transport by tanker to Japan. The Japanese were sceptical of Soviet capacity to undertake these operations, or of the costs of the special type of tanker required. Equally important, they were unprepared at this stage to accept the much higher capital cost of exploiting this

Yakutsk gas and the unadvantageous credit terms demanded by Moscow. Commercial circles in Japan were also reported to be dubious about Japan's capacity to utilise the immense quantities of gas which eventually would be forthcoming from Yakutiya and were concerned about the lack of assurances about the time, price, or volume of deliveries, as well as the strategic danger of Japan becoming dependent on a single source of supply.

Mr. Brezhnev's interview with the Japanese Ambassador to Moscow, in March 1973, and the letter from Prime Minister Tanaka conveyed to him at this interview, were significant events suggesting that the unsatisfactory situation regarding Soviet-Japanese economic cooperation was moving into a more constructive phase. Though the Tanaka letter was not published, the Japanese Foreign Ministry reported that the Japanese government had expressed willingness to withdraw its former objections and to cooperate actively in the Tyumen' oil development scheme, and it was suggested that a compromise solution of the long-outstanding problem of the four Kuril islands claimed by Japan might now be possible. It was also agreed to resume the peace treaty talks which had broken down in 1972, on Japan's firm refusal to abandon its demand for the return of these islands. These talks (which had not taken place at the time of writing), should provide a proper forum for an adjustment of the controversial Northern Territories issue. Simultaneously, there was strong support for the three Siberian oil and natural gas development projects: as proposed at various times by Moscow: Tyumen' oil, Yakutsk natural gas and the natural gas of the Sakhalin continental shelf, from the private Soviet-Japanese Economic Committee. If agreed, these projects or any one of them would involve many Japanese firms and require the employment of large numbers of highly trained Japanese engineers and other technicians, as the Japanese maintain that only their own engineers are qualified to supervise their advanced equipment (an attitude disputed by the Soviets). Latterly, Japanese participation seems less feasible in the Tyumen' oil project. The final details of the Japanese agreement to participate in the development of Yakutsk natural gas, remain to be worked out. The subject came to the fore again in 1972–73 during the Soviet discussions on the development of Siberian oil and natural gas, when Dr. Hammer's Occidental Petroleum Corporation Consortium expressed American interest in the Yakutsk natural gas project. It was further reported that the Japanese also agreed to participate, on condition that there was American participation in this very costly, complex development scheme. According to the memorandum signed in Tokyo by Japanese and Soviet officials, in July 1973, the Soviet Union would receive $150 million in U.S. and Japanese bank loans and supply 1.5 million tons of liquefied natural gas over 20 years, to the U.S. and Japan. Japan and the U.S. should begin to receive supplies of this liquefied natural gas in about 3–5 years, when commercial production at Yakutsk might be expected to begin (see Postscript).

In spite of some tempting economic advantages for Japan arising from these Siberian copartnership schemes, especially in regard to bulk oil and gas supplies, Japan's final decisions in this matter will no doubt be carefully balanced, so as not to disturb the present delicate relations with China (though already Japanese involvement in Siberian development has been severely criticised by the Chinese).

Moreover, the Siberian venture is far from generally popular among bankers and businessmen in Tokyo, who are opposed to sinking such large amounts of Japanese capital in the Soviet Union, a country they profoundly distrust. But these attitudes have been greatly modified by the effect of the energy crisis in Japan.

Soviet-Japanese Barter Trade. Barter trade between the Soviet Far Eastern mainland and Japan is an important element in Soviet-Japanese relations in this part of the Soviet Union, though it represents only a small fraction of total Soviet-Japanese trade. It was first regularised by a separate Protocol, attached to the long term Soviet-Japanese trade agreement of 1963. Since then, according to local Soviet and Japanese statements, it has been rapidly expanding. This barter trade is no longer separately mentioned in Soviet foreign trade statistics dealing with Soviet-Japanese trade as a whole, so its exact volume remains rather obscure and largely based on press reports.

This barter-based exchange of goods is highly valued by both sides and the more so recently by Moscow, since the Far Eastern region's trade with Manchuria over the Amur–Heilungkiang frontier has been severely affected and at times entirely disrupted by the Sino-Soviet conflict. The main Japanese exports to the Soviet Far East are consumer goods and machinery which are in very short supply in the region, while the Soviet Far East exports fish products, lumber and oil (the latter at present only 10% of total Soviet oil exports to Japan, but likely to increase when the Trans-Siberian pipeline is built). The bilateral barter agreement signed with the Japanese-Soviet Association of exporters and importers in Hokkaido, in 1972, is typical of these arrangements. Under the Agreement, the Association will import Soviet goods to the value of $1,871,000 consisting of $1,116,000 timber; $60,000 tomato paste; $60,000 honey; $200,000 tallow; and $435,000 cotton-seed, while it will export $1,871,000 worth of goods consisting of fishing nets ($1,000,000); furniture ($300,000); sweaters ($200,000); shoes and textiles ($371,000). Fish and marine products are also among Soviet exports to Japan. This trade reached its highest level, since it started ten years earlier, in 1972, with reciprocal shipments totalling about $25,000,000. In spite of its increasing value and local importance, the volume of this coastal trade is still only a very small proportion (about 10%) of the total Soviet-Japanese trade. In 1964, a special Soviet office *Dalintorg* (Far Eastern Trade) was set up in Nakhodka to handle these Japanese coastal trade relations and was, exceptionally, authorised to sign contracts with Japanese firms, thus avoiding the often frustrating delays involved in negotiations with distant Moscow. And in addition, a joint Soviet-Japanese Economic Committee meets regularly to discuss Far Eastern trade problems.

The Japanese are in a unique position compared to other non-communist countries in regard to the Soviet Far East. They are permitted to indulge in 'promotional' activities, like trade fairs and exhibitions for their goods in Khabarovsk and other towns in the region, while Japanese businessmen can move about in areas in the Soviet Far East closed to other nationals. Moreover, Japan is the only foreign country with diplomatic representation in the Soviet Far East, and her Consul-General has his establishment in Nakhodka, to look after Japanese interests.

In view of the proximity of Japan to the Soviet mainland, it is not surprising that she should occupy a relatively favourable position there, economically. The rudimentary state of the Region's manufacturing industries (the Primor'ye for example produces only 15% of its cultural-economic requirements) means that Japanese goods fill various acute needs among the local population.

There is also a very much smaller border trade with the adjoining Democratic People's Republic of Korea. Agreements were signed in 1960 and 1967 by the Soviet Union with the Republic, with a view to expanding economic cooperation and commodity exchange between the two countries, but on the whole North Korea has had much the best of the bargain. Soviet exports between 1966–71 (oil products, manganese and chrome ores as well as machines) were intended to strengthen the sagging Korean economy while some Korean foodstuffs, pig iron and metal goods passed into the Soviet Far Eastern region. On the whole, North Korea has been a disappointing area for Soviet economic efforts and the main interest of the relationship (about which little, in fact, is known in the west) would seem to be to ensure that Chinese influence does not dominate the country.

It is interesting, however, to note that, like the Japanese, the Koreans are permitted to organise trade exhibitions in the Soviet Far Eastern towns. There was also a fleeting suggestion in 1973 that some form of economic copartnership might be organised in the Soviet Far East with the Koreans, perhaps in agriculture, where labour is so scarce. In this connection it may be recalled that, according to an agreement of 1957, North Korean labour was imported to cut coniferous timber in the Khabarovsk kray between 1957–62.[2] The agreement does not seem to have been renewed and nothing is known about how it worked out in practice.

Soviet-Australian Trade. Events in 1972–73, suggested that a new bid was being made to increase Soviet trade with Australia within the narrow limits now possible, owing to Soviet policy restricting the imports of consumer goods. Apart from fluctuating imports of Australian grain *via* Far Eastern ports and some exports of Soviet Far Eastern timber to Australia, the first trade agreement in 1965 did not lead to any substantial trade increase to improve the adverse Soviet trade balance with Australia (mainly owing to the regular large Soviet imports of Australian wool to European Russia). But, should the Soviets decide to open the door to Australian consumer goods, especially meat, fruit and other foods, there should be a ready market for them in the Soviet Far East where all food except fish has to be brought in, often over long distances, from other parts of the Soviet Union.

A supplementary trade agreement to that of 1965 was signed in Canberra in 1973 and provided a number of practical measures aimed at stimulating Soviet-Australian trade. The U.S.S.R. Minister for Foreign Trade, N. S. Patolichev, one of the signatories to this agreement, stressed at the time of signature that particular attention should be paid to trade between Australia and the Soviet Far East. And for the first time the question of 'joint ventures in the mineral and industrial fields' was raised in these trade discussions and figures among the tasks allotted to the

[2] cf. P. Dibb., op. cit., p. 112.

joint commission, set up to explore ways of increasing trade between Australia and the Soviet Union. The possible nature of these 'joint ventures' was not disclosed, but it is intriguing to think that Australia might be either linked with Soviet-Japanese-American copartnership projects in the Soviet Far East or cooperate in some other scheme independently. But however Soviet-Australian trade develops, it is unlikely to match the scale of the well-established Soviet-Japanese coastal barter trade, and co-partnership prospects.

The development of Far Eastern trade with other countries of the 'Pacific Rim' (a term dear to Moscow), in the south Pacific and south-east Asia, is also being seriously studied in the Soviet Union and is regarded as a matter of considerable importance for the future. An Import-Export Laboratory was established in the sixties, at the Complex Research Institute of the U.S.S.R. Academy of Sciences in Khabarovsk, for the special purpose of studying trade possibilities and conditions in Pacific Rim countries and the new Economic Institute of the Far Eastern Scientific Centre is also working on these problems. The idea seems to be to ascertain the extent to which the trade now conducted between European Russia and countries of south and south-east Asia, like India or Malaya, might eventually be profitably diverted to the Far East (a route which from the transport point of view at least has some advantages as long as the Suez Canal remains closed). At the moment, the exporting capacity of the Soviet Far East is extremely limited. This capacity could gradually expand with the more efficient development of the territory's resources and the establishment of some associated manufacturing industries. Under these circumstances, this Pacific Rim trade might become a more realistic proposition than it is at present.[3]

Soviet-American Economic Cooperation in Siberia and the Soviet Far East. While Soviet-Japanese negotiations on the Trans-Siberian pipeline and other Siberian projects were still hanging fire, a dramatic change took place in Soviet-American economic relations following President Nixon's visit to Moscow in May 1972. The subsequent, comprehensive new trade agreement signed between the two countries in Washington in October 1972 opened the door to large-scale American participation in Soviet industrial development and notably in the natural gas industry of west Siberia and the Soviet Far East (Yakutiya).

The American intervention in Siberia had the incidental effect of undermining Japan's former position as the sole foreign country engaged in joint Soviet economic projects in Siberia, though in general Soviet-Japanese cooperation does not seem to have been impaired by the appearance of the Americans on the scene. As it is now developing, American economic cooperation could revolutionise the lagging technological-investment situation, as it has been described above, in the Siberian natural gas and oil industries, and in other areas of development which may be suggested by the Soviet government.

First in the field to take advantage of the prospective vision of participation in

[3] A detailed study of Soviet-Pacific Rim trade will be found in P. Dibb, op. cit., 'Commodity Outlook for Pacific Trade.'

Siberian and other economic development projects, even before the Soviet-American trade agreement was signed, was Dr. Armand Hammer, chief executive of the big, fully-integrated oil business, the Occidental Petroleum Corporation, but regarded as something of a 'rogue-elephant' in the international oil world. He is a man of great knowledge and experience in the energy field and likely to be attracted rather than daunted by the complexity of the Siberian projects. He lost no time in opening an office in Moscow to promote his multi-million dollar Siberian and other Soviet schemes. These latter included participation in the development and export to the United States of Yakut natural gas (virtually untapped hitherto) and the construction of fertiliser and chemical plants in European Russia, as well as a large hotel in Moscow.

Dr. Hammer's exuberant announcement of his plans and reception in Moscow were at first received with some scepticism in the west and even interpreted as a propaganda ruse to raise the value of his company's shares on the New York Stock Exchange. But in spite of his standing as a millionaire capitalist tycoon, all doubts regarding his status as a privileged partner in Soviet economic development plans were dispelled by a long article in *Pravda* (9.11.1972), definitely setting the seal of approval on him. This was done by recalling Lenin's approbation of Hammer's aid to Russia during the famine in the Urals in 1921 when, in exchange for an asbestos concession in the Urals and a monopoly agency for the sale of Ford cars, tractors, etc., he had arranged large shipments of American grain to Russia and produced a hospital train loaded with medical supplies and staff to relieve the famine. Lenin put the full weight of his personal authority behind the swift implementation of this Hammer mutual aid scheme. At the same time, Lenin admitted the necessity to grant foreign concessions in order to re-establish the Soviet economy, and dismissed the idea that the workers accustomed to 'regard capitalists as their enemies' would cause trouble to these foreign concessionaires. 'The workers will not cut the branch on which they are sitting', he affirmed.

The prominence given to these Leninist pronouncements in *Pravda* (9.11.1972) and a later article by the influential Soviet journalist Yuri Zhukov (*Pravda* 28.11. 1972), stressing the 'common sense' of the new Soviet-American trade relationship, might also be seen as a move to forestall possible ideological objections to this *volte face* in Soviet policy towards the U.S.A., by more militant elements in the Party ranks. Unless therefore some unforeseen hitch crops up in his negotiations with Moscow, Dr. Hammer would seem to have the edge at present on other competitors (such as Tenneco Inc., Texas Eastern Transmission Corporation and Brown Root Inc.) as Moscow's 'favourite son' in the new Soviet-American oil and gas development projects, in Siberia. He was the first American businessman to open an office in Moscow in 1972 and had an interview with Mr. Brezhnev, early in 1973, a signal honour not yet granted to any other American businessman.

Particularly relevant to the present situation is the Leninist dictum recalled by Dr. Hammer: 'Our two countries, Russia and the U.S.A., complement each other. Russia remains a society with enormous unutilised resources. We need machinery, advanced methods of production, engineers . . . Everything valuable we should take from you'. *Mutatis mutandis*, this is the underlying, realistic Soviet basis of the new

Soviet-American trade Agreement of 1972 and the ensuing many-sided impact of advanced American technology on the Soviet economy.

As far as Siberian energy projects are concerned, Dr. Hammer and his Occidental Petroleum Corporation have so far concentrated on participation in the development of Yakutsk natural gas. A letter of intent was signed by this Corporation, in association with El Paso Natural Gas, in June 1973, for a $10-billion scheme to move up to 2 billion cu.ft/day of this gas through an estimated 3,300 km. long pipeline to Vladivostok (or some other Soviet Pacific port) where a liquefaction plant 'the largest ever envisaged' would be built and 20 cryogenic tankers would carry the gas to the U.S. West Coast.[4] This contract will run for 25 years and deliveries begin by 1979–80 at earliest, according to optimistic American reports. It is an enormous venture into largely unknown terrain and even the exact volume of this gas is something of a mystery (even to the Russians). Much still remains to be agreed between Dr. Hammer and the Soviet government, regarding credits to the Soviet Union and other expenditure, apart altogether from the complex technical matters involved in actually producing the natural gas, and constructing the 3,300 km. long pipeline through Yakutiya to Olga Bay on the Pacific coast (the exact track of which has not yet been announced). Nor is it yet clear how the triangular Soviet-American-Japanese cooperation in this project will be organised.

Participation in the development of west Siberian natural gas involves, not Dr. Hammer, but a consortium consisting of three major Houston companies – Tenneco, Texas Eastern Transmission and Brown and Root. In a letter of intent signed a month after Dr. Hammer's Yakutsk letter, in July 1973, the group made known their intention to engage in the so-called 'North Star' project, also a very difficult and expensive enterprise, for the extraction, liquefaction and export of 2 billion cu.ft/day for 25 years, from the huge Urengoiskoy field of west Siberia, at a cost of an estimated $1.25 per 1,000 cu. ft. A Soviet credit of 3 billion dollars (U.S.) would finance purchase of American-made transmission equipment (compressors and 1,500 miles of 48 in. steel pipe, capable of withstanding temperatures of minus 60°F.) and the construction of a plant at the ice-free port of Murmansk, to liquefy the gas for shipment to the east coast of the United States, in a special fleet of tankers (built and owned by the Americans). Thence it will be distributed for sale in the consortium's pipelines to eastern and southern American utilities. The construction of these liquefied natural gas (L.N.G.) tankers may incidentally help to solve the problem of the 'sick' U.S. shipbuilding industry as they are 'immensely expensive, extremely complicated and highly automated' to construct, but a special feature of American shipyards.

All this would need large dollar loans from the Export-Import Bank or various other U.S. banks and industrial companies, guaranteed by the Export-Import Bank. In view of the magnitude of this undertaking, the need for Western technological know-how, and the adverse effects on American lenders of any interruptions or delays in the supply of west Siberian natural gas, one American expert is of the

[4] Although not mentioned in the Soviet announcement of this letter of intent regarding the development of Yakutsk natural gas, Bechtel, a leading American firm of consultants on the construction of L.N.G. plants is also stated by American sources to be a member of Dr. Hammer's consortium.

opinion 'that the American parties to the deal will expect and require a considerable measure of direct participation in Soviet operations. In the first place, there is the issue of on-site inspection to assure western investors of the adequacy of gas reserves and to permit them to estimate extraction costs ... There is a distinct need for Western technicians to share in decision-making with their Soviet counterparts, in order to insure proper installation and operation of specialised Western technical facilities in severe climatic conditions'.[5] But how far the Soviet government will agree to these requests remains a matter for conjecture at this stage. Like the Yakut natural gas project, 'North Star' is only at the letter of intent state of negotiation and at the best the United States is unlikely to receive gas from either project before 1980. It is interesting to note that these first major Soviet-American joint development schemes in Siberia are both concerned with natural gas, not oil. This is natural from the American point of view, because at the present time natural gas is the immediate requirement of the American energy industry. From the Soviet standpoint, American technical assistance and capital must be specially welcome in developing the remote gas deposits of north Tyumen' and of Yakutiya, both of which are extremely expensive and technically difficult operations, and which, unaided, would have sorely taxed Soviet resources. In fact, it seems most unlikely that, at this time, Moscow would have decided to develop the Yakutsk gas deposits if Dr. Hammer had not opted to do so.

These Soviet moves to attract American capital and advanced technology into the Siberian energy industries coincide with a phase of acute anxiety in the United States about the 'energy crisis'. This situation was surely seen by the Soviet government as a trump card 'to attract a barter deal for the U.S. technology their economy needs.[6] Apart from these joint development projects, American technical aid could be very useful in supplying wide diameter pipe of 40 in. or 48 in. or wider now urgently needed by the Soviet oil and gas industries. Soviet industry has had great difficulty in producing the large quantity of high quality, large diameter pipe required, because of the remoteness and difficult climate of the west Siberian oil and gas fields and was faced with even heavier demands for the long haul of west Siberian oil to the Far East and the projected gas exports from the north of the region, westwards to European Russia already under way, before the American joint projects were concluded. For some years past, German and Italian firms have also been commissioned to supply wide diameter pipe for Siberian gas, but the demand for this pipe is likely to rise for gas and for oil, for at least another ten–fifteen years.

Up to the time of writing the further implementation of the joint Soviet-American Siberian projects has been blocked by the refusal of the U.S. Congress to sanction the export of the huge capital funds required to finance these deals until more satisfactory assurances are forthcoming from the Soviet government about the free emigration of Jews from the Soviet Union. (See appendix on The Jackson Amendment to the East-West Trade Relations Act). It is also not without interest to note that according to the *Gas World* (20.1.1973), various sectional interests in

[5] cf. West Siberia: The Quest for Energy. By John P. Hardt (*Problems of Communism* May-June 1973). This is a well documented article on which I have relied here.
[6] FORBES July 1, 1972.

the U.S.A. were having second thoughts (after a period of euphoria) about the 'high cost of Soviet gas of $1.50 per 1,000 cu. ft. compared to the current U.S. price of 20 cents' (in fact this Soviet gas price is only dear when compared to the price, at the moment, of American domestic gas, it is even cheap, if the estimated costs of extraction, liquefaction and transmission to the U.S. are taken into account, while by 1979–80, the price of American natural gas may have risen highly). *Gas World* also reported that there were doubts about the accuracy of Russian estimates of Siberian gas reserves and the Soviet government's refusal to permit independent testing of the deposits, and about the national security impact of excessive U.S. reliance on Soviet gas. This last fear would appear to be quite groundless, because even when both the Tyumen' and Yakut supplies of natural gas are being delivered as per contract to the east and west coasts of the United States, they will, it is estimated, only form a small percentage of total U.S. requirements. Meanwhile, both American and Japanese experts have visited the Yakut gas fields.

In view of the probably unparalleled financial-economic magnitude of these Siberian natural gas deals, it was to be expected that they would arouse controversy among sectional interests such as the U.S. coal industry, while Soviet sources would uniformly follow the Party leader in approving them. Any such controversies should be regarded as inevitable, but ephemeral, teething troubles and not of lasting significance in a matter of such importance, and even national prestige, to both partners.

The Japanese and the Americans have, so far, mutually accepted each other's participation in Siberian economic development with good grace. As these partnership projects develop, both will no doubt be on the alert to ensure that each enjoys the same footing of equality in their business dealings with the Soviet government. It was noticeable that the opening of a Japanese bank office in Moscow in 1972, for example, was soon followed in 1973 by the announcement that the Chase Manhattan bank had got permission to open a U.S. office, also, in Moscow. The opening of these bank offices represents an exceptional departure from the usual Soviet practice of not permitting banks of foreign capital countries to operate in the Soviet Union. Both are closely connected with financing business deals of their respective countries in the Soviet Union, and their presence is a reflection of the new Soviet interest in attracting foreign capital and technical assistance, not only to Siberia, but to the sagging Soviet economy as a whole. From the American point of view, it remains to be seen how much further the rigid Soviet system will be bent, from above, to facilitate their difficult work in the Siberian environment, how they can adjust to Soviet conditions and how the local difficulties which will almost certainly arise (including some degree of bureaucratic obstruction) will be overcome.

chapter fourteen

Far Eastern Frontier Problems

The Soviet Far Eastern frontier extends over a vast area by land and sea, the coastal area alone stretching from Vladivostok to the north-eastern tip of the region at Uelen and north-west into the Arctic Ocean, being in all about 6,000 miles. It was further enlarged after World War II, by the annexation of the Kuril chain of islands and the southern half of the island of Sakhalin from Japan. The remoteness of this frontier from the defence headquarters in European Russia creates serious defence and supply problems for Moscow. These problems were exacerbated along the land frontier by the outbreak of hostilities with China in the sixties. The Vladivostok naval base and the coastal defences have assumed a new significance in the emerging Soviet plans for the containment of China, extending into the south Pacific and Indian Oceans, by showing the flag if nothing more.

The Sino-Soviet frontier consists of two stretches divided by the Mongolian People's Republic: the Soviet Far Eastern and the Central Asian. The Far Eastern stretch is formed by the 2,000 mile long Amur river and its two tributaries, the Argun and the Ussuri. The continuing dispute over this section of the frontier largely results from the fact that, since the Chinese Communists came to power in 1949, no boundary agreement with the Soviet Union has been signed and the frontier remained demarcated by treaties drawn up in the nineteenth century between Tsarist Russia and the Chinese Emperors. The frontier problem emerged as a source of conflict between the two Communist countries only when their relations declined into bitter ideological hostility, in the mid-sixties.

Sino-Russian rivalry for control of these Far-Eastern borderlands has a long history. A crucial struggle for domination of the Amur basin lands in the mid-seventeenth century ended with the conclusion of the Treaty of Nerchinsk, in 1689. It forced the Russians to abandon this area for 150 years, and it is the only treaty between Tsarist Russia and China recognised as 'equal' and valid today by Peking. The three subsequent treaties, by which Tsarist Russia was established as the sovereign power in these lands, are repudiated as 'unequal' by the Chinese Communists because they regard them as forced on China at a time when, through internal weakness, she was powerless to resist Russian aggression. The treaties in question are the Treaties of Aigun and Tientsin (May and June 1858 respectively), by which China lost some 185,000 sq. miles of territory to Russia in the Amur basin, and the subsequent Treaty of Peking (1860) which extended Russian sovereignty southwards along the Ussuri river frontier, to the borders of Korea. Thus, another 133,000 sq. miles of territory came under the Russian flag, including the important site of the future city of Vladivostok and other Pacific outposts.

A good deal of confusion regarding the actual Chinese position on this frontier has been created, both by misleading Soviet statements and the discrepancies between wildly-inflated Chinese estimates of territories seized by Russia, put out for propaganda purposes, and the more realistic basis on which the Chinese are still apparently prepared to renegotiate this frontier with the Soviet Union. In fact, it seems that these far-reaching Chinese 'claims' amount to little more than an attempt to expose the aggressive policies of both Tsarist and Soviet Russia against these Chinese borderlands. The official Chinese position on this issue, as defined in 1964, and frequently re-stated subsequently, is that if Moscow would formally acknowledge that the nineteenth-century Tsarist treaties were 'unequal', China would be prepared, in turn, to take them as the basis for an overall settlement of these frontier problems and, until this was reached, they would remain in force. This proposal was met with an adamant refusal by Moscow to discuss the present Soviet-Chinese frontiers, on no better grounds than Khrushchev's specious argument that 'historically formed boundaries now exist' and as such could not be changed. Meanwhile both sides have rigidly maintained their respective positions.

Acrimonious charges and counter charges of frontier violations led to talks in 1964 in Peking, which soon broke down, while the situation continued to deteriorate along the Amur-Ussuri frontier. The violent activities of young Red Guard hooligans, during the Cultural Revolution, culminated in the notorious bloody Sino-Soviet clashes around the Ussuri river island of Damanskiy, in 1969. When these eventually halted, border negotiations were resumed, but with no more positive result than in 1964. Simultaneously, in view of the dispute about the lie of the Damanskiy island frontier line, a meeting of the Sino-Soviet Navigation Commission (set up in 1951) was held in Khabarovsk, also with no result. Nor was the meeting of this Commission, in March 1972, on the boundary rivers, any more successful in dealing with the important problems requiring solution.

Though the joint navigation treaty between the Soviet Union and the C.P.R. is still in existence, new problems have arisen for Soviet shipping following the 'Measures for Controlling Foreign Vessels on Border Rivers', issued unilaterally by the Chinese in 1966. These regulations are, apparently, extremely complicated and difficult for Russian skippers to interpret, providing loopholes for the Chinese to refuse entry to river ports on their side of the boundary, or to detain non-Chinese ships. They still await clarification if more navigational troubles in this area are to be avoided.

The 1969 armed clashes between the Soviet and Chinese forces brought into the limelight the urgent need for agreement about the disputed position of the river frontier in relation to Damanskiy island.

The Soviet position, briefly, is that according to the Sino-Russian Treaty of Peking of 1860, the Ussuri river was named as the border between Russia and China and in the area of Damanskiy island this border was drawn directly along the Chinese bank of the river so that, as it is situated on the Soviet side of this 'border line', the island belongs to the Soviet Union and not to China. Moscow categorically denied that there is any principle in international law which 'established the border on border-rivers as passing through the middle of the river's mainstream'.

Equally categorically, the Chinese maintain that the map attached to the 1860 Treaty does not and cannot possibly show the boundary line in the rivers. More pertinent, they claimed, was an explicit regulation issued in 1960 by the Supreme Soviet of the U.S.S.R. on the State frontier of the U.S.S.R. which stated: 'The State boundary of the U.S.S.R. on navigable rivers runs along the centre of the main channel, or thalweg, of the river'. The Chinese would seem to have a trump card in that regulation, but it has so far made no impact on the Soviet attitude. Against a background of mutually offensive Sino-Soviet recriminations, throughout 1972, a Soviet commentary, in standard Chinese, recalled that in 1966 the U.S.S.R. had met Peking's demands for Chinese citizens to be allowed to 'engage in productive activities' on islands and waters under Soviet jurisdiction, along the boundary rivers, and to herd livestock on Soviet territory. It may be presumed, as there is apparently no information to the contrary, that this unusually accommodating regulation was still in force in 1974 and that actual border conditions for the inhabitants are better, in fact, than suggested by the bitter polemics between Moscow and Peking.

This is also the situation in regard to Sino-Soviet trade. Though it has sharply declined since its peak in early sixties, it has nevertheless continued with only occasional interruptions coinciding with the armed clashes in frontier areas. It was agreed in 1970 that the two countries would substantially increase supplies to each other in 1971. This 'forward step' was reinforced by a trade and payments agreement in 1972. As a result of these agreements the total volume of trade between the two countries greatly increased, according to Soviet sources. Nevertheless, it was still far below the pre-conflict level, in 1972–73. More than 70% of Soviet exports to China were machinery and other equipment, including aviation products, aviation equipment and aircraft parts, ferrous and non-ferrous metals and chemicals. It is not clear whether this aviation equipment included military aircraft, but this is most unlikely.

According to an interview given by a staff member of the Soviet Ministry of Foreign Affairs in 1972, the Soviet Union has also trained personnel for China and helped the Chinese to operate the latest Soviet aircraft and helicopters, improbable though it may seem. Soviet imports from China included some non-ferrous metals and finished goods. 'Traditional Chinese exports also increased remarkably, so that more new items can be found in Soviet retail markets. This is conducive to the further meeting of the Soviet people's increasing demands.' The return to more normal trade exchanges promised by this latest Sino-Soviet trade agreement might suggest a bid by the Russians to forestall the anticipated renewal of Sino-American trade, in 1972. This idea seems to inspire the following words from the above-mentioned Soviet official interview: 'The Soviet Union has for long provided China with machinery and other equipment and has in fact met most of China's demands for such commodities. In China, people have long known that Soviet machinery and other equipment are dependable and are wanted by users. Moreover, the terms of trade offered to China are favourable compared with those offered by capitalist countries which provide China with the same sorts of commodities'. There was no mention in these trade reports of the usually small, but important, Chinese border trade with the Soviet Far Eastern region, but as far as is known, it was only briefly interrupted, during the more violent Ussuri-Amur frontier clashes.

Soviet relations with Japan, since World War II, reflect a delicate balance of conflicting political and economic interests in the Far East. Though after 1945, the Soviet Far Eastern frontier territory was no longer threatened from occupied Manchuria (Manchukuo), Soviet suspicion of Japan and of the Japanese-American alliance continued to exist and while Okinawa remained under American occupation, Soviet pressure was often exerted on Japan aimed at undermining the American connection. On her side, Japan continued to press her claim to the four southernmost Kuril islands, her 'northern territories', annexed with the rest of this island chain after the last war, claims which were uncompromisingly rejected by the Soviet Union.

The Kuril island chain formed the official frontier between Russia and Japan for seventy years, from 1875, when the entire archipelago was awarded to Japan by the Treaty of St. Petersburg (1875) and remained Japanese until annexed by Soviet Russia in 1945. These islands thus became part of the new Soviet Far Eastern frontier territory. They were never easily accessible under Japanese rule, but the Soviet security barriers to any foreign visitors are even more exclusive than the Japanese. Consequently, the only information about developments there, since 1945, comes from a thin trickle of Soviet news items impossible to check at first hand. There seems no doubt, however, that the rich fisheries and canneries in the Kurils, in which the Japanese invested large capital sums in the first half of the twentieth century, have been further developed under Soviet auspices. The fur-bearing seal and other mammals found round these islands are also very valuable.

Moscow would seem of recent years to be endeavouring to forge closer bonds with the Kuril island chain and especially the contentious four southern islands, forming the sensitive tip of her Far Eastern frontier, nearest to Japan. Visits of Soviet ornithologists and other scientists occasionally take place and the Islands are now included in tourist cruises for Soviet citizens from the mainland. Girls from the Ukraine were reported to be planning to settle there and details of the climate and job opportunities in Kunashir and Shikotan were broadcast for them in 1973, by Moscow in a glamorous propaganda appeal.

The major interest of the Kurils to the Soviets is, however, their strategic position as a protective shield around the great sweep of the Sea of Okhotsk and its coastline, now to all intents and purposes a closed Soviet sea. These islands would be of still greater defensive importance to the Soviet Union if Japan ever decided to become neutral and all bases were removed from her territory. In such a case, the strategic position of the Soviet Far East and of the Vladivostok naval base would be strengthened by the freeing of the exits to the Sea of Japan, on which Vladivostok is situated, from possible threats, as at present, from bases in Japan. A more northerly route might then have to be planned for any attacks on the Soviet Far East and as a result the Kuril islands would assume a bigger role in its defence.[1]

From mid-1972, the Soviet attitude towards Japan became increasingly friendly. Apprehension about the possible threat to the Soviet Far Eastern region of a consolidation of China's new relationship with both the U.S.A. and Japan, may well have prompted Moscow to aim at a better political understanding with Tokyo and the conclusion of the long-deferred peace treaty. At the same time, the energy position was arousing deep concern in Japan and the importance of securing a closer source of oil, in Siberia, than the present long-haul supply line from the Middle East, was of considerable concern. In this situation, the idea of a peace treaty with the Soviet Union, long repugnant to the Japanese, assumed a new significance as a more stable political basis for cooperation in the Siberian oil industry. A turning point seemed to have been reached in March, 1973, by the high level exchange of messages between Prime Minister Tanaka and Mr. Brezhnev, in which the Japanese Prime Minister agreed to the resumption of the peace treaty talks which had previously broken down on the 'Northern Territories' issue. The Soviet Union had provided a basis for compromise on this thorny problem by suggesting that it be left 'for a later settlement', instead of reiterating the usual, frigid 'no discussion of this issue' formula – but contrary to expectations, nothing was changed by Mr. Tanaka's Moscow visit in October 1973.

The criss-cross of conflicting political interests around the frontiers of the Soviet Far Eastern region, compounded by the outbreak of hostilities on the Amur-Ussuri border in 1969, necessitated a massive strengthening of the Soviet defence forces. Though exact information about these defence measures is a carefully guarded secret, Western military experts have no doubt that the Soviet armed forces on land and sea in the Amur-Ussuri frontier area have been heavily reinforced in recent years. The island of Sakhalin is also reliably reported to have become a veritable arsenal of sophisticated weaponry and to have acquired powerful air and naval bases. And the Soviet Pacific fleet based on Vladivostok has been strengthened.

These defence measures have had their psychological counterpart in the Soviet Far East, where it is apparently official policy to maintain an atmosphere of tension and military preparedness among the local population. Moscow seems acutely preoccupied with ensuring that there is no slackening of Soviet patriotism among its citizens. And no opportunity is missed to stimulate these sentiments. The annual military parades in Vladivostok, Khabarovsk and Blagoveshtchensk, and the naval display in Zolotoy Rog Bay, adjoining the Far Eastern naval base of Vladivostok, provide well-publicised occasions for the speeches of the G.O.C. Far Eastern Military Okrug and the G.O.C. Pacific Fleet, invariably denouncing the enemies of the Soviet Union and rallying their audiences to deeds of valour if attacked. There

[1] For a close analysis of the Soviet military position in the Far East see Geoffrey Jukes: *The Soviet Union in Asia*, pp. 187-96 to which I am indebted for insights on the Kuril islands.

is also an impressive array of Soviet military and naval equipment during these parades. The equipment shown during the October Anniversary parade in 1971 included field rocket launchers, while the official Soviet commentator boasted that 'the soldiers are aware that no bogs, hills or glens, nothing at all is an obstacle for these wonderful machines.'

The 50th anniversary of the Far Eastern Frontier Military District was celebrated as a special event. 'Cordial meetings took place between workers, war veterans, and border guards at frontier posts along the Amur and the Ussuri', to mark the occasion. In his address, the District G.O.C. reminded the Far East Frontier Troops of the 'necessity constantly to increase political watchfulness' and stated that there had been an increase in personnel, in the number of ships, units, combat posts, crews and patrols as a result of the competition in honour of the jubilee of the formation of the U.S.S.R., in 1972. It would appear from his statement that 'every day the frontier provides numerous examples of courage, bravery, toughness and great alertness', and that it is no sinecure to be posted there, even when conditions are relatively peaceful.

The unshakable loyalty and endurance of the frontier guards are constantly eulogised in Soviet press notices, illustrated by the bleak frontier posts which they man, 'undaunted by blizzards or other dangers'. The people are encouraged to honour and respect these frontier guards. 'Friendship with them and the soldiers has a great significance for the education of youth in the spirit of socialist patriotism and preparation for the defence of the motherland', according to the First Secretary of the Vladivostok city Party Committee (*Gorkom*). *Esprit de corps* within the ranks of these Frontier Guards has been fostered by 'a magnificent tradition' whereby elder son succeeds father and younger son elder brother. Whether this 'tradition' is common to all the frontier guards of the Soviet Union, or peculiar to those of the Far Eastern Military Okrug, is not clear.

In this patriotic drive, the native peoples have their place. They are constantly reminded of the benefits they have received from the Soviet system and what they owe to Lenin's nationalities policy, and their duty to defend it. For their part, many native men of letters express their feelings of affection and gratitude to the 'Otechestvo' (Fatherland) in prose and verse which is widely publicised in Russian translation. In the Amur villages in 1972, a series of talks was organised on the Leninist nationalities policy for the Nanaytsy, Ul'chi, Nivkhi, Negidal'tsy and Udegeytsy, the traditional fishermen and hunters of the area. There were also 1,000 lecture rooms throughout the Khabarovsk kray in 1972, in which 'the talks would be devoted to the benefits conferred by the 50 years period of liberation of the Far East from interventionists and White guards' and 'the full-blooded life enjoyed by all the peoples of the country of the Soviets compared to the pre-Revolutionary period, when they had no written language'.

Rallies and plaques commemorate the valiant deeds of Far Eastern participants in the Soviet Civil War and World War II, and it is assumed in these activities that the Far Eastern native peoples to a man welcomed the advent of Soviet power in 1917–20; awkward facts like the difficulties in forcing the Yakuts and other Siberian peoples to accept the new system are simply ignored. Apart from the metropolitan press, the local magazine *Dal'niy Vostok* (Khabarovsk) regularly digs up faded photographs to illustrate its stories of Far Eastern 'war heroes'.

This build-up of patriotism in the Far East has its counterpart in a calculated Soviet propaganda campaign, to forestall the effects of anti-Soviet Chinese propaganda from Manchuria, which dwells on the earlier allegiance of the indigenous border tribes to China. Soviet historians and archaeologists have produced learned evidence from artefacts etc., to show that far from being influenced by China, the Amur tribes 'who are endowed with a distinctive independent culture', 'inhabited a sort of political no-man's-land until the arrival of the Russians'. This is not the place to argue the pros and cons of this *ex-parte* statement, save to note that it is not generally accepted by non-Soviet experts in this field.

A rather petty example of the effort to remove any traces of former Chinese influence in the Far Eastern border regions was the decree of the R.S.F.S.R. Supreme Soviet, in 1973, changing the long-familiar names of a number of towns in the Han and Manchu dialects in the Far Eastern area, to Russian. Thus, some of the places listed by this decree were renamed as follows:

In the Maritime Kray:
Iman (town and rayon) – renamed Dalnerechensk
Lifudzin (settlement) – renamed Rudnyy
Severnyy Suchan (settlement) – renamed Uglekamensk
Sinancha (settlement) – renamed Cheremshany
Suchan (town) – renamed Partizansk
Tetyukhe (settlement and rayon) – renamed Dalnegorsk
Tetyukhe-Pristan' (settlement)– renamed Rudnaya-Pristan',
In Khabarovsk Kray:
Khungari (settlement) – renamed Gurskoye.

Under the same decree, ships bearing non-Russian names were also renamed.

Looking across the narrow Bering Strait, once connected with the north American mainland by a land bridge, the excavations carried out in Chukotka, by Academician Okladnikov, allegedly refute 'certain American scientists' opinion that the ancient culture of Siberia and the Far East originated in America; stone instruments up to 30,000 years old have been found in Siberia, whereas the oldest so far found in America were made between 1,000 and 2,000 B.C.' And so Siberian culture has been given another boost by Soviet scientists, the implication being that the indigenous peoples, e.g. the Eskimos, Indians of north America and Canada and their cultures, originated in north-east Siberia and not vice-versa.

The strident Soviet attitude in all that pertains to the Sino-Soviet frontier in the Far East contrasts sharply with the increasingly amicable tone used in the presentation of the idea of economic cooperation with Japan, the United States and other foreign countries in developing its natural resources. The idea of involving these Pacific countries in the development of the Soviet Far Eastern mainland, apart from its obvious economic significance, could well also be part of the Kremlin's long-term strategy of containing China in this part of the world. The expectation would be that once this copartnership was operating in the Far Eastern region, it would give the countries concerned a certain vested interest in stabilising the present Soviet frontier with China's N. Eastern territories, remote though this aim might be from their direct interests. Under present political conditions, it is not, therefore, surprising that the Chinese have been consistently hostile to the economic build-up of Siberia and the Soviet Far East, with the assistance of Japan and other countries.

chapter fifteen

Postscript

Economically, Siberia is now in a state of flux, as it passes from the belated early stages of industrialisation in the thirties, through many complex development problems towards the brighter prospects now looming on the economic horizon. The remarkable advances on the economic front since World War II have been surveyed in the previous pages, but geographically and industrially this development remains patchy. In particular, the level of management is generally poor, there are costly inter-regional imbalances in production and the manufacture of consumer goods has been neglected in favour of the expansion of heavy industry and mining. It is all too easy in surveying the buoyant list of industrial projects and constructions in this huge territory, to forget that there are still great tracts of geologically unexplored taiga and tundra, and that even in the relatively developed south of the country, the main industrial centres, Tyumen', Omsk, Krasnoyarsk, Irkutsk and Chita, are hundreds of kilometres apart.

Siberia today presents such a rapidly changing kaleidoscope of new geological finds, mines being opened up, industries and towns established and great electrification schemes in a former wilderness, that it eludes a 'fix' accurate for any length of time. It has proved to be the richest of the developing countries of the world, being amply endowed with energy resources, a wide range of other minerals including gold and other precious metals, tin, nickel, copper, tungsten and diamonds. In addition, great timber stocks and most of Russia's valuable fur are found in Siberia, while the Soviet north Pacific fishing grounds are among the most prolific in the world.

Soviet experts and workers have proved their ability to exploit Siberian minerals and other natural resources and build modern cities under the harshest Arctic conditions and not only with concentration camp labour, as at Noril'sk, but also with free labour further east in the now emerging towns of Bilibino and Cherskiy, far beyond the Arctic Circle. All forms of energy: hydropower, oil and natural gas have been very actively developed in recent years. The largest hydropower stations in the U.S.S.R. are in Siberia at Bratsk (4.1 million kw.), Krasnoyarsk (6 million kw.), and a still more powerful station is now being built south of Krasnoyarsk, also on the Yenisey, at Sayan (6.4 million kw.). There is abundant electric power in

Siberia for any foreseeable industrial development. Several important new industries, in the first place the big aluminium and wood-chemical industries in east Siberia, have been established on the basis of this electric power. And when the present technological problems are overcome, it is planned to link the European and Siberian electricity grids in an all-Union grid and thus make this Siberian power also available in European Russia, where it is much needed.

The west Siberian oil and natural gas reserves are proving a most valuable reinforcement of the Soviet energy position, at a moment when dwindling supplies in the former main oil-gas source in the Volga-Urals region was causing concern in the Soviet Union. The major 48 trunk pipeline, long under discussion as a joint Soviet-Japanese project to link the Tyumen' oil-fields with Nakhodka, was abruptly cancelled by Moscow in 1974 and replaced by the Baykal-Amur railway project (see map p. 168). Only the Tyumen'-Irkutsk section of the original trans-continental pipe is now being built and by the Soviets without Japanese assistance. But, it is likely that a similar pipeline may be built later on. Tyumen' oil and natural gas is being fed into other trunk pipelines which will shortly reach European Russia and Samotlor oil is also planned to be carried to Eastern Europe *via* the *Druzhba* (Friendship) pipeline and also to the Volga industrial region. Though the north Tyumen' natural gas deposits are exceptionally rich, gas output there is constantly lagging behind production targets owing to lack of pipe and other essential equipment, while the oil targets are regularly overfulfilled. But, within a decade, Tyumen' oil and natural gas have become resources of exceptional national and potential international importance and relieved the Soviet Union of immediate concern about these sources of energy.

The attitude of the Japanese towards participation in the Tyumen' oil industry perceptibly cooled when confronted with the Soviet decision to cancel the Irkutsk-Nakhodka pipeline, on which their hopes of deliveries of Tyumen' oil were originally based, compounding as it did earlier disappointment with the reduction of these promised deliveries from 40 million to 20-25 million tons. Moscow's somewhat off-hand alternative proposal to the Japanese, to the effect that they might contribute a $3,300 million loan towards the construction of the new Baykal-Amur railway which it was alleged could also supply Tyumen' oil to Japan, was not alluring in the light of the heavy costs envisaged. The proposal will obviously be the subject of much hard bargaining between Moscow and Tokyo about prices, credit rates, carrying capacity of the new Railway etc., before it is accepted in Tokyo, if, in fact, it is eventually acceptable.

While Japan was hesitating about participation in the B.A.M. railway enterprise, she almost simultaneously made provision for a $450 million bank loan to Moscow for the acquisition of Japanese equipment for the development of the Chul'man Neyungra coal mines, in south Yakutiya, and other natural resources in this area. As a *quid pro quo*, Japan is to receive 5,500,000 tons of coking annually for 20 years, beginning in 1978. Soviet-Japanese negotiations about these coking coal arrangements had been hanging fire for about seven years, owing to failure to agree about credit terms, as well as Soviet unwillingness to supply coking coal alone, as demanded by the Japanese, uncombined with other coal. These matters having been at last settled to the satisfaction of the Japanese, the ensuing coking coal memorandum arranged for the South Yakutsk Coal Development Co-operation (*sic*) to be set up to deal with matters arising from Japanese participation in this industry. Japan will also supply equipment and consumption goods for the railway (and its builders) now under construction between the Trans-Siberian railway station of Bam and the Chul'man coal mines. This technical assistance should expedite its completion.

Moreover, about this time in 1974, Japan and the Soviet Union signed an inter-governmental protocol defining the terms under which the Soviet Union could acquire an additional $1,050 million, long-term Japanese bank credit for other but undefined Siberian development schemes. This credit was stated by Soviet sources to be the largest in the history of Soviet foreign trade. It is also of interest to note 'the agreement in principle' in this protocol for Japanese co-operation in oil and natural gas prospecting on the Sakhalin shelf, in return for potential deliveries of this fuel. Should these shelf reserves prove as rich as anticipated by some Soviet sources, they could be important for energy-hungry Japan and literally on her doorstep.

Soviet-American co-operation in the development of Siberian natural resources has so far been confined to the proposed natural gas projects in north Tyumen' and Yakutiya, while Japan has for some time been discussing participation in both Tyumen' oil and Yakut natural gas development, the latter with the Americans. If these complicated Soviet-American-Japanese enterprises eventually get off the ground, they could be technologically and financially very advantageous to the Soviet Union. But little or no information is yet available about how the triangular partnership will operate in the Yakut natural gas scheme, or to what extent it has in fact been finalised.

A stumbling block to these American natural gas schemes was at first Senator Jackson's Amendment to the Congressional Trade Bill barring 'most favoured' trading status to the Soviet Union. The State guaranteed loans, normally necessary to finance enterprises of this magnitude, could not be granted while the Amendment remained in force. But in October 1974, this Amendment was withdrawn and the U.S.S.R. was conditionally granted most-favoured nation trade status by the United States.

American involvement in Siberian natural gas developments became a practical proposition originally as a result of Nixon-Brezhnev Agreements of 1972 initiating the so-called 'open door' policy. This switch in the Kremlin's former 'closed door' approach to foreign investment in Siberia (or elsewhere in the Soviet Union) coincided with growing concern in the United States and Japan about their respective energy positions and the need to seek out new sources of fuel supply. Simultaneously, the Soviet leaders had cause for concern about the state of the U.S.S.R. economy and recognised that large injections of American advanced technology and investment could go far to raise the low levels of production and answer the need for re-structuring and modernisation of the Soviet industrial system. The advantages of Japanese-American technical cooperation in the development of the Siberian oil-gas industries were frankly recognised.

The cancellation of the long projected Irkutsk-Nakhodka pipeline was accompanied by the announcement, out of the blue, by Brezhnev of the construction of the great Baykal-Amur (B.A.M.)[1] trunk railway at the 20th Anniversary Conference of the Virgin Lands, in Alma Ata in March 1974. The arguments put forward for this unexpected switch in policy were that a railway would be more 'versatile', that is, capable of carrying more diversified products than a pipeline and that it would be the 'key to opening up yet untouched, inestimable treasures in Siberia and the Far East'. This may well prove to be the case in the long run but the resource endowment of this largely 'wild' railway zone must remain to some extent in the realm of speculation until the present intensive geological investigations are completed.

In Siberia, however, where communications are of such crucial importance for economic-social development, 'grandiose' B.A.M. must rank as a project of major significance and bids fair to rival, in time, the dynamic influence of the old Trans-Siberian railway, still the sole arterial railway traversing the Siberian mainland, from west to east. The B.A.M. has had a curious history since its still rather obscure origin as a concentration construction, pre-1939. Its postwar existence, or even the extent to which work on the track may have advanced, was shrouded in mystery until it was revived, in principle, in 1966 as the eastern branch of the new north Siberian railway (*Sevsib*). But subsequently little more was heard of it, until it emerged in Brezhnev's statement as a project of urgent national importance.

The 3,145 km. long B.A.M. is planned to connect the western rail head at Ust'Kut (Lena station) with Komsomol'sk-na-Amure (whence there are connections with Khabarovsk and Vladivostok on the Trans-Siberian railway). The problems confronting the builders of this track are enormous.

Apart from supply difficulties over vast distances mostly in uninhabited country lacking organised road, air or rail communications, the track itself will have to be hacked out of virgin taiga and traverse many high mountains, permafrost and seismic zones as well as large areas of bog and marsh. Bridges will have to be built over the Lena, the Olekma, the Vitim, the Amur and many smaller rivers where in many cases the surrounding permafrost ground creates complicated bridge support problems. A number of tunnels will also have to be built and that through the Severo-Muyskiy range will be about 15 km. long. In all, the B.A.M. will be a most costly construction.

It is planned as a trunk line of the 'first category' for which 'the most advanced Soviet equipment' and 'a high level of automation' is to be provided, including high speed diesel engines and oil tankers for 'large scale oil transport'. The main stations along the new line are to be built at Nizhneangarsk, Chara, Tynda and Urgal proceeding from the western terminal at Ust' Kut. But the pioneer Komsomol' workers have already named the first temporary station beyond Ust'Kut, Zvezdnyy, a point at the junction of the east Siberian rivers Taura and Niya, not yet marked on Soviet maps. These main railway station sites, now only insignificant villages, are planned to become much larger urban centres according as the local resources are

---

[1] This BAM abbreviation should not be confused with Bam, the name of a station on the Amur railway.

developed. Thus Chara, the future centre of the big Udokan copper mines, is planned soon to have a population of 50-60,000. In spite of these optimistic forecasts, the settlement of this vast territory may in fact prove a major future problem and very difficult to solve under present Soviet population conditions.

Construction on this 'second road to the Ocean' is to proceed simultaneously from the eastern and western terminals. Only the first 700 km. of this line, eastwards from Lake Baykal, is to be electrified in the first place and electricity for this stretch will be supplied from the now partly completed Ust'Ilim hydro-electric station. A large supply base to serve both the eastern and western branches of the B.A.M. is being established at the half-way station of Tynda (in the Amur oblast). Tynda will soon, it is expected, be connected with the Trans-Siberian railway *via* a branch-line from Bam station (180 km.). According to the present timetable, the B.A.M. should be entirely completed by 1982-84. Individual sectors are to be put into operation as soon as commissioned. *Pravda* (25/7/74), at least, 'has no doubt that the trunk line will be completed at the stated times'.

The labour force for the B.A.M. construction is being supplied by thousands of young Komsomol' 'volunteers' who are reported to have rushed to the future track sites 'from all the Soviet republics' as soon as they were informed of Brezhnev's appeal for their cooperation and the B.A.M. was declared an all-Union shock Komsomol' enterprise at the XVII Komsomol' Congress in April 1974. These Komsomol' pioneers are reinforced by demobilised service men and reservists and student construction teams from various Soviet cities throughout the Soviet Union. All these people started work in 'tent settlements' in the virgin taiga under very primitive conditions. Their 'enthusiasm' apparently carried them through the first summer months of 1974 but it remains to be seen how they will fare during the very severe winter frosts of this region, unless their conditions rapidly improve.

Meanwhile, the Soviet media are putting out glamorous accounts of what the future holds for these workers. They are promised 'living quarters supplied with hot water, gas, clubs, cinemas, schools' and many other amenities. But it is difficult to foresee how or when these attractions can be provided along 3,145 km. of track by the usually inefficient Soviet social service. And if conditions do not improve, a labour problem could easily halt progress on the B.A.M., as the weaker brethren slip away to less arduous sites.

This capital and labour intensive B.A.M. project is undoubtedly motivated both by overt Soviet economic objectives and by strategic considerations which Soviet sources prefer to ignore. Though the exact nature of the 'untapped' natural riches of the B.A.M. zone must await confirmation by the geological surveys now under way, there is nevertheless no doubt about the existence of a number of valuable resources. In the first place, the virgin taiga traversed by the B.A.M. contains vast stands of unexploited timber and large new industrial timber complexes are planned, although there is plenty of uncut timber in west and east Siberia and the Far Eastern region, where labour and equipment still remain constant problems. The new line will certainly facilitate the development of the 'unique' Udokan copper mines, 'the largest in the Soviet Union' but whether with or without foreign technical-financial assistance is still not clear. The long-discussed Far Eastern metallurgical complex based on Chul'man coking coals and Aldan iron ores may now get off the ground, owing to the approach of the new railway from Bam to Tynda-Berkakit, in the vicinity of the mines. Moreover, Soviet geologists assert that the B.A.M. zones is rich in nickel, manganese, molybdenum, wolfram, mercury and asbestos (so far there has been no mention of the long-sought bauxite ore). There are also Soviet anticipations that the area may eventually prove as rich in oil and natural gas as the north Tyumen' reserves. Of course, should these still rather tentative surmises be confirmed, the national economic significance of the B.A.M. territory would be enormously increased. In any case, a huge hitherto 'silent' area of the Soviet Union should eventually be vitalised by the railway, though the costs, as in the case of the Trans-Siberian and Amur railways, will be enormous. It is in many ways an exciting prospect.

These reassuring economic prognostications notwithstanding, it is likely that at this particular juncture, the *strategic* case for sinking so much scarce labour and capital in the B.A.M. construction was decisive in Moscow. Facing a bitterly hostile China beyond the Far Eastern frontier, the vulnerability of the Trans-Siberian railway, running for hundreds of miles parallel to this frontier, must have been of increasing concern to Moscow. The construction of the Baykal-Amur railway, to be built 180-500 kms. north of the Trans-Siberian track, provided at least a relatively safer means of transport for military and non-military supplies (in the first place Tyumen' oil, as well as other commodities for the Far Eastern region), certainly an important advantage in the event of armed hostilities in the Far East with China. The trans-continental pipeline should not be regarded as finally eliminated from future Soviet plans but rather postponed, to be later revived along probably another route to feed the projected big new refinery at Nakhodka.

The strategic aspects of the B.A.M. construction are foremost in Peking's sharply critical comments on the matter. In turn, before deciding to participate in this costly enterprise, the Japanese will no doubt carefully balance the risk of incurring Chinese disfavour against the economic advantages of facilitating deliveries of Tyumen' oil and a number of raw materials of interest to Japan from the area being opened up by the B.A.M. The outcome of these deliberations is not yet known.

Siberia's progress as a developing industrial country is to a considerable extent retarded by the low levels of agricultural production, in which defective planning and expertise, poor managerial skills and serious labour problems all play a part. As a result of low agricultural production, many parts of Siberia cannot feed themselves and large and costly imports of grain, meat, sugar and butter are necessary, notably to the Soviet Far Eastern region. The soil and climatic conditions of Siberia are not normally good for agriculture, apart from the traditional so-called 'breadbasket' of southern west Siberia, but even there, much better results could be achieved by more efficient organisation and more intensive mechanisation. It is not yet clear how effective in improving this situation the Soviet-U.S. Agreement of 1973 on agricultural cooperation will be as it is heavily weighted on research and information rather than on actual farm work. The Russians obviously have nothing to teach the Americans about large-scale farming, which they have practised very sucessfully for years, so the opportunities for the mutual exchange of information etc., could be of much greater use to Soviet than American agriculture, if American experience and knowledge is in fact fed down to the farms, including the Siberian farms. The notoriously backward Soviet agriculture now has a great opportunity of learning from the American exemplar, but whether the peculiar Soviet agrarian concepts underlying Siberian (and all Soviet agriculture) will prove an insuperable barrier to American ideas of good farming practice remains to be seen. Some indications of increased Soviet interest in the needs of agriculture, however, may be noted. Dr. Hammer's first big business deal concluded with the Soviet Union for the 'sale of the highest quality chemical fertiliser amounting to approximately $200,000,000 annually' and the construction of fertiliser plants within the Soviet Union reflect, both the acute need for fertiliser on Soviet farms, which is also frequently mentioned in Siberia. Commenting on the new 'business atmosphere' between the U.S. and the Soviet Union, *Pravda* mentioned the big contracts concluded with American agricultural machinery firms such as International Harvester, Caterpillar Tractor, Hewlett-Packard Corporation, etc., and that many other contracts were under discussion. Presumably, some of these machines will also find their way to help to mechanise the under-mechanised Siberian farms. Thus as a result of Soviet-American economic cooperation the Siberian energy industries and possibly also agriculture stand to benefit substantially from American technical assistance, provided always that Soviet-American relations remain friendly and the present financial barriers surmounted.

The Soviet government has signally failed, as in agriculture, to deal with the serious population and labour problems confronting them for years in Siberia. The population in west Siberia, east Siberia and the Far Eastern region remains relatively low in regard both to industrial and agricultural labour requirements and the respective size of these areas. Flight of labour is high from the more arduous construction sites, owing to the low living standards, and especially the wholly inadequate housing and social-domestic services, including schools and medical care. The government has repeatedly called for improvements but took little effective action until quite recently, when it seems at last to have awakened to the seriousness of the problem. It was interesting in this connection to note a Soviet report, early in 1973, that whereas the towns of Bratsk and Angarsk started from tents and dugouts, the new town for the Zima electro-chemical plant (planned population 250,000), will be provided from the start with well-constructed flats or communal dwellings as well as food enterprises and a clothes factory. Such optimistic forecasts are not entirely new, but if this approach becomes general policy, it could go far to reduce the present high outward flow of the settled Siberian population as well as of 'one-time' migrants. It may also be anticipated that, if American experts move into the west Siberian gas fields in any numbers, they would find much of the housing there intolerable and improvements might follow from their own housing plans and standards. The so-called 'narrow departmental attitudes' of the central industrial ministries and planning agencies cannot be overlooked, among the adverse factors hampering Siberian economic development, and also giving rise to much local frustration and economic dislocation. The defects of over-centralisation of the economic administration in the main branches of the Siberian economy have been illustrated in the preceding chapters and the case for some decentralisation, on the score of efficiency, for this great and rich landmass is well founded. Many difficulties are created simply because the Moscow bureaucrats are too remote from the area of their decisions to be properly aware of the state of affairs on the construction sites, until there is a crisis.

Yet, all things considered, none of these defects in the Soviet handling of Siberian economic development is irremediable. In the new pragmatic attitude to the economy in the Kremlin, embodied in the *volte-face* regarding American technical assistance in Siberia, it is surely no longer quite Utopian to anticipate the gradual emergence of a more efficient approach to Siberian economic affairs, and the elimination of the grosser failings of hyper-centralisation. Nevertheless, however faulty the economic organisation of Siberia, it cannot in the end destroy, though it may retard, her great future based on an almost unique wealth of resources.

The impact of Siberian gold and precious metals, diamonds, oil and natural gas, a wide range of other valuable minerals, timber and timber products must be increasingly felt on international commodity markets. And as a result of this progress, it may be anticipated that Siberia will, in time, be recognised as an economic entity in its own right (while remaining an inalienable part of the Soviet Union). Moreover, if the multi-national economic cooperation now in favour in the Kremlin continues to flourish, Siberia should become much better known in the western world, rather than the closed book it mostly is today.

China's attitude to developments in the Soviet Far East, with possible implications westwards for Siberia, is important but entirely unpredictable. A protracted Sino-Soviet armed confrontation provoked by China is on balance highly unlikely while Soviet strategic strength is so overwhelmingly stronger than Chinese. It could, however, be argued that this situation might well change with the rapid build-up now taking place of Chinese military power, including a nuclear weapons system, already capable of striking at many southern cities of Siberia. But these are questions for the unforeseeable future and in any case far beyond the scope of this book, or my competence. Nevertheless, there is little doubt that Peking's original suspicions of Moscow's attitude in the Far Eastern frontier regions have been deepened by the reinforcement of Soviet military positions and also, to some extent, by the proposed economic cooperation with Japan and the United States. But this is a far cry from a deliberate head-on Sino-Soviet confrontation, which could imperil the economic future of the Far Eastern region and even the Siberian hinterland. The Soviet embroilment with China does, however, enhance the role of the Far Eastern region and in particular the Pacific Fleet base at Vladivostok in Soviet strategy, because of the new Soviet interest in the containment of China in areas of traditional, or potential, Chinese influence bordering on the Pacific and Indian Oceans.

Thus Siberia, extending to the Far Eastern region, is emerging as a focal point in Soviet politics and international commerce, as well as being a vital source of supply of most raw materials, oil and natural gas, for the major manufacturing industries of European Russia. It is in fact the future base of Soviet economic power.

Short Reading List

This list is necessarily short because it is confined to books in English and the number of books worth recommending in English on Siberia is extremely small. The best sources of information for contemporary economic developments in Siberia are in Russian and I have relied on them almost exclusively in this book. One important exception is Theodore Shabad's *Basic Industrial Resources of the U.S.S.R.*, an impeccably accurate reference work on the progress of the fuels, electric power, metals and chemical raw materials in Siberia (and elsewhere in the Soviet Union) to whom (like so many working in this field), I am deeply indebted.

Apart from works dealing specifically with Siberia, I have included some more general works on the Soviet political-economic system which may be found useful by the reader new to this field.

Armstrong, T., Russian Settlement in the North. Cambridge University Press, 1965.

The Northern Sea Route. Cambridge University Press, 1952.

Botting, Douglas, One Chilly Siberian Morning. Hodder and Stoughton, 1965.

Campbell, Robert W., The Economics of Soviet Oil and Gas. Published for Resources for the Future, Inc. by The Johns Hopkins Press, Baltimore, 1968.

Conolly, Violet, Beyond The Urals. Oxford University Press, 1967. *Soviet Trade from the Pacific to the Levant.* Oxford, 1935.

Czaplicka, M. A., Aboriginal Siberia. Clarendon Press, Oxford 1914. *My Siberian Year.* Mills and Boon, London 1916.

Dibb, Paul, Siberia and the Pacific. A Study of Economic Development and Trade Prospects. Praeger N.Y. 1972.

Fisher, R. H., The Russian Fur Trade, 1550, 1700. University of California Publications in History, vol. 31, XI, 1943.

Gibson, James R., Feeding the Russian Fur Trade. Provisionment of the Okhotsk Seaboard and the Kamchatka Peninsula. 1939-1856. University of Wisconsin Press, 1970.

Gregory, James S., Russian Land Soviet People. A Geographical Approach to the U.S.S.R., George G. Harrap and Co. Ltd., London, 1968.

Hooson, David S. M., A New Soviet Heartland? Van Nostrand, N.Y. 1964.

Jasny, Naum, The Socialized Agriculture of the U.S.S.R. Stanford University Press, California 1949.

Jukes, Geoffrey, The Soviet Union in Asia. Angus and Robertson in association with The Australian Institute of International Affairs, 1973.

Katkov, George (ed.), *Russia Enters the 20th Century.* Temple Smith, London, 1971.

Kolarz, Walter, The Peoples of the Soviet Far East. George Philip and Son, London 1954.

Levin, M. G., and Potapov, L. P. (eds.), *Peoples of Siberia*

Mellor, R. E. H., Geography of the U.S.S.R. Macmillan, London 1964.

N.A.T.O., Direction of Economic Affairs, Round-table Exploitation of Siberia's Natural Resources, Brussels, 1974.

Nove, Alec, The Soviet Economy (revised edition). George Allen and Unwin, London 1965.

Pipes, Richard, The Formation of the Soviet Union. Revised edition. Harvard University Press, Cambridge, Mass. 1964.

Post, Laurens Van der, Journey into Russia. Hogarth Press, London 1964.

Schapiro, Leonard, The Government and Politics of the Soviet Union. Hutchinson University Library, London 1965.

Scott, John, Behind The Urals. Secker and Warburg, London 1942.

Shabad, Theodore, Basic Resources of the U.S.S.R. Columbia University Press, N.Y. 1969. *Geography of the U.S.S.R.* Columbia University Press, 1951.

Shimkin, Demitri B., Minerals: A Key to Soviet Power. Harvard University Press, Cambridge, Mass. 1953.

Stephan, John J., Sakhalin, A History. Clarendon Press, Oxford. 1971.

Sutton, Anthony C., Western Technology and Soviet Economic Development 1917 to 1930. Stanford University, California, 1968.

Swianiewicz, S., Forced Labour and Economic Development. An Enquiry into the Experience of Soviet Industrialisation. Oxford University Press, London 1965.

Thiel, Erich, The Soviet Far East. Methuen, London 1957. Translated by Annelie and Ralph Rookwood.

Tupper, Harmon, To the Great Ocean. Secker and Warburg, London 1965.

Utechin, S. V., Everyman's Concise Encyclopaedia of Russia. Dent, London 1961.

Appendix

The Jackson amendment

East-West Trade Relations Act—Amendment. At the end of the bill, add the following new section: East-West Trade and Fundamental Human Rights

Sec. 10 (a) To assure the continued dedication of the United States to fundamental human rights and notwithstanding any other provision of this Act or any other law, after October 15, 1972 no nonmarket economy country shall be eligible to receive most-favoured-nation treatment or to participate in any programme of the Government of the United States which extends credits or credit guarantees or investment guarantees, directly or indirectly, during the period beginning with the date on which the President of the United States determines that such country:

(1) denies its citizens the right or opportunity to emigrate, or;

(2) imposes more than a nominal tax on emigration or on the visas or other documents required for emigration, for any purpose or cause whatsoever; or

(3) imposes more than a nominal tax, levy, fine, fee, or other charge on any citizen, as a consequence of the desire of such citizen to emigrate to the country of his choice,

and ending on the date on which the President determines that such country is no longer in violation of paragraph (1), (2) or (3).

(b) After October 15, 1972 a nonmarket economy country may participate in a programme of the Government of the United States which extends credits or credit guarantees or investment guarantees, and the authority conferred by sections 3 and 6(a) of this Act may be exercised with respect to such country, only after the President of the United States has submitted to the Congress a report indicating that such country is not in violation of paragraph (1), (2) or (3) of subsection (a). Such report with respect to such country, shall include information as to the nature and implementation of emigration laws and policies and restrictions or discrimination applied to or against persons wishing to emigrate. The report required by this subsection shall be submitted initially as provided herein and semi-annually thereafter so long as any agreement entered into pursuant to the exercise of such authority is in effect.

index

index